Good Reasons
Designing and Writing Effective Arguments

Second Edition

■ **Lester Faigley**
University of Texas at Austin

■ **Jack Selzer**
The Pennsylvania State University

New York San Francisco Boston
London Toronto Sydney Tokyo Singapore Madrid
Mexico City Munich Paris Cape Town Hong Kong Montreal

Vice President and Editor-in-Chief: Joseph Opiela
Vice President: Eben W. Ludlow
Supplements Editor: Donna Campion
Media Supplements Editor: Nancy Garcia
Executive Marketing Manager: Ann Stypuloski
Senior Production Manager: Bob Ginsberg
Project Coordination, Text Design, and Electronic Page Makeup: Pre-Press Company, Inc.
Cover Design Manager and Designer: Nancy Danahy
Cover/Photo: © Getty Images, Inc.
Senior Manufacturing Buyer: Dennis J. Para
Printer and Binder: RR Donnelley & Sons Company
Cover Printer: Phoenix Color Corporation

For permission to use copyrighted textual material, grateful acknowledgment is made to the copyright holders on page 329, which are hereby made part of this copyright page.

Photos: pp. 2, 32, 36, 59, 108, 137, 171, 201, 286, 289: Lester Faigley Photos; p. 5: Erich Hartman / Magnum Photos Inc.; p. 72: Heinz Kluetmeier / *Sports Illustrated*; p. 87: *Washington Star* Archive / Martin Luther King Memorial Library, Washington, DC; p. 111: Library of Congress; p. 157: Doc Pele / Stills / Retna Ltd.; p. 159: Colonial Williamsburg Foundation; p. 191: *Austin American Statesman*

Library of Congress Cataloging-in-Publication Data

Faigley, Lester, date
    Good reasons: designing and writing effective arguments / Lester Faigley, Jack Selzer.—2nd ed.
        p. cm.
    Includes bibliographical references and index.
    ISBN 0-321-10531-1
    1. English language—Rhetoric. 2. Persuasion (Rhetoric) 3. Report writing. I. Selzer, Jack. II. Title.

    PE1431 .F35 2003
    808'.042—dc21

2002022674

Please visit our Web site at http://www.ablongman.com/faigley

ISBN 0-321-10531-1

2 3 4 5 6 7 8 9 10—DOH—05 04 03 02

In memory of our teacher and friend,
James L. Kinneavy (1920–1999)

Contents

Preface

Like many other college writing teachers, we have come to believe that a course focusing on argument is an essential part of a college writing curriculum. Most students come to college with very little experience in reading and writing extended arguments. Because so much writing in college concerns arguments in the disciplines, a basic course in writing arguments is foundational for an undergraduate education. You will find that college courses frequently require you to analyze the structure of arguments, to identify competing claims, to weigh the evidence offered, to recognize assumptions, to locate contradictions, and to anticipate opposing views. The ability to write cogent arguments is also highly valued in most occupations that require college degrees. Just as important, you need to be able to read arguments critically and write arguments skillfully if you are to participate in public life after you leave college. The long-term issues that will affect your life after your college years—education, the environment, social justice, and the quality of life, to name a few—have many diverse stakeholders and long, complex histories. They cannot be reduced to slogans and sound bites. If you are to help make your views prevail in your communities, you must be able to participate in sustained give-and-take on a range of civic issues.

We find that other argument textbooks spend too much time on complicated schemes and terminology for analyzing arguments and too little time thinking about helping students produce real arguments that work. This book begins by considering why people take the time to write arguments in the first place. People write arguments because they want things to change. They want to change attitudes and beliefs about particular issues, and they want things done about problems they identify. We start out by making you examine exactly why you might want to write an argument and how what you write can lead to extended discussion and long-term results. We then provide you with practical means to find good reasons that support convincingly the positions you want to advocate. *Good Reasons* is also distinctive in its attention to the delivery and presentation of arguments—to the visual aspects of argument, in other words—and to arguments in electronic media. It encourages you to formulate arguments in different genres and different media.

Several textbooks on writing arguments have appeared in recent years that use Stephen Toulmin's method of analyzing arguments. We take a simpler approach. Toulmin's method provides useful analytic tools, but we do not find it a necessary one to teach the practical art of making arguments. In fact, our experience is that Toulmin's terminology is often more confusing than helpful. The key to the Toulmin method is understanding how warrants work. *Warrants,* in the Toulmin scheme, are the assumptions, knowledge, and beliefs that allow an audience to connect evidence with a claim. We feel that you will understand this concept better if you focus not on "Toulminizing" an argument but on conceptualizing the rhetorical situation—examining what assumptions, knowledge, and beliefs a particular audience might have about a specific issue. The only technical terms this book uses are the general classical concepts of *pathos, ethos,* and *logos:* sources of good reasons that emerge from the audience's most passionately held values, from the speaker's expertise and credibility, or from reasonable, commonsense thinking.

Likewise, you will not find explicit discussions of syllogisms or enthymemes in *Good Reasons.* We have avoided introducing these terms because, like the Toulmin terminology, they too often hinder rather than help. The crux of teaching argument, in our view, is to get you to appreciate its rhetorical nature. What makes a good reason *good* in public debate is not that it follows logically from a set of truth claims arranged in syllogisms but that the audience accepts the writer or speaker as credible and accepts the assumptions, knowledge, and beliefs on which the argument is based—and thus accepts the reasons given as *good reasons.*

Another difference is that our book does not make a sharp distinction between what some people think of as rational and irrational arguments. Rationality is a socially constructed concept. Until the twentieth century, it was rational to believe that women should not participate in politics. To question the absolute nature of rationality is not to say that rationality does not exist. Driving on the right side of the road is rational in North, South, and Central America and most of western Europe, just as driving on the left side is rational in Great Britain, Ireland, India, and Japan. But insisting on a dichotomy between rational and irrational has some unfortunate consequences, including a sharp division between argument and persuasion. Advertisements are often held up as typifying persuasion that plays to emotion rather than reason. Other pieces of writing, however, are not so easy to classify as either argument or persuasion. For example, personal and fictional narratives often include arguments or have an argumentative aim. Personal narratives are critical in many essays because they supply cultural knowledge of other perspectives and group experiences, which in turn enables the writer to advance good reasons in support of an argumentative purpose. We treat narratives in *Good Reasons* as an important aspect of argument. We also pay attention to ads and other genres of persuasion that are usually not represented in textbooks on argument. In short, you will find examples in the readings that illustrate the wide range of argument.

The dichotomy between rational and irrational also leads to an almost total neglect of the visual nature of writing. Visual thinking remains excluded from the mainstream literacy curriculum in the schools, and it is taught only in specialized courses in college in disciplines such as architecture and art history. This exclusion might be justified (though we would argue otherwise) if writing courses were still bound by the technology of the typewriter, but the great majority of college students today prepare their work on personal computers. Commonly used word processing programs and Web page editors now allow you to include pictures, icons, charts, and graphs, making design an important part of an argument. While we still believe that the heart of an argument course should be the critical reading and critical writing of prose, we also believe that the basics of visual persuasion should be included as well. In Part III, therefore, you will find an extensive discussion of visual design and how good design can support good reasons in both written and oral arguments.

If our goal is to help you become an active citizen in a participatory democracy, then it would be counterproductive for us to ignore that most of the writing you will do in your future public and private life will be electronically mediated. Most students now have access to the most powerful publishing technology ever invented—the World Wide Web. Until very recently, students who published on the Web had to learn HTML and had to manipulate cumbersome file transfer programs. But current word processing programs and WYSIWYG ("what you see is what you get") editors now bypass the step of coding HTML, and the process of putting a Web page on a server has become almost as simple as opening a file on a PC. The Web has become a vast arena of argument, with nearly every interest group maintaining a Web presence. Chapter 13 provides an introduction to arguments on the Web.

The popularity of argument courses is not an accident. Even though we hear frequently that people have become cynical about politics, they are producing self-sponsored writing in quantities never before seen. It's almost as if people have rediscovered writing. While writing personal letters is perhaps becoming a lost art, participating in online discussion groups, putting up Web sites, and sending email have become commonplace. Citizen participation in local and national government forums, in a multitude of issue-related online discussions, and in other forms such as online magazines is increasing daily. You already have many opportunities to speak in the electronic polis. We want you to recognize and value the breadth of information available on the Internet and to evaluate, analyze, and synthesize that information. And we want to prepare you for the changing demands of the professions and public citizenship in your future.

COMPANION WEB SITE AND INSTRUCTOR'S MANUAL

The Companion Web site to accompany *Good Reasons*, Second Edition, (http://www.ablongman.com/faigley) offers a wealth of resources for both students and instructors. Students can access detailed chapter summaries and objectives, writing exercises, chapter review quizzes, and links to additional Web resources for further study. Instructors will find sample syllabus, additional activities for in-classroom use, Web resources, and the Instructor's Manual available for download.

The Instructor's Manual that accompanies this text was revised by Eric Lupfer and Victoria Davis and is designed to be useful for new and experienced instructors alike. The Instructor's Manual briefly discusses the ins and outs of teaching the material in each chapter. Also provided are in-class exercises, homework assignments, discussion questions for each reading selection, and model paper assignments and syllabi. This revised Instructor's Manual will make your work as a teacher a bit easier. Teaching argumentation and composition becomes a process that has genuine—and often surprising—rewards.

Acknowledgments

We are much indebted to the work of many outstanding scholars of argument and to our colleagues who teach argument at Texas and at Penn State. In particular, we thank the following reviewers for sharing their expertise: William A. Covino, Florida Atlantic University; Caley O'Dwyer Feagin, University of California, Irvine; Richard Fulkerson, Texas A&M University–Commerce; David Harvey, Central Arkansas University; Joe Law, Wright State University; Elizabeth Losh, University of California, Irvine; Rise A. Quay, Heartland Community College; Gardner Rogers, University of Illinois at Urbana-Champaign; Jeffrey Walker, Emory University; Maria W. Warren, The University of West Florida; Patricia J. Webb, Maysville Community College; and Stephen Wilhoit, University of Dayton. We are especially grateful to our students, who have given us opportunities to test these materials in class and who have taught us a great deal about the nature of argument.

Our editor, Eben Ludlow, convinced us we should write this book and gave us wise guidance throughout. Elsa van Bergen and Willie DeFord at Pre-Press, Bob Ginsberg and Bill Russo at Longman, and our copy editor, Carol Noble, all did splendid work in preparing our book for publication. Finally we thank our families, who make it all possible.

LESTER FAIGLEY
JACK SELZER

PART 1

Persuading with Good Reasons

What Do We Mean by Argument?

For over thirty years, the debate over legalized abortion has raged in the United States. The following scene is a familiar one: Outside an abortion clinic, a crowd of pro-life activists has gathered to try to stop women from entering the clinic. They carry signs that read "ABORTION = MURDER" and "A BABY'S LIFE IS A HUMAN LIFE." Pro-choice supporters are also present in a counterdemonstration. Their signs read "KEEP YOUR LAWS OFF MY BODY" and "WOMEN HAVE THE RIGHT TO CONTROL THEIR BODIES." Police keep the two sides apart, but they do not stop the shouts of "Murderer!" from the pro-life side and "If you're anti-abortion, don't have one!" from the pro-choice side.

When you imagine an argument, you might think of two people engaged in a heated exchange or two groups of people with different views, shouting back and forth at each other like the pro-choice and pro-life demonstrators. Or you might think of the arguing that occurs in the courthouse, where district attorneys and defense lawyers debate strenuously. Written arguments can resemble these oral arguments in being heated and one sided. For example, the signs that the pro-choice and pro-life demonstrators carry might be considered written arguments.

But in college courses, in public life, and in professional careers, written arguments are not thought of as slogans. Bumper stickers require no supporting evidence or reasons. Many other kinds of writing do not offer reasons either. An instruction manual, for example, does not try to persuade you. It assumes that you want to do whatever the manual tells you how to do; indeed, most people are willing to follow the advice, or else they would not be consulting the manual. Likewise, an article written by someone who is totally committed to a particular cause or belief often assumes that everyone should think the same way. These writers can count on certain phrases and words to produce predictable responses.

Effective arguments do not make the assumption that everyone should think the same way or hold the same beliefs. They attempt to change people's minds by convincing them of the validity of new ideas or that a particular course of action is the best one to take. Written arguments not only offer evidence and reasons but also often examine the assumptions on which they are based, think through opposing arguments, and anticipate objections. They explore positions thoroughly and take opposing views into account.

Extended written arguments make more demands on their readers than most other kinds of writing. Like bumper stickers, they often appeal to our emotions. But they typically do much more. They expand our knowledge with the depth of their analysis and lead us through a complex set of claims by providing networks of logical relations and appropriate evidence. They explicitly build on what has been written before by offering trails of sources, which also demonstrates that they can be trusted because the writers have done their homework. They cause us to reflect on what we read, in a process that we will shortly describe as critical reading.

Our culture is a competitive culture, and often the goal is to win. If you are a professional athlete, a top trial lawyer, or a candidate for president of the United States, it really is win big or lose. But most of us live in a world in which the opponents don't go away when the game is over. Even professional athletes have to play the team they beat in the championship game the next year.

In real life, most of us have to deal with the people who disagree with us at times but with whom we have to continue to work and live in the same communities. The idea of winning in such situations can only be temporary. Other situations will come up soon enough in which we will need the support of those who were on the other side of the current issue. Probably you can think of times when friendly arguments ended up with everyone involved coming to a better understanding of the others' views. And probably you can think of other times when someone was so concerned with winning an argument that even though the person might have been technically right, hard feelings were created that lasted for years.

Usually, listeners and readers are more willing to consider your argument seriously if you cast yourself as a respectful partner rather than as a competitor and put forth your arguments in the spirit of mutual support and negotiation—in the interest of finding the *best* way, not "my way." How can you be the person that your reader will want to cooperate with rather than resist? Here are a few suggestions, both for your writing and for discussing controversial issues in class:

- **Try to think of yourself as engaged not so much in winning over your audience as in courting your audience's cooperation.** It is important to argue vigorously, but you don't want to argue so vigorously that opposing views are vanquished or silenced. Remember that your goal is to invite a response that creates a dialog.

- **Show that you understand and genuinely respect your listener's or reader's position even if you think the position is ultimately wrong.** Often, that amounts to remembering to argue against an opponent's position, not against the opponent himself or herself. It often means representing your opponent's position in terms that your opponent would accept. Look for ground that you already share with your reader, and search for even more. See yourself as a mediator. Consider that neither you nor the other person has arrived at a best solution, and carry on in the hope that dialog will lead to an even better course of action than the one you now recommend. Expect and assume the best of your listener or reader, and deliver your own best yourself.

Cultivate a sense of humor and a distinctive voice. Many textbooks on argument emphasize using a reasonable voice. But a reasonable voice doesn't have to be a dull one. Humor is a legitimate tool of argument. Although playing an issue strictly for laughs risks not having the reader take it seriously, nothing creates a sense of goodwill quite so much as good humor. You will be seen as open to new possibilities and to cooperation if you occasionally show a sense of humor. And a sense of humor can sometimes be especially welcome when the stakes are high, the sides have been chosen, and tempers are flaring.

Consider that your argument might be just one move in a larger process that might end up helping *you*. Most times we argue because we think we have something to offer. But in the process of developing and presenting your views, realize also that you might learn something in the course of your research or from an argument that answers your own. Holding onto that attitude will keep you from becoming too overbearing and dogmatic.

CHAPTER 1

What to Argue About

A Book That Changed the World

In 1958, Rachel Carson received a copy of a letter that her friend Olga Huckens had sent to the *Boston Herald*. The letter described what had happened during the previous summer when Duxbury, Massachusetts, a small town just north of Cape Cod where Huckens lived, was sprayed several times from an airplane with the chemical pesticide DDT to kill mosquitoes. The mosquitoes came back as hungry as ever, but the songbirds, bees, and other insects vanished except for a few dead birds that Huckens had to pick up out of her yard. Huckens asked Carson if she knew anyone in Washington who could help to stop the spraying.

Rachel Carson

The letter from Olga Huckens struck a nerve with Rachel Carson. Carson was a marine biologist who had worked for many years for the U.S. Fish and Wildlife Service and who had written three highly acclaimed books about the sea and wetlands. In 1944, she published an article on how bats use radarlike echoes to find insects, which was reprinted in *Reader's Digest* in 1945. The editors at *Reader's Digest* asked whether she could write something else for them, and Carson replied in a letter that she wanted to write about experiments using DDT. DDT was being hyped as the solution for controlling insect pests, but Carson knew in 1945 that fish, waterfowl, and other animals would also be poisoned by widespread spraying and that eventually people could die too. *Reader's Digest* was not interested in Carson's proposed article, so she dropped the idea and went on to write about other things.

Huckens's letter brought Carson back to the subject of chemical spraying. In the late 1940s and 1950s, pesticides—especially the chlorinated hydrocarbons DDT, aldrin, and dieldrin—were sprayed on a massive scale throughout the United States and were hailed as a panacea for world hunger and famine. In 1957, much of the greater New York City area, including Long Island, was sprayed with DDT to kill gypsy moths. But there were noticeable side effects. Many people complained about not only birds, fish, and useful insects being killed but also their plants, shrubs, and pets. Other scientists had written about the dangers of massive spraying of pesticides, but they had not convinced the public of the hazards of pesticides and of the urgency for change.

Rachel Carson decided that she needed to write a magazine article about the facts of DDT. When she contacted *Reader's Digest* and other magazines, she found that they still would not consider publishing on the subject. Carson then concluded that she should write a short book. She knew that her job was not going to be an easy one because people in the United States still trusted science to solve all problems. Science had brought the "green revolution" that greatly increased crop yields through the use of chemical fertilizers and chemical pesticides. Carson's subject matter was also technical and difficult to communicate to the general public. The public did not think much at that time about air and water pollution, and most people were unaware that pesticides could poison humans as well as insects. And she was sure to face opposition from the pesticide industry, which had become a multimillion-dollar business. Carson knew the pesticide industry would do everything it could to stop her from publishing and to discredit her if she did.

Rachel Carson nonetheless wrote her book, *Silent Spring*. It sounded the alarm about the dangers caused by the overuse of pesticides, and the controversy it raised has still not ended. No book has had a greater impact on our thinking about the environment. *Silent Spring* was first published in installments in *The New Yorker* in the summer of 1962, and it created an immediate furor. Chemical companies threatened to sue Carson, and the trade associations that they sponsored launched full-scale attacks against the book in pamphlets and magazine articles. The chemical companies treated *Silent Spring* as a public relations problem; they hired scientists whose only job was to ridicule the book and to dismiss Carson as a "hysterical woman." Some even accused *Silent Spring* of being part of a communist plot to ruin U.S. agriculture.

But the public controversy over *Silent Spring* had another effect. It helped to make the book a success shortly after it was published in September 1962. A half million hardcover copies of *Silent Spring* were sold, keeping it on the best-seller list for thirty-one weeks. President John F. Kennedy read *Silent Spring* and met with Carson and other scientists to discuss the pesticide problem. Kennedy requested that the President's Scientific Advisory Committee study the effects of pesticides and make a report.

> **That we still talk so much about the environment is testimony to the lasting power of *Silent Spring*.**

This report found evidence around the world of high levels of pesticides in the environment, including the tissues of humans. The report confirmed what Carson had described in *Silent Spring*.

In the words of a news commentator at the time, *Silent Spring* "lit a fire" under the government. Many congressional hearings were held on the effects of pesticides and other pollutants on the environment. In 1967, the Environmental Defense Fund was formed; it developed the guidelines under which DDT was eventually banned. Three years later, President Richard Nixon became convinced that only an independent agency within the executive branch could operate with enough independence to enforce environmental regulations. Nixon created the Environmental Protection Agency (EPA) in December 1970, and he named William Ruckelshaus as its first head. One of the missions of the EPA, according to Ruckelshaus, was to develop an environmental ethic.

The United States was not the only country to respond to *Silent Spring*. The book was widely translated and inspired legislation on the environment in nearly all industrialized nations. Moreover, it changed the way we think about the environment. Carson pointed out that the nerve gases that were developed for use on our enemies in World War II were being used as pesticides after the war. She criticized the view of the environment as a battlefield where people make war on those natural forces that they believe impede their progress. Instead, she advocated living in coexistence with the environment because we are part of it. She was not totally opposed to pesticides, but she wanted to make people more aware of the environment as a whole and how changing one part would affect other parts. Her message was to try to live in balance with nature. That we still talk so much about the environment is testimony to the lasting power of *Silent Spring*. In 1980, Rachel Carson was posthumously awarded the highest civilian decoration in the nation, the Presidential Medal of Freedom. The citation accompanying the award expresses the way she is remembered:

> Never silent herself in the face of destructive trends, Rachel Carson fed a spring of awareness across America and beyond. A biologist with a gentle, clear voice, she welcomed her audiences to her love of the sea, while with an equally clear voice she warned Americans of the dangers human beings themselves pose for their own environment. Always concerned, always eloquent, she created a tide of environmental consciousness that has not ebbed.

Why *Silent Spring* Became a Classic

A book that covered much of the same ground as *Silent Spring*, titled *Our Synthetic Environment*, had been published six months earlier. The author, Murray Bookchin, writing under the pen name Lewis Herber, also wrote about the pollution of the natural world and the effects on people. Bookchin was as committed to warning people about the hazards of pesticides as Carson, but *Our Synthetic Environment* was read only by a small community of scientists. Why, then, did Carson succeed in reaching a larger audience?

Rachel Carson had far more impact than Murray Bookchin not simply because she was a more talented writer or because she was a scientist while Bookchin was not. She also thought a great deal about who she was writing for—her **audience.** If she was going to stop the widespread spraying of dangerous pesticides, she knew she would have to connect with the values of a wide audience, an audience that included a large segment of the public as well as other scientists.

The opening chapter in *Silent Spring* begins not by announcing Carson's thesis or giving a list of facts. Instead, the book starts out with a short fable about a small town located in the middle of prosperous farmland, where wildflowers bloomed much of the year, trout swam in the streams, and wildlife was abundant. Suddenly, a strange blight came on the town, as if an evil spell had been cast upon it. The chickens, sheep, and cattle on the farms grew sick and died. The families of the townspeople and farmers alike developed mysterious illnesses. Most of the birds disappeared, and the few that remained could neither sing nor fly. The apple trees bloomed, but there were no bees to pollinate the trees, and so they bore no fruit. The wildflowers withered as if they had been burned. Fishermen quit going to the streams because the fish had all died.

But it wasn't witchcraft that caused everything to grow sick and die. Carson writes that "the people had done it to themselves." She continues, "I know of no community that has experienced all the misfortunes I describe. Yet every one of these disasters has actually happened somewhere, and many real communities have already suffered a substantial number of them. A grim specter has crept upon us almost unnoticed, and this imagined tragedy may easily become a stark reality." Carson's fable did happen several times after the book was published. In July 1976, a chemical reaction went out of control at a plant near Seveso, Italy, and a cloud of powdery white crystals of almost pure dioxin fell on the town. The children ran out to play in the powder because it looked like snow. Within four days, plants, birds, and animals began dying, and the next week, people started getting sick. Most of the people had to go to the hospital, and everyone had to move out of the town. An even worse disaster happened in December 1982, when a storage tank in a pesticide plant exploded near Bhopal, India, showering the town. Two thousand people died quickly, and another fifty thousand became sick for the rest of their lives.

Perhaps if Rachel Carson were alive today and writing a book about the dangers of pesticides, she might begin differently. But remember that at the time she was writing, people trusted pesticides and believed that DDT was a miracle solution for all sorts of insect pests. She first had to make people aware that DDT could be harmful to them. In the second chapter of *Silent Spring* (reprinted at the end of this chapter), Carson continued appealing to the emotions of her audience. People in 1962 knew about the dangers of radiation even if they were ignorant about pesticides. They knew that the atomic bombs that had been dropped on Hiroshima and Nagasaki at the end of World War II were still killing Japanese people through the effects of radiation many years later, and they feared the fallout from nuclear bombs that were still being tested and stockpiled in the United States and Soviet Union.

Getting people's attention by exposing the threat of pesticides wasn't enough by itself. There are always people writing about various kinds of threats, and most aren't taken seriously except by those who already believe that the threats exist. Carson wanted to reach people who didn't think that pesticides were a threat but might be persuaded to take this view. To convince these people, she had to explain why pesticides are potentially dangerous, and she had to make readers believe that she could be trusted.

Rachel Carson was an expert marine biologist. To write *Silent Spring*, she had to read widely in sciences that she had not studied, including research about insects, toxic chemicals, cell physiology, biochemistry, plant and soil science, and public health. Then she had to explain complex scientific processes to people who had very little or no background in science. It was a very difficult and frustrating task. While writing *Silent Spring*, Carson confided in a letter to a friend the problems she was having: "How to reveal

Tactics of *Silent Spring*

Chapter 1 of *Silent Spring* tells a parable of a rural town where the birds, fish, flowers, and plants die and people become sick after a white powder is sprayed on the town. At the beginning of Chapter 2, Rachel Carson begins her argument against the mass aerial spraying of pesticides. Most of her readers were not aware of the dangers of pesticides, but they were well aware of the harmful effects of radiation. Let's look at her tactics:

The history of life on earth has been a history of interaction between living things and their surroundings. To a large extent, the physical form and the habits of earth's vegetation and its animal life have been molded by the environment. Considering the whole span of earthly time, the opposite effect, in which life actually modifies its surroundings, has been relatively slight. Only within the moment of time represented by the present century has one species—man—acquired significant power to alter the nature of his world.

> The interrelationship of people and the environment provides the basis for Carson's argument.

During the past quarter century this power has not only increased to one of disturbing magnitude but it has changed in character. The most alarming of all man's assaults upon the environment is the contamination of air, earth, rivers, and sea with dangerous and even lethal materials. This pollution is for the most part irrecoverable; the chain of life it initiates not only in the world that must support life but in living tissues is for the most part irreversible. In this now universal contamination of the environment, chemicals are the sinister and little-recognized partners of radiation in changing the very nature of the world—the very nature of its life. Strontium 90, released through nuclear explosions into the air, comes to earth in rain or drifts down as fallout, lodges in the soil, enters into the grass or corn or wheat grown there, and in time takes its abode in the

> Carson shifts her language to a metaphor of war against the environment rather than interaction with the natural world.

> In 1963 the first treaty was signed by the United States and the Soviet Union that banned the testing of nuclear weapons above ground, under water, and in space.

(continued)

Tactics of *Silent Spring* (continued)

The key move: Carson associates the dangers of chemical pesticides with those of radiation.

bones of a human being, there to remain until his death. Similarly, chemicals sprayed on croplands or forests or gardens lie long in soil, entering into living organisms, passing from one to another in a chain of poisoning and death. Or they pass mysteriously by underground streams until they emerge and, through the alchemy of air and sunlight, combine into new forms that kill vegetation, sicken cattle, and work unknown harm on those who drink from once-pure wells. As Albert Schweitzer has said, "Man can hardly even recognize the devils of his own creation."

Albert Schweitzer (1875–1965) was a concert musician, philosopher, and doctor who spent most of his life as a medical missionary in Africa.

enough to give understanding of the most serious effects of the chemicals without being technical, how to simplify without error—these have been problems of rather monumental proportions."

To make people understand the bad effects of pesticides required explaining what is not common sense: why very tiny amounts of pesticides can be so harmful. The reason lies in how pesticides are absorbed by the body. DDT is fat-soluble and gets stored in organs such as the adrenals, thyroid, liver, and kidneys. Carson explains how pesticides build up in the body:

> This storage of DDT begins with the smallest conceivable intake of the chemical (which is present as residues on most foodstuffs) and continues until quite high levels are reached. The fatty storage deposits act as biological magnifiers, so that an intake of as little as $\frac{1}{10}$ of 1 part per million in the diet results in storage of about 10 to 15 parts per million, an increase of one hundredfold or more. These terms of reference, so commonplace to the chemist or the pharmacologist, are unfamiliar to most of us. One part in a million sounds like a very small amount—and so it is. But such substances are so potent that a minute quantity can bring about vast changes in the body. In animal experiments, 3 parts per million has been found to inhibit an essential enzyme in the heart muscle; only 5 parts per million has brought about necrosis or disintegration of liver cells.

Throughout the book, Carson succeeds in translating scientific facts into language that, to use her words, "most of us" can understand. Of course Carson was a scientist and quite capable of reading scientific articles. She establishes her credibility as a scientist by using technical terms such as *necrosis*. But at the same time she identifies herself with people who are not scientists and gains our trust by taking our point of view.

To accompany these facts, Carson tells about places that have been affected by pesticides. One of the more memorable stories is about Clear Lake, California, in the mountainous country north of San Francisco. Clear Lake is popular for fishing, but it is also an ideal habitat for a species of gnat. In the late 1940s the state of California began spraying the lake with DDD, a close relative of DDT. Spraying had to be repeated because the gnats kept coming back. The western grebes that lived on the lake began to die, and when scientists examined their bodies, the grebes were loaded with extraordinary levels of DDD. Microscopic plants and animals filtered the lake water for nutrients and concentrated the pesticides at 20 times their level in the lake water. Small fish ate these tiny plants and animals and again concentrated the DDD at levels 10 to 100 times that of their microscopic food. The grebes that ate the fish suffered the effects of this huge magnification.

Although DDT is still used in parts of the developing world, the influence of *Silent Spring* led to the banning of it and most other similar pesticides in the United States and Canada. Rachel Carson's book eventually led people to stop relying only on pesticides and to look instead to other methods of controlling pests, such as planting crops that are resistant to insects and disease. When pesticides are used today, they typically are applied much more selectively and in lower amounts than was common when Carson was writing.

Rachel Carson's more lasting legacy is our awareness of our environment. She urges us to be aware that we share this planet with other creatures and that "we are dealing with life—with living populations and all their pressures and counterpressures, their surges and recessions." She warns against dismissing the balance of nature. She writes:

> The balance of nature is not the same today as in Pleistocene times, but it is still there: a complex, precise, and highly integrated system of relationships between living things which cannot safely be ignored any more than the law of gravity can be defied with impunity by a man perched on the edge of a cliff. The balance of nature is not a *status quo*; it is fluid, ever shifting, in a constant state of adjustment.

Since the publication of *Silent Spring*, we have grown much more conscious of large-scale effects on ecosystems caused by global warming, acid rain, and the depleted ozone layer in addition to the local effects of pesticides described in Carson's book. The cooperation of nations today in attempting to control air and water pollution, in encouraging more efficient use of energy and natural resources, and in promoting sustainable patterns of consumption is due in no small part to the long-term influence of *Silent Spring*.

Analyzing Arguments: Pathos, Ethos, and Logos

When the modern concept of democracy was developed in Greece in the fifth century B.C.E., the study of rhetoric also began. It's not a coincidence that the teaching of rhetoric was closely tied to the rise of democracy. In the Greek city-states, all citizens had the right to speak and vote at the popular assembly and in the committees of the assembly that functioned as the criminal courts. Citizens took turns serving as the officials of government. Because the citizens of Athens and other city-states took their responsibilities quite seriously, they highly valued the ability to speak effectively in public. Teachers of rhetoric were held in great esteem.

In the next century, the most important teacher of rhetoric in ancient Greece, Aristotle (384–323 B.C.E.), made the study of rhetoric systematic. He defined *rhetoric* as the art of finding the best available means of persuasion in any situation. Aristotle set out three primary tactics of argument: appeals to the emotions and deepest-held values of the audience (*pathos*), appeals based on the trustworthiness of the speaker (*ethos*), and appeals to good reasons (*logos*).

Carson makes these appeals with great skill in *Silent Spring*. Very simply, her purpose is to stop pesticide pollution. She first appeals to *pathos*, engaging her readers in her subject. She gives many specific examples of how pesticides have accumulated in the bodies of animals and people. But she also engages her readers through her skill as a writer, making us care about nature as well as be concerned about our own safety. She uses the fate of robins to symbolize her crusade. Robins were the victims of spraying for Dutch elm disease. Robins feed on earthworms, which in turn process fallen elm leaves. The earthworms act as magnifiers of the pesticide, which either kills the robins outright or renders them sterile. Thus when no robins sang, it was indeed a silent spring.

Carson is also successful in creating a credible *ethos*. We believe her not just because she establishes her expertise. She convinces us also because she establishes her ethos as a person with her audience's best interests at heart. She anticipates possible objections, demonstrating that she has thought about opposing positions. She takes time to explain concepts that most people do not understand fully, and she discusses how everyone can benefit if we take a different attitude toward nature. She shows that she has done her homework on the topic. By creating a credible ethos,

(continued)

Analyzing Arguments: Pathos, Ethos, and Logos (continued)

Carson makes an effective moral argument that humans as a species have a responsibility not to destroy the world they live in.

Finally, Carson supports her argument with good reasons, what Aristotle called *logos*. She offers "because clauses" to support her main claims. She describes webs of relationships among the earth, plants, animals, and humans, and she explains how changing one part will affect the others. Her point is not that we should never disturb these relationships but that we should be as aware as possible of the consequences.

Reading Arguments

If you have ever been coached in a sport or have been taught an art such as dancing or playing a musical instrument, you likely have viewed a game or a performance in two ways. You might enjoy the game or performance like everyone else, but at the same time, you might be especially aware of something that you know from your experience is difficult to do and therefore appreciated the skill and the practice necessary to develop it. A similar distinction can be made about two kinds of reading. For the sake of convenience, the first can be called *ordinary reading*, although we don't really think there is a single kind of ordinary reading. In ordinary reading, on the first time through, the reader forms a sense of content and gets an initial impression: whether it's interesting, whether the author has something important to say, whether you agree or disagree.

For most of what you read, one time through is enough. When you read for the second or third time, you start to use different strategies because you have some reason to do so. You are no longer reading to form a sense of the overall content. Often, you are looking for something in particular. If you reread a textbook chapter, you might want to make sure you understand how a key concept is being used. When you reread your apartment contract, you might want to know what is required to get your deposit back. This second kind of reading can be called *critical reading*. Critical reading does not mean criticizing what the writer has to say (although that's certainly possible). Critical reading begins with questions and specific goals.

Writers of arguments engage in critical reading even on the first time through. They know that they will have to acknowledge what else has been written about a particular issue. If the issue is new (and few are), then the writer will need to establish its significance by comparing it to other issues on

Become a Critical Reader

The best way to read arguments is with a pencil—not a pen or highlighter. Pens don't erase, and highlighters are distracting. Much of the time, you don't know what is important the first time through an argument, and highlighters don't tell you why something is important. Use a pencil instead, and write in the margins.

If you are reading on a computer screen, open a new window in your word processing program so that you can write while you read. Reading on a computer has the advantage of letting you copy parts of what you read to your file. You just have to be careful to distinguish what you copy from what you write. Always remember to include the information about where it came from. (Your Web browser allows you to copy text and paste it in a new file. Look in the Edit menu on Netscape or Internet Explorer.)

Before you start reading, find out when the argument was written, where it first appeared, and who wrote it. Arguments don't appear in vacuums. They most often occur in response to something else that has been written or some event that has happened. In this book, you'll find this information in the headnotes. You also have a title, which suggests what the argument might be about. This information will help you to form an initial impression about why the writer wrote this particular argument, who the writer imagined as the readers, and what purposes the writer might have had in mind. Then pick up your pencil and start reading.

Ask Questions

On the first time through, you need to understand what's in the argument. So circle the words and references that you don't know and look them up. If a statement part of the argument isn't clear, note that section in the margin. You might figure out what the writer is arguing later, or you might have to work through it slowly a second time through.

Analyze

On your second reading, you should start analyzing the structure of the argument. Here's how to do it:

- Identify the writer's main claim or claims. You should be able to paraphrase it if it doesn't appear explicitly.

(continued)

Become a Critical Reader (continued)

- What are the reasons that support the claim? List them by number in the margins. There might be only one reason, or there could be several (and some reasons could be supported by others).

- Where is the evidence? Does it really support the reasons? Can you think of contradictory evidence?

- Does the writer refer to expert opinion or research about this subject? Do other experts see this issue differently?

- Does the writer acknowledge opposing views? Does the writer deal fairly with opposing views?

Respond

Write your thoughts as you read. Often you will find that something you read reminds you of something else. Jot that down. It might be something to think about later, and it might give you ideas for writing. Think also about what else you should read if you want to write about this topic. Or you might want to write down whether you are persuaded by the argument and why.

which much has been written. Writers of argument, therefore, begin reading with **questions.** They want to know *why* a particular argument was written. They want to know *what* the writer's basic assumptions are. They want to know *who* the writer had in mind when the argument was written. Critical readers most often read with pen or pencil in hand or with a window open on their computer in which they can write. They write their questions in the margins or in the file.

Critical readers do more than just question what they read. They **analyze** how the argument works. Critical readers look at how an argument is laid out. They identify key terms and examine how the writer is using them. They consider how the writer appeals to our emotions, represents himself or herself, and uses good reasons. They analyze the structure of an argument—the organization—and the way in which it is written—the style.

Finally, critical readers often **respond** as they read. They don't just take in what they read in a passive way. They jot down notes to themselves in the margins or on the blank pages at the front and back of a book. They use these notes later when they start writing. Reading is often the best way to get started writing.

Finding Arguments

Rachel Carson did not so much find the subject for *Silent Spring* as the subject found her. She wrote about a subject that she had cared about for many years. Subjects that we argue about often find us. There are enough of them in daily life. We're late for work because the traffic is bad or the bus doesn't run on time. We can't find a place to park when we get to school or work. We have to negotiate through various bureaucracies for almost anything we do—making an appointment to see a doctor, getting a course added or dropped, or correcting a mistake on a bill. Most of the time, we grumble and let it go at that.

But sometimes, like Rachel Carson, we stick with a subject. Neighborhood groups in cities and towns have been especially effective in getting things done by writing about them—from stopping a new road from being built to getting better police and fire protection to having a vacant lot turned into a park. Most jobs that require college degrees sooner or later demand the ability to write extended arguments. Usually, it is sooner; the primary cause of new employees being fired during their first year at *Fortune* 500 companies is poor communications skills. If your writing skills are not up to speed, you may pay heavily down the road.

Being either inspired or required to write an argument is only the beginning. Once Rachel Carson decided that she wanted to write a book about the hazards of pesticides, she did her homework before she started writing. She used these questions as guides to her research:

- How do pesticides work?
- Why are pesticides used?
- Who and what benefits from the use of pesticides?
- Who or what is harmed by the use of pesticides?
- Who creates pesticides?
- Who supports the use of pesticides?
- When can pesticides be used beneficially? When is their use harmful?
- What alternatives to pesticides are feasible?

Position and Proposal Arguments

In *Silent Spring,* Rachel Carson made an effective argument against the massive use of synthetic pesticides. Arguing against the indiscriminate use of pesticides, however, did not solve the problem of what to do about harmful insects that destroy crops and spread disease. Carson also did the harder job of offering solutions. In her final chapter, "The Other Road," Carson gives alternatives to the massive use of pesticides. She describes how a pest organism's natural enemies can be used against it instead.

These two kinds of arguments can be characterized as **position** and **proposal** arguments.

Position Arguments

In a position argument, the writer makes a claim about a controversial issue.

- **The writer first has to define the issue.** Carson had to explain what synthetic pesticides are in chemical terms and how they work, and she had to give a history of their increasing use after World War II before she could begin arguing against pesticides.

- **The writer should take a clear position.** Carson wasted no time setting out her position by describing the threat that high levels of pesticides pose to people worldwide.

- **The writer should make a convincing argument and acknowledge opposing views.** Carson used a variety of strategies in support of her position, including research studies, quotes from authorities, and her own analyses and observations. She took into account opposing views by acknowledging that harmful insects needed to be controlled and conceded that selective spraying is necessary and desirable.

Proposal Arguments

In a proposal argument, the writer proposes a course of action in response to a recognizable problem situation. The proposal says what can be done to improve the situation or change it altogether.

- **The writer first has to define the problem.** The problem Carson had to define was complex. Not only was the overuse of pesticides

(continued)

Position and Proposal Arguments (continued)

killing helpful insects, plants, and animals and threatening people, but the harmful insects the pesticides were intended to eliminate were becoming increasingly resistant. More spraying and more frequent spraying produced pesticide-resistant "superbugs." Mass spraying resulted in actually helping bad bugs such as fire ants by killing off their competition.

- **The writer has to propose a solution or solutions.** Carson did not hold out for one particular approach to controlling insects, but she did advocate biological solutions. She proposed biological alternatives to pesticides, such as sterilizing and releasing large numbers of male insects and introducing predators of pest insects. Above all, she urged that we work with nature rather than being at war with it.

- **The solution or solutions must work, and they must be feasible.** The projected consequences should be set out, arguing that good things will happen, bad things will be avoided, or both. Carson discussed research studies that indicated her solutions would work, and she argued that they would be less expensive than massive spraying. Today, we can look at Carson's book with the benefit of hindsight. Not everything Carson proposed ended up working, but her primary solution—learn to live with nature—has been a powerful one. Mass spraying of pesticides has stopped in the United States, and species that were threatened by the excessive use of pesticides, including falcons, eagles, and brown pelicans, have made remarkable comebacks.

In much the same way, you can explore a topic by asking questions.

Carson also kept in mind what had been written before about the environment. She was trained as a scientist, and she could have written only for other scientists. But she wanted to reach a much wider audience, and she wanted people to think about more than just the hazards of pesticides. She wanted to create a revolution in the way we think about the environment. Carson's respect for the integrity and interconnectedness of life contributed a great deal to the power of her argument. Her goal was not so much to make chemical companies into the Evil Ones as it was to promote a different way of thinking that would reconnect people with the world around them. She

alludes to Robert Frost's poem "The Road Not Taken" for her concluding chapter, "The Other Road." "We stand now where two roads diverge,"
she says, the one "a smooth superhighway on which we progress with great
speed" but on which disaster lies at the end, the other the road "less-traveled"
but on which is our chance to preserve the earth. The greatest legacy of *Silent
Spring* is that we are still concerned with and actively discussing the issues she
raised.

RACHEL CARSON

The Obligation to Endure

*Rachel Carson (1907–1964) was born and grew up in Springdale,
Pennsylvania, eighteen miles up the Allegheny River from Pittsburgh.
When Carson was in elementary school, her mother was fearful of
infectious diseases that were sweeping through the nation and often
kept young Rachel out of school. In her wandering on the family farm,
Rachel developed the love of nature that she maintained throughout
her life. At twenty-two she began her career as a marine biologist at
Woods Hole, Massachusetts, and she later went to graduate school at
Johns Hopkins University in Baltimore. She began working for the U.S.
government in 1936 in the agency that later became the Fish and
Wildlife Service, and she was soon recognized as a talented writer as
well as a meticulous scientist. She wrote three highly praised books
about the sea and wetlands:* Under the Sea Wind *(1941),* The Sea
around Us *(1951), and* The Edge of the Sea *(1954).*

Carson's decision to write Silent Spring *marked a great change in
her life. For the first time, she became an environmental activist rather
than an inspired and enthusiastic writer about nature. She had written
about the interconnectedness of life in her previous three books, but with*
Silent Spring *she had to convince people that hazards lie in what had
seemed familiar and harmless. Although many people think of birds
when they hear Rachel Carson's name, she was the first scientist to
make a comprehensive argument that links cancer to environmental
causes. Earlier in this chapter, you saw how Carson associated pesticides
with the dangers of radiation from nuclear weapons. Notice how else
she gets her readers to think differently about pesticides in this selection,
which begins Chapter 2 of* Silent Spring.*

1   **THE** history of life on earth has been a history of interaction between living things and their surroundings. To a large extent, the physical form and the habits of the earth's vegetation and its animal life have been molded by the environment. Considering the whole span of earthly time, the opposite effect, in which life actually modifies its surroundings, has been relatively slight. Only within the moment of time represented by the present century has one species—man—acquired significant power to alter the nature of his world.

2   During the past quarter century this power has not only increased to one of disturbing magnitude but it has changed in character. The most alarming of all man's assaults upon the environment is the contamination of air, earth, rivers, and sea with dangerous and even lethal materials. This pollution is for the most part irrecoverable; the chain of evil it initiates not only in the world that must support life but in living tissues is for the most part irreversible. In this now universal contamination of the environment, chemicals are the sinister and little recognized partners of radiation in changing the very nature of the world—the very nature of its life. Strontium 90, released through nuclear explosions into the air, comes to earth in rain or drifts down as fallout, lodges in soil, enters into the grass or corn or wheat grown there, and in time takes up its abode in the bones of a human being, there to remain until his death. Similarly, chemicals sprayed on croplands or forests or gardens lie long in soil, entering into living organisms, passing from one to another in a chain of poisoning and death. Or they pass mysteriously by underground streams until they emerge and, through the alchemy of air and sunlight, combine into new forms that kill vegetation, sicken cattle, and work unknown harm on those who drink from once-pure wells. As Albert Schweitzer has said, "Man can hardly even recognize the devils of his own creation."

3   It took hundreds of millions of years to produce the life that now inhabits the earth—eons of time in which that developing and evolving and diversifying life reached a state of adjustment and balance with its surroundings. The environment, rigorously shaping and directing the life it supported, contained elements that were hostile as well as supporting. Certain rocks gave out dangerous radiation; even within the light of the sun, from which all life draws its energy, there were short-wave radiations with power to injure. Given time—time not in years but in millennia—life adjusts, and a balance has been reached. For time is the essential ingredient; but in the modern world there is no time.

4   The rapidity of change and the speed with which new situations are created follow the impetuous and heedless pace of man rather than the deliberate pace of nature. Radiation is no longer merely the background radiation of rocks, the bombardment of cosmic rays, the ultraviolet of the sun that have existed before there was any life on earth; radiation is now the unnatural creation of man's tampering with the atom. The chemicals to which life is asked to make its adjustment are no longer merely the calcium and silica and copper and all the rest of the minerals washed out of the rocks and carried in rivers to the sea; they are the synthetic creations of man's inventive mind, brewed in his laboratories, and having no counterparts in nature.

5   To adjust to these chemicals would require time on the scale that is nature's; it would require not merely the years of a man's life but the life of generations. And even this, were it by some miracle possible, would be futile, for the new chemicals come from our laboratories in an endless stream; almost five hundred annually find their way into actual use in the United States alone. The figure is staggering and its implications are not easily grasped—500 new chemicals to which the bodies of men and animals are required somehow to adapt each year, chemicals totally outside the limits of biologic experience.

6   Among them are many that are used in man's war against nature. Since the mid-1940s over 200 basic chemicals have been created for use in killing insects, weeds, rodents, and other organisms described in the modern vernacular as "pests"; and they are sold under several thousand different brand names.

7   These sprays, dusts, and aerosols are now applied almost universally to farms, gardens, forests, and homes—nonselective chemicals that have the power to kill every insect, the "good" and the "bad," to still the song of birds and the leaping of fish in the streams, to coat the leaves with a deadly film, and to linger on in soil—all this though the intended target may be only a few weeds or insects. Can anyone believe it is possible to lay down such a barrage of poisons on the surface of the earth without making it unfit for all life? They should not be called "insecticides," but "biocides."

8   The whole process of spraying seems caught up in an endless spiral. Since DDT was released for civilian use, a process of escalation has been going on in which ever more toxic materials must be found. This has happened because insects, in a triumphant vindication of Darwin's principle of the survival of the fittest, have evolved super races immune to the par-

ticular insecticide used, hence a deadlier one has always to be developed—and then a deadlier one than that. It has happened also because, for reasons to be described later, destructive insects often undergo a "flareback," or resurgence, after spraying, in numbers greater than before. Thus the chemical war is never won, and all life is caught in its violent crossfire.

9   Along with the possibility of the extinction of mankind by nuclear war, the central problem of our age has therefore become the contamination of man's total environment with such substances of incredible potential for harm—substances that accumulate in the tissues of plants and animals and even penetrate the germ cells to shatter or alter the very material of heredity upon which the shape of the future depends.

10   Some would-be architects of our future look toward a time when it will be possible to alter the human germ plasm by design. But we may easily be doing so now by inadvertence, for many chemicals, like radiation, bring about gene mutations. It is ironic to think that man might determine his own future by something so seemingly trivial as the choice of an insect spray.

11   All this has been risked—for what? Future historians may well be amazed by our distorted sense of proportion. How could intelligent beings seek to control a few unwanted species by a method that contaminated the entire environment and brought the threat of disease and death even to their own kind? Yet this is precisely what we have done. We have done it, moreover, for reasons that collapse the moment we examine them. We are told that the enormous and expanding use of pesticides is necessary to maintain farm production. Yet is our real problem not one of *overproduc - tion?* Our farms, despite measures to remove acreages from production and to pay farmers *not* to produce, have yielded such a staggering excess of crops that the American taxpayer in 1962 is paying out more than one billion dollars a year as the total carrying cost of the surplus-food storage program. And is the situation helped when one branch of the Agriculture Department tries to reduce production while another states, as it did in 1958, "It is believed generally that reduction of crop acreages under provisions of the Soil Bank will stimulate interest in use of chemicals to obtain maximum production on the land retained in crops."

12   All this is not to say there is no insect problem and no need of control. I am saying, rather, that control must be geared to realities, not to mythical situations, and that the methods employed must be such that they do not destroy us along with the insects.

Getting Started: Listing and Analyzing Issues

A good way to get started is to list possible issues to write about. Make a list of questions that can be answered "YES because . . ." or "NO because . . ." (Following is a list to get you started.) These questions all ask whether we should do something, and therefore they are all phrased as arguments of policy. You'll find out that often before you can make recommendations of policy, you first have to analyze exactly what is meant by a phrase like *censorship of the Internet*. Does it mean censorship of the World Wide Web or of everything that goes over the Internet, including private email? To be convincing, you'll have to argue that one thing causes another, for good or bad.

Think about issues that affect your campus, the place where you live, the nation, and the world. Which ones interest you? In which could you make a contribution to the larger discussion?

Campus

- Should students be required to pay fees for access to computers on campus?
- Should smoking be banned on campus?
- Should varsity athletes get paid for playing sports that bring in revenue?
- Should admissions decisions be based exclusively on academic achievement?
- Should knowledge of a foreign language be required for all degree plans?
- Should your college or university have a computer literacy requirement?
- Should fraternities be banned from campuses if they are caught encouraging alcohol abuse?

Community

- Should people who ride bicycles and motorcycles be required to wear helmets?
- Should high schools be allowed to search students for drugs at any time?
- Should high schools distribute condoms?
- Should bilingual education programs be eliminated?
- Should the public schools be privatized?
- Should bike lanes be built throughout your community to encourage more people to ride bicycles?
- Should more tax dollars be shifted from building highways to public transportation?

Nation/World

- Should advertising be banned on television shows aimed at preschool children?
- Should capital punishment be abolished?
- Should the Internet be censored?
- Should the government be allowed to monitor all phone calls and all email to combat terrorism?
- Should handguns be outlawed?
- Should beef and poultry be free of growth hormones?
- Should a law be passed requiring that the parents of teenagers who have abortions be informed?
- Should people who are terminally ill be allowed to end their lives?
- Should it be made illegal to kill animals for their fur?
- Should the United States punish nations with poor human rights records?

After You Make a List

1. Put a check beside the issues that look most interesting to write about or the ones that mean the most to you.
2. Put a question mark beside the issues that you don't know very much about. If you choose one of these issues, you will probably have to do in-depth research—by talking to people, by using the Internet, or by going to the library.
3. Select the two or three issues that look most promising. For each issue, make another list:
   - Who is most interested in this issue?
   - Whom or what does this issue affect?
   - What are the pros and cons of this issue? Make two columns. At the top of the left one, write "YES because." At the top of the right one, write "NO because."
   - What has been written about this issue? How can you find out what has been written?

Getting Started: Making an Idea Map

When you identify an issue that looks promising and interests you, the next step is to discover how much you know about it and how many different aspects of it you can think of. One way to take this inventory is to make an *idea map* that describes visually how the many aspects of a particular issue relate to each other. Idea maps are useful because you can see everything at once and make connections among the different aspects of an issue—definitions, causes, effects, proposed solutions, and your personal experience.

A good way to get started is to write down ideas on sticky notes. Then you can move the sticky notes around until you figure out which ideas fit together.

As an example, let's say you pick binge drinking among college students. Several stories have been in your campus newspaper this year about binge drinking. You read an article recently that reported the results of an annual study of student drinking behavior done by Harvard University's School of Public Health. From this article you have a few statistics and facts to go with your knowledge of binge drinking. Figure 1.1 shows what your idea map might look like after you assemble your notes.

Causes of binge drinking
- Binge drinking is a part of college culture
- Alumni and students binge at tailgate parties at sporting events
- Many bars and liquor stores close to campus
- Many alcohol promotions such as 2-for-1 happy hours and free nights for women
- Administrators condone drinking
- No exams on Friday allow students to binge Thursday through Sunday

Harvard survey released March 2000
- 44% of 14,000 students surveyed at 119 schools reported that they had binged at least once in the preceding 2 weeks
- 23% are frequent bingers
- Little change in drinking patterns since 1994
- Increase in drinking deliberately to get drunk, and in alcohol-related problems—including injuries, drunk driving, violence, and academic difficulties

Definition of binge drinking
- More than 5 drinks a night for men
- More than 4 drinks a night for women

Experience with binge drinking
- Three students on my dorm floor are regular binge drinkers and become obnoxious
- Not enough alcohol-free alternatives at my school
- Legal drinking age of 21 leads to more drinking rather than less because it gives alcohol a mystique
- Students under much pressure and look for a release

Binge Drinking

Fraternities and sororities
- Harvard study reports 4 of 5 residents in fraternities and sororities binge
- Most recent alcohol-related deaths of college students involved fraternity parties
- High school seniors often go to fraternity parties
- Administrators hesitant to regulate fraternities for fear of angering alumni donors

Effects of binge drinking
- Rise in alcohol-related deaths on campus
- Colleges are being sued by families of students injured by excessive drinking
- Rise in alcohol-related problems including drunk driving and academic difficulties
- Binge drinkers harm nonbingers, interrupting sleep, committing violent acts, driving drunk

Proposed solutions to binge drinking
- Education campaigns about risks of binge drinking
- Ban alcohol in residence halls and in fraternities and sororities
- Ban alcohol and alcohol ads at sporting events
- Punish disruptive behavior
- Notify parents when students binge
- Provide alcohol-free alternatives

Figure 1.1 Idea Map on Binge Drinking

CHAPTER 2

Finding Good Reasons

The Basics of Arguments

Many people think of the term *argument* as a synonym for *debate*. College courses and professional careers, however, require a different kind of argument—one that, most of the time, is cooler in emotion and much more elaborate in detail than oral debate. At first glance an **argument** in writing doesn't seem to have much in common with debate. But the basic elements and ways of reasoning used in written arguments are similar to those we use in everyday conversations. Let's look at an example of an informal debate:

> **JEFF:** I think students should not have to pay tuition to go to state colleges and universities.
>
> **MARIA:** Cool idea, but why should students not have to pay?
>
> **JEFF:** Because you don't have to pay to go to high school.
>
> **MARIA:** Yeah, but that's different. The law says that everyone has to go to high school, at least to age 16. Everyone doesn't have to go to college.
>
> **JEFF:** Well, in some other countries like the United Kingdom, students don't have to pay tuition.

MARIA: The whole system of education is different in Britain from the United States. Plus you're wrong. Students started paying tuition at British universities in fall 1998.

JEFF: OK, maybe the United Kingdom isn't a good example. But students should have a right to go to college, just like they have the right to drive on the highway.

MARIA: Jeff, you pay for driving through taxes. Everyone who buys gas and has a driver's license helps pay for the highways. Going to college isn't necessary, and not everyone does it. Only people who go to college should pay. Why should everyone have to pay taxes for some people to go to college?

JEFF: Because our nation would be better if everyone had the opportunity to go to college free of charge.

MARIA: Why? What evidence do you have that things would be better if everyone went to college? It would put an enormous drain on the economy. People would have to pay a lot more in taxes.

JEFF: The way to help poor people is to provide them with a good education. That's what's wrong now: Poor people don't get a good education and can't afford to go to college.

In this discussion, Jeff starts out by making a **claim** that students should not have to pay tuition. Maria immediately asks him why students should not have to pay tuition. She wants a **good reason** to accept his claim. A reason is typically offered in a **because clause** that begins with the word *because* and then provides a supporting reason for the claim. Jeff's first attempt is to argue that students shouldn't have to pay to go to college *because* they don't have to pay to go to high school.

> **A good reason works because it includes a link to your claim that your readers will find valid.**

The word *because* signals a **link** between the reason and the claim. When Jeff tells Maria that students don't have to pay to go to public high schools, Maria does not accept the link. Maria asks **"So what?"** every time Jeff presents a new reason. She will accept Jeff's evidence only if she accepts that his reason supports his claim.

In this small discussion, we find the basics of arguments. Jeff makes a claim for which he offers a reason.

CLAIM ◀■■ REASON

Every argument that is more than a shouting match or a simple assertion has to be supported by one or more reasons. That reason in turn has to be linked to the claim if it is to become a *good reason*.

CLAIM ◀━━ *LINK (because)* ◀━━ REASON

Jeff's problem in convincing Maria is that he can't convince her to link his reasons to his claim. Maria challenges Jeff's links and keeps asking "So what?" For her, Jeff's reasons are not good reasons.

CLAIM ◀━━ *LINK (because)* ◀━━ REASON
               ↑
      CHALLENGES (So what?)

By the end of this short discussion, Jeff has begun to build an argument. He has had to come up with another claim to support his main claim, and if he is to convince Maria, he will probably have to provide a **series of claims** that she will accept as linked to his primary claim. He will also need to find evidence to support these claims.

CLAIM ◀━━ *LINK (because)* ◀━━ REASON ◀━━ EVIDENCE
               ↑
      CHALLENGES (So what?)

Benjamin Franklin observed that "so convenient a thing it is to be a rational creature, since it enables us to find or make a reason for every thing one has a mind to do." It is not hard to think of reasons. What is difficult is to convince your audience that your reasons are *good reasons*. In a conversation, you get immediate feedback that tells you whether your listener agrees or disagrees. When you are writing, you usually don't have someone reading who can question you immediately unless you are writing on a computer connected to other computers. Consequently, you have to be more specific about what you are claiming, you have to connect with the values you hold in common with your readers, and you have to anticipate what questions and objections your readers might have if you are going to convince someone who doesn't agree with you or know what you know already.

When you write an argument, imagine a reader like Maria who is going to listen carefully to what you have to say but is not going to agree with you automatically. When you present a reason, she will ask, "So what?" You will have to have evidence, and you will have to link it to your claim in ways she will accept if she is to agree that your reason is a good one.

To begin, you must make a claim. If that claim is very general, it is often hard to argue. For example, Jeff's assertion that our nation would be better off if everyone went to college is almost like saying our nation would be better if everyone obeyed traffic laws. Jeff's claim seems unrealistic because it doesn't

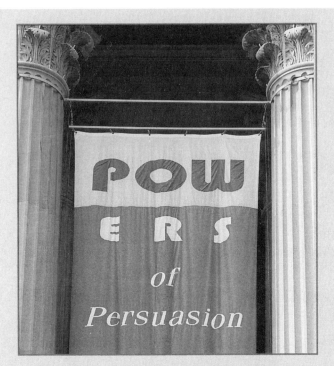

National Archives building, Washington, D.C.

take into account what it would take to accomplish the goal or why things would be better as a result. He makes a more specific claim in response to Maria that education is the route out of poverty, but that claim too is very broad.

Your claim should be specific, and it should be contestable. If you claim that you like sour cream on a baked potato, your claim is specific but not contestable. Someone could tell you that a baked potato is less fattening without sour cream, but it still doesn't change the fact that you like sour cream. Besides, you might want to gain weight.

What Is Not Arguable

Just about everything is arguable, but much of the time certain types of argument are not advanced. Statements of **facts** are usually not considered arguable. Jeff's claim that students at universities in the United Kingdom do

(continued)

What Is Not Arguable (continued)

not pay tuition is a statement of fact that turned out not to be true. Most facts can be verified by doing research. But even simple facts can sometimes be argued. For example, Mount Everest is usually acknowledged to be the highest mountain in the world at 29,028 feet above sea level. But if the total height of a mountain from base to summit is the measure, then the volcano Mauna Loa in Hawaii is the highest mountain in the world. Although the top of Mauna Loa is 13,667 feet above sea level, the summit is 31,784 above the ocean floor. Thus the "fact" that Mount Everest is the highest mountain on the earth depends on a definition of *highest* being the point farthest above sea level. You could argue for this definition.

Another category of claims that are not arguable are those of **personal taste.** Your favorite food and your favorite color are examples of personal taste. If you hate fresh tomatoes, no one can convince you that you actually like them. But many claims of personal taste turn out to be value judgments using arguable criteria. For example, if you think that *Alien* is the best science fiction movie ever made, you can argue that claim using evaluative criteria that other people can consider as good reasons (see Chapter 7). Indeed, you might not even like science fiction and still argue that *Alien* is the best science fiction movie ever.

Finally, many claims rest on **beliefs** or **faith**. If someone accepts a claim as a matter of religious belief, then for that person, the claim is true and cannot be refuted. Of course, people still make arguments about the existence of God and which religion reflects the will of God. Any time an audience will not consider an idea, it's possible but very difficult to construct an argument. Many people claim to have evidence that UFOs exist, but most people refuse to acknowledge that evidence as even being possibly factual.

The Basics of Reasoning

You decide to pick up a new pair of prescription sunglasses at the mall on your way to class. The company promises that it can make your glasses in an hour, but what you hadn't counted on was how long it would take you to park and how long you would wait in line at the counter. You jog into the mall, drop off your prescription, and go out of the store to wait. There's a booth nearby where volunteers are checking blood pressure. You don't have anything better to do, so you have your blood pressure checked.

After the volunteer takes the blood pressure cuff off your arm, he asks how old you are. He asks you whether you smoke, and you say no. He tells you that your reading is 150 over 100. He says that's high for a person your age and that you ought to have it checked again. "This is all I need," you think. "I have a test coming up tomorrow, a term paper due Friday, and if I don't make it to class, I won't get my homework turned in on time. And now something bad is wrong with me."

When you get your blood pressure checked again at the student health center after your test the next day, it turns out to be 120/80, which the nurse says is normal. When you think about it, you realize that you probably had a high reading because of stress and jogging into the mall.

Your blood pressure is one of the most important indicators of your health. When the volunteer checking your blood pressure tells you that you might have a serious health problem because your blood pressure is too high, he is relying on his knowledge of how the human body works. If your blood pressure is too high, it eventually damages your arteries and puts a strain on your entire body. But he used the word *might* because your blood pressure is not the same all the time. It can go up when you are under stress or even when you eat too much salt. And blood pressure varies from person to person and even in different parts of your body. For example, your blood pressure is higher in your legs than in your arms.

Doctors use blood pressure and other information to make diagnoses. Diagnoses are claims based on evidence. But as the blood pressure example shows, often the link is not clear, at least from a single reading. A doctor will collect several blood pressure readings over many weeks or even years before concluding that a patient has a condition of high blood pressure called *hypertension*. These readings will be compared to readings from thousands of other patients in making a diagnosis. Doctors are trained to rely on **generalizations** from thousands of past observations in medical science and to make diagnoses based on **probability.** In everyday life, you learn to make similar generalizations from which you make decisions based on probability. If you are in a hurry in the grocery store, you likely will go to the line that looks the shortest. You pick the shortest line because you think it will probably be the fastest.

Sometimes we don't have past experience to rely on, and we have to reason in other ways. When we claim that one thing is like something else, we make a link by **analogy.** Jeff's attempt to argue that American colleges and universities should be tuition free because British universities are tuition free is an argument by analogy. Analogies work only if the resemblances are more convincing than the dissimilarities. Maria pointed out that Jeff simply didn't know the facts.

Another way we reason is by using **cultural assumptions,** which we often think of as common sense. For example, you walk down the street and see a 280Z speed around a car that is double-parked, cross the double line, and side-swipe a truck coming the other way. A police officer arrives shortly, and you tell her that the 280Z is at fault. Maybe you've seen many accidents before, but the reason you think the 280Z is at fault is because in the United States, drivers are supposed to stay on the right side of two-way roads. It is part of our culture that you take for granted—that is, until you try to drive in Japan, Great Britain, or India, where people drive on the left. Driving on the left will seem unnatural to you, but it's natural for the people in those countries.

Driving on the right or left side of a street is a cultural assumption. Many assumptions are formally written down as laws. Others are simply part of cultural knowledge. There is no law that people who are waiting should stand in a line or that people who are first in line should receive attention first, but we think someone is rude who cuts in front of us when we stand in a line. In some other cultures, people don't stand in line when they wait. Crowding up to the counter, which seems rude to us, is the norm for them. Other cultures sometimes find the informality of Americans rude. For example, in some cultures, calling people by their first name when you first meet them is considered rude instead of friendly.

Particular cultural assumptions can be hard to challenge because you often have to take on an entire system of belief. The metric system is much easier to use to calculate distances than the English system of miles, feet, and inches. Nonetheless, people in the United States have strongly resisted efforts to convert to metric measures. When cultural assumptions become common sense, people accept them as true even though they often can be questioned. It seems like common sense to say that salad is good for you, but in reality it depends on what's in the salad. A salad consisting of lettuce and a mayonnaise-based dressing has little nutritional value and much fat.

Finding Good Reasons

A good reason works because it includes a link to your claim that your readers will find valid. Your readers are almost like a jury that passes judgment on your good reasons. If they accept them and cannot think of other, more compelling good reasons that oppose your position, you will convince them.

Most good reasons derive from mulling things over "reasonably," or, to use the technical term, from logos. *Logos* refers to the logic of what you communicate; in fact, logos is the root of our modern word *logic*. Good reasons

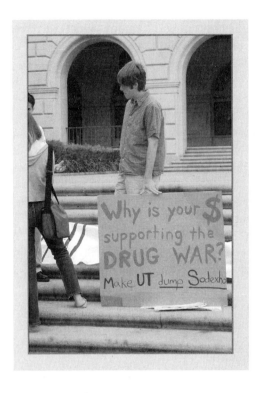

are thus commonly associated with logical appeals. Over the years, professional rhetoricians have devised a number of informal methods, known as *heuristics*, to help speakers and writers find good reasons to support their arguments. (The word *heuristics* comes from the same root as the Greek word *eureka*, which means "I have found it!") In the rest of this section, you will find a set of heuristics for developing good reasons for your arguments. Think of them as a series of questions that can help you to develop persuasive arguments.

These questions will equip you to communicate more effectively when you are speaking before a group as well as writing an argument. But do not expect every question to be productive in every case. Sometimes, a certain question won't get you very far; and often, the questions will develop so many good reasons and strategies that you will not be able to use them all. You will ultimately have to select from among the best of your good reasons to find the ones that are most likely to work in a given case.

If a certain question does not seem to work for you at first, do not give up on it the next time. Get in the habit of asking these questions in the course of developing your arguments. If you ask them systematically, you will probably have more good reasons than you need for your arguments.

Can You Argue by Definition?

Probably the most powerful kind of good reason is an **argument from definition.** You can think of a definition as a simple statement: _____ *is a* _____. You use these statements all the time. When you need a course to fulfill your social science requirement, you look at the list of courses that are defined as social science courses. You find out that the anthropology class you want to take is one of them. It's just as important when _____ is not a _____. Suppose you are taking College Algebra this semester, which is a math course taught by the math department, yet it doesn't count for the math requirement. The reason it doesn't count is because College Algebra is not defined as a college-level math class. So you have to enroll next semester in Calculus I.

Many definitions are not nearly as clear cut as the math requirement. If you want to argue that figure skaters are athletes, you will need to define what an athlete is. You start thinking. An athlete competes in an activity, but that definition alone is too broad, since many competitions do not require physical activity. Thus, an athlete must participate in a competitive physical activity and must train for it. But that definition is still not quite narrow enough, since soldiers train for competitive physical activity. You decide to add that the activity must be a sport and that it must require special competence and precision. Your because clause turns out as follows: *Figure skaters are athletes because true athletes train for and compete in physical sporting competitions that require special competence and precision.*

If you can get your audience to accept your definitions of things, you've gone a long way toward convincing them of the validity of your claim. That is why the most controversial issues in our culture—abortion, affirmative action, gay rights, pornography, women's rights, gun control, the death penalty—are argued from definition. Is abortion a crime or a medical procedure? Is pornography protected by the First Amendment, or is it a violation of women's rights? Is the death penalty just or cruel and inhuman? You can see from these examples that definitions often rely on cultural assumptions for their links.

Because cultural assumptions about controversial issues are strongly held, people usually don't care about the practical consequences. Arguing that it is much cheaper to execute prisoners who have been convicted of first-degree murder than to keep them in prison for life does not convince those who believe that it is morally wrong to kill anyone, no matter what they have done.

CAN YOU ARGUE FROM VALUE?

A special kind of argument from definition, one that often implies consequences, is the **argument from value.** You can support your claim with a because clause (or several of them) that includes a sense of evaluation.

Arguments from value follow from claims like _____ *is a good* _____ or
_____ *is not a good* _____.

You make arguments from value every day. Your old TV set breaks, so
you go to your local discount store to buy a new one. When you get there, you
find too many choices. You have to decide which one to buy. You have only
$230 to spend, but there are still a lot of choices. Which is the best TV for
$230 or less? The more you look, the more confusing it gets. There are several
19-inch TVs in your price range. All have remote control. Some have features such as front surround sound, multilingual on-screen display, and A/V
inputs. But you realize that there is one test that will determine the best TV
for you: the picture quality. You buy the one with the best picture.

Evaluative arguments usually proceed from the presentation of certain
criteria. These criteria come from the definitions of good and bad, of poor and
not so poor, that prevail in a given case. A really good 19-inch TV fulfills certain criteria; so does an outstanding movie, an excellent class, or, if you work
in an office, an effective telephone system. Sometimes the criteria are
straightforward, as in the TV example. The TV that you select has to be under a certain cost, equipped with a remote, and ready to hook up to your cable. After those criteria are met, the big ones are picture and sound quality.
But if your boss asks you to recommend a new telephone system, then it's not
quite so straightforward. You are presented with many options, and you have
to decide which of them are worth paying for. You have to decide how the
phone system is going to be used, examine which features will be important
for your office, and then rate the systems according to the criteria you have
set out. The key to evaluation arguments is identifying and arguing for the
right criteria. If you can convince your readers that you have the right criteria
and that your assessments are correct, then you will be convincing.

CAN YOU COMPARE OR CONTRAST?

Evaluative arguments can generate comparisons often enough. But even if
they don't generate comparisons, your argument might profit if you get in
the habit of thinking in comparative terms—in terms of what things are like
or unlike the topic you are discussing. **Claims of comparisons** take the form
_____ *is like* _____ or _____ *is not like* _____. If you are having trouble coming up with good reasons, think of comparisons that help your readers agree with you. If you want to argue that figure skaters are athletes, you
might think about how their training and competitions resemble those of
other athletes. Making comparisons is an effective way of building common
ground.

A particular kind of comparison is an analogy. An **analogy** is an extended comparison—one that is developed over several sentences or paragraphs for explanatory or persuasive purposes. Analogies take different forms. A **historical analogy** compares something that is going on now with a similar case in the past. One of the most frequent historical analogies is to compare a current situation in which one country attacks or threatens another with Germany's seizing of Czechoslovakia in 1938 and then invading Poland in 1939, starting World War II. The difficulty with this analogy is that circumstances today are not the same as those in 1939, and it is easy to point out how the analogy fails.

Other analogies make literal comparisons. A **literal analogy** is a comparison between current situations, in which you argue what is true or works in one situation should be true or work in another. Most advanced nations provide basic health care to all their citizens either free or at minimal charge. All citizens of Canada are covered by the same comprehensive health care system, which is free for both rich and poor. Canadians go to the doctor more frequently than citizens of the United States do, and they receive what is generally regarded as better care than their southern neighbors, who pay the most expensive health care bills on the planet.

The Canadian analogy has failed to convince members of the U.S. Congress to vote for a similar system in the United States. Opponents of adopting the Canadian system argue that health care costs are also high in Canada, but Canadians pay the costs in different ways. They pay high taxes, and the Canadian national debt has increased since the universal health system was approved. These opponents of adopting the Canadian system for the United States believe that the best care can be obtained for the lowest cost if health care is treated like any other service and consumers decide what they are willing to pay. Comparisons can always work both ways.

Analogies are especially valuable when you are trying to explain a concept to a willing listener or reader, but analogies are far from foolproof if the reader does not agree with you from the outset. Using an analogy can be risky if the entire argument depends on the reader's accepting it.

CAN YOU ARGUE FROM CONSEQUENCE?

Another powerful source of good reasons comes from considering the possible consequences of your position: Can you sketch out the good things that will follow from your position? Can you establish that certain bad things will be avoided if your position is adopted? If so, you will have other good reasons to use.

Arguments from consequence take the basic form of _____ *causes* _____ (or _____ *does not cause* _____). Very often, arguments from consequence are more complicated, taking the form _____ *causes* _____ *which, in turn, causes* _____ and so on. In Chapter 1 we describe how *Silent Spring* makes powerful arguments from consequence. Rachel Carson's primary claim is that *DDT should not be sprayed on a massive scale because it will poison animals and people.* The key to her argument is the causal chain that explains how animals and people are poisoned. Carson describes how nothing exists alone in nature. When a potato field is sprayed with chemical poison such as DDT, some of that poison is absorbed by the skin of the potatoes and some washes into the groundwater, where it contaminates drinking water. Other poisonous residue is absorbed into streams, where it is ingested by insect larvae, which in turn are eaten by fish. Fish are eaten by other fish, which are then eaten by waterfowl and people. At each stage, the poisons become more concentrated. Carson shows why people are in danger from drinking contaminated water and eating contaminated vegetables and fish. Even today, over thirty years after DDT stopped being used in the United States, dangerous levels exist in the sediment at the bottom of many lakes and bays.

Proposal arguments are future-oriented arguments from consequence. In a proposal argument, you cannot stop with naming good reasons; you also have to show that these consequences would follow from the idea or course of action that you are arguing. As an example, let's say you want to argue that all high school graduates in your state should be computer literate. You want a computer requirement more substantial than the one computer literacy course you had in the eighth grade. You want all high school graduates to be familiar with basic computer concepts and terminology, to be able to use a word processing application and at least two other applications, and to understand issues of ethics and privacy raised by new electronic technologies.

Your strongest good reason is that high school graduates should be competent in the use of computers, the tool that they will most certainly use for most writing tasks and many other activities during their lifetime. Even if your readers accept that good reason, you still have to prove that the requirement will actually give students the competency they require. Many students pass language requirements without being able to speak, read, or write the language they have studied.

Furthermore, you have to consider the feasibility of any proposal that you make. A good idea has to be a practical one. If you want to impose a computer literacy requirement, you have to argue for increased funding for expensive technology. High school students in poor communities cannot become computer literate unless they have access to computers. More teachers might also need to be hired. And you will need to figure out how to fit the computer requirement into an already crowded curriculum. Sometimes, feasibility is not a major issue (for example, if you're proposing that the starting time for basketball games be changed by thirty minutes); but if it is, you must address it.

CAN YOU COUNTER OBJECTIONS TO YOUR POSITION?

Another good way to find convincing good reasons is to think about possible objections to your position. If you can imagine how your audience might counter or respond to your argument, you will probably include in your argument precisely the points that will address your readers' particular needs and objections. If you are successful, your readers will be convinced that you are right. You've no doubt had the experience yourself of mentally saying to a writer in the course of your reading, "Yeah, but what about this other idea?"—only to have the writer address precisely this objection.

You can impress your readers that you've thought about why anyone would oppose your position and exactly how that opposition would be expressed. If you are writing a proposal argument for a computer literacy requirement for all high school graduates, you might think about why anyone would object, since computers are becoming increasingly important to our jobs and lives. What will the practical objections be? What philosophical ones? Why hasn't such a requirement been put in place already? By asking such questions in your own arguments, you are likely to develop robust because clauses that may be the ones that most affect your readers.

Sometimes, writers actually create an objector by posing rhetorical questions such as "You might say, 'But won't that make my taxes go up to pay for computers for all students?'" Stating objections explicitly can be effective if you make the objections as those of a reasonable person with an alternative point of view. But if the objections you state are ridiculous ones, then you risk being accused of setting up a *straw man*, that is, making the position opposing your own so simplistic that no one would likely identify with it.

Supporting Good Reasons

Good reasons are essential ingredients of good arguments, but they don't do the job alone. You must support or verify good reasons with evidence. Evidence consists of hard data or examples or narratives or episodes or tabulations of

Questions for Finding Good Reasons

1. **Can you argue by definition—from "the nature of the thing"?**

   ■ Can you argue that while many (most) people think X is a Y, X is better thought of as a Z?

   Example: Most people do not think of humans as an endangered species, but small farmers have been successful in comparing their way of life to an endangered species and thus have extended the definition of an endangered species to include themselves.

   ■ Can you argue that while X is a Y, X differs from other Ys and might be thought of as a Z?

   Example: Colleges and universities are similar to public schools in having education as their primary mission, but unlike public schools, colleges and universities receive only part of their operating costs from tax revenues and therefore, like a business, must generate much of their own revenue.

2. **Can you argue from value?**

   ■ Can you grade a few examples of the kind of thing you are evaluating as good, better, and best (or bad and worse)?

   Example: There have been lots of great actors in detective films, but none compare to Humphrey Bogart.

   ■ Can you list the features you use to determine whether something is good or bad and then show why one is most important?

   Example: Coach Powers taught me a great deal about the skills and strategy of playing tennis, but most of all, she taught me that the game is fun.

3. **Can you compare or contrast?**

   ■ Can you think of items, events, or situations that are similar or dissimilar to the one you are writing about?

   Example: We should require a foreign language for all students at our college because our main competitor does not have such a requirement.

   ■ Can you distinguish why your subject is different than one usually thought of as similar?

(continued)

Questions for Finding Good Reasons *(continued)*

Example: While poor people are often lumped in with the unemployed and those on welfare, the majority of poor people do work in low-paying jobs.

4. **Can you argue from consequence?**

   ■ Can you argue that good things will happen if a certain course of action is followed or that bad things will be avoided?

   Example: Eliminating all income tax deductions would save every taxpayer many hours and would create a system of taxation that does not reward people for cheating.

   ■ Can you argue that while there were obvious causes of Y, Y would not have occurred had it not been for X?

   Example: A seventeen-year-old driver is killed when her car skids across the grass median of an interstate highway and collides with a pickup truck going the other direction. Even though a slick road and excessive speed were the immediate causes, the driver would be alive today if the median had had a concrete barrier.

   ■ Can you argue for an alternative cause rather than the one many people assume?

   Example: Politicians take credit for reducing the violent crime rate because of "get-tough" police policies, but in fact, the rate of violent crime is decreasing because more people are working.

5. **Can you counter objections to your position?**

   ■ Can you think of the most likely objections to your claim and turn them into your own good reasons?

   Example: High school administrators might object to requiring computer literacy because of cost, but schools can now lease computers and put them on a statewide system at a cost less than they now pay for textbooks.

   ■ Can the *reverse* or opposite of an opposing claim be argued?

   Example: A proposed expressway through a city is claimed to help traffic, but it also could make traffic worse by encouraging more people to drive to the city.

episodes (known as *statistics*) that are seen as relevant to the good reasons that you are putting forward. To put it another way, a writer of arguments puts forward not only claims and good reasons but also evidence that those good reasons are true. And that evidence consists of examples, personal experiences, comparisons, statistics, calculations, quotations, and other kinds of data that a reader will find relevant and compelling.

How much supporting evidence should you supply? How much evidence is enough? That is difficult to generalize about; as is usual in the case of rhetoric, the best answer is to say, "It depends." If a reader is likely to find one of your good reasons hard to believe, then you should be aggressive in offering support. You should present detailed evidence in a patient and painstaking way. As one presenting an argument, you have a responsibility not just to *state* a case but to *make* a case with evidence. Arguments that are unsuccessful tend to fail not because of a shortage of good reasons; more often, they fail because the reader doesn't agree that there is enough evidence to support the good reason that is being presented.

If your good reason isn't especially controversial, you probably should not belabor it. Think of your own experiences as a reader. How often do you recall saying to yourself, as you read a passage or listened to a speaker, "OK! OK! I get the point! Don't keep piling up all of this evidence for me because I don't want it or need it." However, such a reaction is rare, isn't it? By contrast, how often do you recall muttering under your breath, "How can you say that? What evidence do you have to back it up?" When in doubt, err on the side of offering too much evidence. It's an error that is seldom made and not often criticized.

When a writer doesn't provide satisfactory evidence for a because clause, readers might feel that there has been a failure in the reasoning process. In fact, in your previous courses in writing and speaking, you may have learned about various fallacies associated with faulty arguments (which are listed at the end of this section).

Strictly speaking, there is nothing false about these so-called logical fallacies. The fallacies most often refer to failures in providing evidence; when you don't provide enough good evidence to convince your audience, you might be accused of committing a fallacy in reasoning. You will usually avoid such accusations if the evidence that you cite is both *relevant* and *sufficient*.

Relevance refers to the appropriateness of the evidence to the case at hand. Some kinds of evidence are seen as more relevant than others for particular audiences. For example, in science and industry, personal testimony is seen as having limited relevance, while experimental procedures and controlled observations have far more credibility. Compare someone who defends the use of a particular piece of computer software because "it worked for me" with someone who defends it because "according to a journal article published last month, 84 percent of the users of the software were satisfied or very satisfied with it." On the other hand, in writing to the general public on controversial issues such as gun control, personal experience is often considered more relevant than other kinds of data. The so-called Brady Bill, which requires a mandatory waiting period for the purchase of handguns, was named for President Ronald Reagan's press secretary, James Brady, who was permanently disabled when John W. Hinckley, Jr., made an assassination attempt on the president in 1981. James Brady's wife, Sarah, effectively told the story of her husband's suffering in lobbying for the bill.

Sufficiency refers to the amount of evidence cited. Sometimes a single piece of evidence, a single instance, will carry the day if it is especially compelling in some way—if it represents the situation well or makes a point that isn't particularly controversial. More often, people expect more than one piece of evidence if they are to be convinced of something. Convincing readers that they should approve a statewide computer literacy requirement for all high school graduates will require much more evidence than the story of a single graduate who succeeded with her computer skills. You will likely need statistical evidence for such a broad proposal.

If you anticipate that your audience might not accept your evidence, face the situation squarely. First, think carefully about the argument you are presenting. If you cannot cite adequate evidence for your assertions, perhaps those assertions must be modified or qualified in some way. If you remain convinced of your assertions, then think about doing more research to come up with additional evidence. If you anticipate that your audience might suspect you have overlooked or minimized important information, reassure them that you have not and deal explicitly with conflicting arguments. Another strategy is to acknowledge explicitly the limitations of your evidence. Acknowledging limitations doesn't shrink the limitations, but it does build your credibility and convinces your audience that alternatives have indeed been explored fully and responsibly. If you are thinking of your reader as a partner rather than as an adversary, it is usually easy to acknowledge limitations because you are looking not for victory and the end of debate but for a mutually satisfactory situation that might emerge as a result of the communication process that you are part of.

Fallacies in Arguments

Reasoning in arguments depends less on *proving* a claim than it does on finding evidence for the claim that readers will accept as valid. Logical fallacies in argument reflect a failure to provide adequate evidence for the

(continued)

Fallacies in Arguments (continued)

claim that is being made. Among the most common fallacies are the
following.

- **Bandwagon appeals.** *It doesn't matter if I cheat on a test because
  everyone else does.* This argument suggests that everyone is doing
  it, so why shouldn't you? Close examination may reveal that in fact
  everyone really isn't doing it—and in any case, it may not be the
  right thing to do.

- **Begging the question.** *People should be able to use land any way
  they want to because using land is an individual right.* The fallacy of
  begging the question occurs when the claim is restated and passed
  off as evidence.

- **Either-or.** *Either we build a new freeway crossing downtown or else
  there will be perpetual gridlock.* The either-or fallacy suggests that
  there are only two choices in a complex situation. This is rarely, if
  ever, the case. (In this example, the writer ignores other transportation options besides freeways.)

- **False analogies.** *The Serbian seizure of Bosnian territory was like
  Hitler's takeover of Czechoslovakia in 1938, and having learned the
  hard way what happens when they give in to dictators, Western
  nations stood up to Serbian aggression.* Analogies always depend on
  the degree of resemblance of one situation to another. In this case,
  the analogy fails to recognize that Serbia in 1993 was hardly like
  Nazi Germany in 1938.

- **Hasty generalization.** *We had three days this summer when the
  temperature reached an all-time high; that's a sure sign of global
  warming.* A hasty generalization is a broad claim made on the basis
  of a few occurrences. The debate over global warming takes into
  account climate data for centuries. Individual climate events such as
  record hot days do not confirm trends.

- **Name calling.** Name calling is as frequent in political argument as
  on the playground. Candidates are "accused" of being tax-and-
  spend liberals, ultraconservatives, radical feminists, and so on. Rarely
  are these terms defined; hence they are meaningless.

(continued)

Fallacies in Arguments *(continued)*

- **Non sequitur.** *A university that can afford to build a new football stadium should not have to raise tuition.* A non sequitur (a Latin term meaning "it does not follow") ties together two unrelated ideas. In this case, the argument fails to recognize that the money for new stadiums is often donated for that purpose and is not part of a university's general revenue.

- **Oversimplification.** *No one would run stop signs if we had a mandatory death penalty for doing it.* This claim may be true, but the argument would be unacceptable to most citizens. More complex, if less definitive, solutions are called for.

- **Polarization.** *Feminists are all man haters.* Polarization, like name calling, exaggerates positions and groups by representing them as extreme and divisive.

- **Post hoc fallacy.** *I ate a hamburger last night and got deathly sick—must have been food poisoning.* The post hoc fallacy (from the Latin *post hoc ergo hoc,* "after this, therefore this") assumes that things that follow in time have a causal relationship. In this example, you may have simply started coming down with the flu—as would be obvious two days later.

- **Rationalization.** *I could have done better on the test if I thought the course mattered to my major.* People frequently come up with excuses and weak explanations for their own and others' behavior that avoid actual causes.

- **Slippery slope.** *We shouldn't grant amnesty to illegal immigrants now living in the United States because it will mean opening our borders to a flood of people from around the world who want to move here.* The slippery slope fallacy assumes that if the first step is taken, other steps necessarily follow.

- **Straw man.** *Environmentalists won't be satisfied until not a single human being is allowed to enter a national park.* A straw man argument is a diversionary tactic that sets up another's position in a way that can be easily rejected. In fact, only a small percentage of environmentalists would make an argument even close to this one.

Deciding Which Good Reasons to Use

Asking a series of questions can generate a list of because clauses, but even if you have plenty, you still have to decide which ones to use. How can you decide which points are likely to be most persuasive? In choosing which good reasons to use in your arguments, consider your readers' attitudes and values and the values that are especially sanctioned by your community.

When people communicate, they tend to present their own thinking—to rely on the lines of thought that have led them to believe as they do. That's natural enough, since it is reasonable to present to others the reasons that make us believe what we are advocating in writing or speech. People have much in common, and it is natural to think that the evidence and patterns of thought that have guided your thinking to a certain point will also guide others to the same conclusions.

But people are also different, and what convinces you might not always convince others. When you are deciding what because clauses to present to others, therefore, try not so much to recapitulate your own thinking process as to influence the thinking of others. Ask yourself not just why you think as you do but also what you need to convince others to see things your way. Don't pick the because clauses that seem compelling to you; pick those that will seem compelling to your audience.

LANI GUINIER

The Tyranny of the Majority

During her college years at Harvard and the Yale Law School, Lani Guinier (1950–   ) became intensely committed to voting rights, one of the long-standing initiatives of the civil rights movement. She grew up in an interracial family—with an African-American father and a white, Jewish mother—and as a young attorney gained a reputation as a coalition builder. In 1988 she became the first African-American woman tenured professor in the Harvard Law School.

This excerpt, taken from her 1994 book The Tyranny of the Majority, *was inspired by the work of one of the founders of the United States, James Madison, who later became the fourth president. Madison believed that the "tyranny of the majority" represented the biggest threat to the system of democracy proposed for the new nation because the majority could become as despotic in its rule as a king. Guinier explores ways in which a majority can work with rather than tyrannize a minority in a diverse society.*

1   I have always wanted to be a civil rights lawyer. This lifelong ambition is based on a deep-seated commitment to democratic fair play—to playing by the rules as long as the rules are fair. When the rules seem unfair, I have worked to change them, not subvert them. When I was eight years old, I was a Brownie. I was especially proud of my uniform, which represented a commitment to good citizenship and good deeds. But one day, when my Brownie group staged a hatmaking contest, I realized that uniforms are only as honorable as the people who wear them. The contest was rigged. The winner was assisted by her milliner mother, who actually made the winning entry in full view of all the participants. At the time, I was too young to be able to change the rules, but I was old enough to resign, which I promptly did.

2   To me, fair play means that the rules encourage everyone to play. They should reward those who win, but they must be acceptable to those who lose. The central theme of my academic writing is that not all rules lead to elemental fair play. Some even commonplace rules work against it.

3   The professional milliner competing with amateur Brownies stands as an example of rules that are patently rigged or patently subverted. Yet, sometimes, even when rules are perfectly fair in form, they serve in practice to exclude particular groups from meaningful participation. When they do not encourage everyone to play, or when, over the long haul, they do not make the losers feel as good about the outcomes as the winners, they can seem as unfair as the milliner who makes the winning hat for her daughter.

4   Sometimes, too, we construct rules that force us to be divided into winners and losers when we might have otherwise joined together. This idea was cogently expressed by my son, Nikolas, when he was four years old, far exceeding the thoughtfulness of his mother when she was an eight-year-old Brownie. While I was writing one of my law journal articles, Nikolas and I had a conversation about voting prompted by a *Sesame Street Magazine* exercise. The magazine pictured six children: four children had raised their hands because they wanted to play tag; two had their hands down because they wanted to play hide-and-seek. The magazine asked its readers to count the number of children whose hands were raised and then decide what game the children would play.

5   Nikolas quite realistically replied, "They will play both. First they will play tag. Then they will play hide-and-seek." Despite the magazine's "rules,"

he was right. To children, it is natural to take turns. The winner may get to play first or more often, but even the "loser" gets something. His was a positive-sum solution that many adult rule-makers ignore.

6   The traditional answer to the magazine's problem would have been a zero-sum solution. "The children—all the children—will play tag, and only tag." As a zero-sum solution, everything is seen in terms of "I win; you lose." The conventional answer relies on winner-take-all majority rule, in which the tag players, as the majority, win the right to decide for all the children what game to play. The hide-and-seek preference becomes irrelevant. The numerically more powerful majority choice simply subsumes minority preferences.

7   In the conventional case, the majority that rules gains all the power and the minority that loses gets none. For example, two years ago Brother Rice High School in Chicago held two senior proms. It was not planned that way. The prom committee at Brother Rice, a boys' Catholic high school, expected just one prom when it hired a disc jockey, picked a rock band, and selected music for the prom by consulting student preferences. Each senior was asked to list his three favorite songs, and the band would play the songs that appeared most frequently on the lists.

8   Seems attractively democratic. But Brother Rice is predominantly white, and the prom committee was all white. That's how they got two proms. The black seniors at Brother Rice felt so shut out by the "democratic process" that they organized their own prom. As one black student put it: "For every vote we had, there were eight votes for what they wanted. . . . [W]ith us being in the minority we're always outvoted. It's as if we don't count."

9   Some embittered white seniors saw things differently. They complained that the black students should have gone along with the majority: "The majority makes a decision. That's the way it works."

10   In a way, both groups were right. From the white students' perspective, this was ordinary decision making. To the black students, majority rule sent the message: "we don't count" is the "way it works" for minorities. In a racially divided society, majority rule may be perceived as majority tyranny.

11   That is a large claim, and I do not rest my case for it solely on the actions of the prom committee in one Chicago high school. To expand the range of the argument, I first consider the ideal of majority rule itself, particularly as reflected in the writings of James Madison and other founding members of our Republic. These early democrats explored the relationship between majority rule and democracy. James Madison warned, "If a majority be united by a common interest, the rights of the minority will be insecure."

The tyranny of the majority, according to Madison, requires safeguards to protect "one part of the society against the injustice of the other part."

12   For Madison, majority tyranny represented the great danger to our early constitutional democracy. Although the American revolution was fought against the tyranny of the British monarch, it soon became clear that there was another tyranny to be avoided. The accumulations of all powers in the same hands, Madison warned, "whether of one, a few, or many, and whether hereditary, self-appointed, or elective, may justly be pronounced the very definition of tyranny."

13   As another colonist suggested in papers published in Philadelphia, "We have been so long habituated to a jealousy of tyranny from monarchy and aristocracy, that we have yet to learn the dangers of it from democracy." Despotism had to be opposed "whether it came from Kings, Lords or the people."

14   The debate about majority tyranny reflected Madison's concern that the majority may not represent the whole. In a homogeneous society, the interest of the majority would likely be that of the minority also. But in a heterogeneous community, the majority may not represent all competing interests. The majority is likely to be self-interested and ignorant or indifferent to the concerns of the minority. In such case, Madison observed, the assumption that the majority represents the minority is "altogether fictitious."

15   Yet even a self-interested majority can govern fairly if it cooperates with the minority. One reason for such cooperation is that the self-interested majority values the principle of reciprocity. The self-interested majority worries that the minority may attract defectors from the majority and become the next governing majority. The Golden Rule principle of reciprocity functions to check the tendency of a self-interested majority to act tyrannically.

16   So the argument for the majority principle connects it with the value of reciprocity: You cooperate when you lose in part because members of the current majority will cooperate when they lose. The conventional case for the fairness of majority rule is that it is not really the rule of a fixed group—The Majority—on all issues; instead it is the rule of shifting majorities, as the losers at one time or on one issue join with others and become part of the governing coalition at another time or on another issue. The result will be a fair system of mutually beneficial cooperation. I call a majority that rules but does not dominate a Madisonian Majority.

17   The problem of majority tyranny arises, however, when the self-interested majority does not need to worry about defections. When the majority is fixed and permanent, there are no checks on its ability to be

overbearing. A majority that does not worry about defectors is a majority with total power.

18   In such a case, Madison's concern about majority tyranny arises. In a heterogeneous community, any faction with total power might subject "the minority to the caprice and arbitrary decisions of the majority, who instead of consulting the interest of the whole community collectively, attend sometimes to partial and local advantages."

19   "What remedy can be found in a republican Government, where the majority must ultimately decide," argued Madison, but to ensure "that no one common interest or passion will be likely to unite a majority of the whole number in an unjust pursuit." The answer was to disaggregate the majority to ensure checks and balances or fluid, rotating interests. The minority needed protection against an overbearing majority, so that "a common sentiment is less likely to be felt, and the requisite concert less likely to be formed, by a majority of the whole."

20   Political struggles would not be simply a contest between rulers and people; the political struggles would be among the people themselves. The work of government was not to transcend different interests but to reconcile them. In an ideal democracy, the people would rule, but the minorities would also be protected against the power of majorities. Again, where the rules of decision making protect the minority, the Madisonian Majority rules without dominating.

21   But if a group is unfairly treated, for example, when it forms a racial minority, *and* if the problems of unfairness are not cured by conventional assumptions about majority rule, then what is to be done? The answer is that we may need an *alternative* to winner-take-all majoritarianism. In this book, a collection of my law review articles, I describe the alternative, which, with Nikolas's help, I now call the "principle of taking turns." In a racially divided society, this principle does better than simple majority rule if it accommodates the values of self-government, fairness, deliberation, compromise, and consensus that lie at the heart of the democratic ideal.

22   In my legal writing, I follow the caveat of James Madison and other early American democrats. I explore decision-making rules that might work in a multiracial society to ensure that majority rule does not become majority tyranny. I pursue voting systems that might disaggregate The Majority so that it does not exercise power unfairly or tyrannically. I aspire to a more cooperative political style of decision making to enable all of the students at Brother Rice to feel comfortable attending the same prom. In looking to create Madisonian Majorities, I pursue a positive-sum, taking-turns solution.

23   Structuring decision making to allow the minority "a turn" may be necessary to restore the reciprocity ideal when a fixed majority refuses to cooperate with the minority. If the fixed majority loses its incentive to follow the Golden Rule principle of shifting majorities, the minority never gets to take a turn. Giving the minority a turn does not mean the minority gets to rule; what it does mean is that the minority gets to influence decision making and the majority rules more legitimately.

24   Instead of automatically rewarding the preferences of the monolithic majority, a taking-turns approach anticipates that the majority rules, but is not overbearing. Because those with 51 percent of the votes are not assured 100 percent of the power, the majority cooperates with, or at least does not tyrannize, the minority.

25   The sports analogy of "I win; you lose" competition within a political hierarchy makes sense when only one team can win; Nikolas's intuition that it is often possible to take turns suggests an alternative approach. Take family decision making, for example. It utilizes a taking-turns approach. When parents sit around the kitchen table deciding on a vacation destination or activities for a rainy day, often they do not simply rely on a show of hands, especially if that means that the older children always prevail or if affinity groups among the children (those who prefer movies to video games, or those who prefer baseball to playing cards) never get to play their activity of choice. Instead of allowing the majority simply to rule, the parents may propose that everyone take turns, going to the movies one night and playing video games the next. Or as Nikolas proposes, they might do both on a given night.

26   Taking turns attempts to build consensus while recognizing political or social differences, and it encourages everyone to play. The taking-turns approach gives those with the most support more turns, but it also legitimates the outcome from each individual's perspective, including those whose views are shared only by a minority.

27   In the end, I do not believe that democracy should encourage rule by the powerful—even a powerful majority. Instead, the idea of democracy promises a fair discussion among self-defined equals about how to achieve our common aspirations. To redeem that promise, we need to put the idea of taking turns and disaggregating the majority at the center of our conception of representation. Particularly as we move into the twenty-first century as a more highly diversified citizenry, it is essential that we consider the ways in which voting and representational systems succeed or fail at encouraging Madisonian Majorities.

28   To use Nikolas's terminology, "it is no fair" if a fixed, tyrannical major-ity excludes or alienates the minority. It is no fair if a fixed, tyrannical ma-jority monopolizes all the power all the time. It is no fair if we engage in the periodic ritual of elections, but only the permanent majority gets to choose who is elected. Where we have tyranny by The Majority, we do not have genuine democracy.

Getting Started on Your Draft

Before You Start Writing Your Draft

1. Pick one of the issues from the list you made in Chapter 1 as a possi-ble candidate. Then write in one sentence your position on this issue. You can change the statement later if you need to, but at this point, you need to know whether you can write a paper using this statement as your thesis.
2. Use the questions on pp. 42–43 to help you think of as many reasons as you can. List your reasons as because clauses after your claim—for example, "Smoking should be banned on campus *because* nonsmokers are endangered by secondhand smoke."
3. When you finish listing your reasons, put checks beside the strongest ones.
4. What evidence do you have to support your strongest reasons? Do you have any facts, statistics, testimony from authority, or personal observations to back up the reasons? Make notes beside your reasons.
5. List as many reasons as you can against your claim. For example, "Smoking should not be banned on campus *because* the risk of sec-ondhand smoke is minimal if smokers go outside and *because* it would discourage or even prevent smokers from working or going to school on campus." Think about how you are going to answer the arguments against your position.
6. Think about who is going to read your argument. How much will they know about the issues involved? Where are they likely to stand on these issues? Will they define the issues the same way you do? On what are they most likely to agree and disagree with you?

Writing Your Draft

Some people write best from detailed outlines; others write from notes. Try making some notes about your beginning, middle, and end to get you started and to give you a sense of where you're headed.

1. **The beginning.** How much do you need to explain the issue before making your claim? How can you get off to a fast start? What can you do to convince your reader to keep reading? Do you need to establish that there's a problem that your paper will address? Are you answering a specific argument by someone else?

2. **The middle.** If you have more than one reason, which reason do you want to put first? Most of the time, you want your strongest reason to be up front or else at the end. Group similar arguments together. Weaker arguments might go in the middle. Next, you have to think about how you are going to bring in the evidence that you have. If you have only one reason, the evidence will make or break your argument. Finally, you need to think about where you are going to acknowledge opposing viewpoints and how much space you need to give to countering those viewpoints. If most of your readers are likely to think differently than you, then you need to spend time anticipating and refuting objections to your claim.

3. **The ending.** Endings are always tricky. Simply stating your claim again isn't the best way to finish. The worst endings say something like "In my essay, I've said this." Is there a summarizing point you can make? Some implication you can draw? Another example you can include that will sum up your position? If you are writing a proposal, your ending might be a call for action.

CHAPTER 3

Thinking More about Your Audience

What Exactly Is an Audience?

The audience is the most important concern in any kind of persuasion—from advertising to the kind of extended written arguments that you write in college. Thinking in advance about your audience pays off when you write. But what exactly is an audience?

Often, the answer is easy to supply. In those cases, *audience* refers to the person or people who actually hear an oral communication or who actually read a written one. Audience denotes the real consumers of communications. The idea of a *real audience* is usually a concrete reality for people who are speaking, because those audiences are actually, visibly present at the scene. When real audiences are present in the flesh, they are hard to ignore. In fact, you do so at your own risk, for audiences who are lost or confused by an oral presentation can make their discomfort known by body language ("If this speech doesn't end soon, I'm going to scream!" their bodies say) or by their verbal responses ("Excuse me, but I'm really confused by what you just said"). Sometimes, the audiences for written communications can be almost as real (and just as responsive) as the ones who take in a verbal performance, especially if you are writing to people whom you know well or who work closely with you. The real audience for this book is certainly immediate to the people who are writing it. The authors are aware of you—the flesh-and-blood student with a real name, a real presence, a student like the ones we work with every semester. And the authors know that you are likely to respond in real ways to what you read.

> *Audience* **is a concrete and useful concept even if you do not know who eventually will read what you write.**

When the term *audience* is used in this book, then, it most often refers to the real audience. But there is also another way of thinking about audience, another way in which you are the audience for this book: The authors had to imagine you reading while they were composing the chapters. In this sense, an audience can be an imaginary concept in the mind of the writer, not just a real, flesh-and-blood presence. You have this sense of audience whenever you think about someone later reading what you are writing as you write. In fact, from the point of view of the writer, it does not even matter whether the person you imagine reading eventually does read what you write. What is important is that this imaginary reader helps you to think about the reasons and supporting evidence you need to write your argument. When you have very little sense of who will eventually read what you write, this imaginary reader becomes especially important.

The goal of this chapter is to help you make the audience in your mind a concrete, useful concept, whether or not you know the real people who will ultimately read what you write. Real audiences exist, and you can think about them in productive ways. But even if your real audience doesn't have a concrete presence for you, you can make *audience* a creative concept in your mind as you write. Whether the audience is a real presence or something in the mind of the writer finally might not make much difference.

To imagine an audience for what you write, think about what readers actually do when they read. Most people are not very aware of how they read because reading is almost like breathing. They have done it so often for so long that they are hardly conscious of how they do it. Think for a moment about the following examples:

▪ A third grader brings his mother a flower he has picked from the yard and a note that says "I love you Mom." Earlier in the day, he was bouncing a ball against the hearth in the living room and broke a lamp. His mother reads the note and realizes that he is trying to gain her forgiveness. She thanks him politely and, even though she is still mad about the lamp, hugs him.

A psychologist finds a reference to an article in a scholarly journal that pertains to her area of research. When she looks up the article in the library, she quickly scans the introduction to learn exactly what question is being investigated. Because she has read many similar articles, she knows where to find what she is looking for. She flips to the "Discussion" section to find out what conclusions the author has drawn and then turns back to the "Methods" and "Results" sections. She decides that the experiment being reported does not test what it claims to test. Later, when she writes a review of research in her field, she criticizes the experiment.

A developer of desert land decides to use the contest gimmick to attract customers. Later, a college student, among many others on a mailing list, receives a card telling him that he will win a new car just for visiting El Rancho Estates. The student has a friend who responded to a similar notice, only to find out that the new car was a toy. He throws the card in the trash.

A financial analyst who works for a large New York holding company reads the annual financial statement of a small bank in Vermont. Her company may be interested in acquiring the bank. She notices a particularly high amount of deposits in comparison to outstanding loans. She turns to the list of depositors to learn more about why so much money is deposited in the rural bank. On the basis of her review of bank documents, she decides that the bank has the potential for increased profits, and she writes a report recommending that the bank be purchased.

These examples suggest that we rely on a great deal more than what is on the page when we read. The mother understood that the note "I love you Mom" really meant something like "Don't be mad at me anymore." In the same way, the college student determined that the announcement that he had just won a contest was a gimmick to get him to visit the real estate development. We don't read just by decoding the

words on the page. We read by connecting what's on the page with what we know about the world. The numbers that the financial analyst looked at were meaningless by themselves. They became meaningful when she connected them with what she knew about banks.

Reading is often represented as if people were machines that decode characters on the page. But people don't function like machines when they read. They are more like artists who turn a sketch into a painting. They transform a plan into a particular form by filling in gaps and imagining a background. They are not passive receivers. They infer motives, make judgments, debate points, and sometimes write responses.

Who Will Read Your Argument?

Many times, you know exactly who you are writing for. If you write a letter to a close friend, you know that only your friend will read it. You and your friend know the same people, so you don't have to explain who they are. In the workplace, you sometimes write memos making arguments to people you know almost as well as close friends. You don't have to fill them in on the background of the issue because you know they are familiar with the subject. Such audiences are called **simple audiences.**

Other times, your real audience might consist of many individuals, but you can conceive of them as a simple audience because their knowledge is very similar. If you write an article for a journal in your field, you can assume that your readers are familiar with the terms and concepts in that field. Although the people who are reading the journal are different individuals, they are similar in their interest in and knowledge about a particular field.

In other situations, the issue of audience is much more complicated. Take as an example the financial statement from the small bank in Vermont that was mentioned in the previous section. Many different people might read that statement for different reasons—officers of the bank, other employees, shareholders, government regulatory officials, financial analysts, and potential investors in the bank. This kind of complex audience—a group of people who read for different reasons—is a **multiple audience.** Multiple audiences are often very difficult to write for.

In writing arguments to multiple audiences, you will have to take into account differing levels of knowledge about your subject among your potential readers and differing attitudes about that subject. Before you begin writing, think carefully about all the people who might read your argument and then analyze what they know and don't know about your subject and what their attitudes toward your subject and you are likely to be.

WHAT DOES YOUR AUDIENCE ALREADY KNOW— AND NOT KNOW?

Critical to your argument is your audience's knowledge of your subject. If they are not familiar with the background information, they probably won't understand your argument fully. If you know that your readers will be unfamiliar with your subject, you will have to supply background information before attempting to convince them of your position. A good tactic is to tie your new information with what your readers already know. Comparisons and analogies can very helpful in linking old and new information.

Another critical factor is your audience's level of expertise. How much technical language can you use? For example, if you are writing a proposal to put high-speed Internet connections into all dormitory rooms, will your readers know the difference between a T1 line and a T3 line? The director of the computation center should know the difference, but the vice president for student affairs might not. If you are unsure of your readers' knowledge level, it's better to include background information and explain technical terms. Few readers will be insulted, and they can skip over this information quickly if they are familiar with your subject.

WHAT ARE YOUR AUDIENCE'S ATTITUDES TOWARD YOU?

Does your audience know you at all, either by reputation or from previous work? Are you considered your reader's equal, superior, or subordinate? How your audience regards you will affect the tone and presentation of your message. Does your audience respect you and trust you? What can you include in your presentation to build trust? In many cases, your audience will know little about you. Especially in those circumstances, you can build trust in your reader by following the advice on ethos, discussed in Chapter 4.

WHAT ARE YOUR AUDIENCE'S ATTITUDES TOWARD YOUR SUBJECT?

People have prior attitudes about controversial issues that you must take into consideration as you write or speak. Imagine, for instance, that you are preparing an argument for a guest editorial in your college newspaper advocating that your state government provide parents with choices among public and private schools. You will argue that the tax dollars that now automatically go to public schools should go to private schools if the parents so choose. You have evidence that the sophomore-to-senior dropout rate in private schools is less than half the rate of public schools. Furthermore, students from private schools attend college at nearly twice the rate of public school graduates. You intend to argue that one of the reasons private schools are more successful is that they spend more money on instruction and less on administration. And you believe that school choice speaks to the American desire for personal freedom.

Not everyone on your campus will agree with your stand. How might the faculty at your college or university feel about this issue? The administrators? The staff? Other students? Interested people in the community who read the student newspaper? What attitudes toward public funding of private schools will they have before they start reading what you have to say? How are you going to deal with the objection that because many students in private schools come from more affluent families, it is not surprising that they do better?

Even when you write about a much less controversial subject, you must think carefully about your audience's attitudes toward what you have to say or write. Sometimes, your audience may share your attitudes; other times, your audience may be neutral; at still other times, your audience will have attitudes that differ sharply from your own. If possible, you should anticipate these various attitudes and act accordingly. You should show awareness of the attitudes of your audience, and if those attitudes are very different from yours, you will have to work hard to counter them without insulting your audience. It's not just a particular attitude that you have to address but also a set of assumptions that follow from that attitude. The next section will include more about identifying assumptions that follow from attitudes.

An even more difficult situation is when your audience is indifferent to what you write. You feel very strongly that your college or university should have a varsity gymnastics team, but most people on campus are indifferent to the issue. The first task, then, is to get your readers engaged in your subject. Sometimes, you can begin by using a particularly striking example to get your readers interested. Another tactic is to add visuals—illustrations, charts, or tables—to catch your readers' attention.

Why People Reach Different Conclusions from the Same Evidence

Some people think that if the facts of an issue are accurately described, then all reasonable people should come to similar conclusions about what course of action should be followed. As you get older, however, you discover that your friends and other people whom you respect often don't agree with your conclusions even when you all agree on the facts. Arguments would be easy to write if reasonable people considered the same facts and came to the same conclusions. But often they don't. Why do reasonable people look at the same facts and come to different conclusions? Let's look at an example.

One set of facts that has caused great concern is the spread of AIDS among young people. A fifth of the people now living with AIDS are in their twenties. Because the incubation period for the disease can be as long as ten years, many contracted AIDS when they were teenagers. Because of the AIDS epidemic, many parents, politicians, clergy, and school board officials have debated whether condoms should be given out to high school students without fees and without parents' consent. In some high schools, condoms are being distributed in school clinics if parents give their consent. In other cities and communities, school boards have voted down proposals to distribute condoms.

The AIDS epidemic is of particular concern in New York City, which has just 3 percent of the nation's thirteen- to twenty-one-year-old population but 20 percent of the nation's AIDS cases for that age group. On November 26, 1991, after almost two years of public controversy, New York City became the first city in the country to make condoms available to students in its 120 high schools.

Let's take a look at how different viewpoints were argued in the condom debate in New York City. The first article, "Clinic Visit" by Anna Quindlen, appeared on the editorial page of the *New York Times*. The second article, "Condom Sense," was first printed as an unsigned editorial in *Commonweal*, a magazine that has a largely Catholic readership. The author's knowledge of the religious and moral values that the Catholic community holds in common shapes the rhetorical strategy. For example, the author does not define morality because he or she can assume an agreed-upon definition.

Quindlen, Anna. "Clinic Visit." *The New York Times* 21 Feb. 1991, sec A: 19.

There are two examining rooms, a nurse practitioner and the three pediatricians who alternate days. There is a social worker and a health educator. The psychiatrist comes on Fridays.

Welcome to the clinic at Martin Luther King Jr. High School. You can check your old notions of the school nurse and the kid with the phony stomachache at the door. Most of the students have no family physician and no insurance coverage. Here they can get treatment for their asthma, their acne or their depression. Dr. Alwyn T. Cohall, who runs 3 of the city's 17 school-based clinics, says they've taken care of everything from a splinter to a stab wound. The happiest thing they ever do is a physical for a kid going to college.

There's a questionnaire for patients, and to read it is both a delight, because it was clearly written by someone who knows adolescents, and a sorrow, because it was written by someone who knows what it's like to be young in 1991. Questions range from "If you were alone on an island, who would you want to visit you?" to "Have you ever been in any trouble with the police?" and "Did you ever try to kill yourself?" There's a poignancy to finding the section on thumbsucking just after the one on sex. Adolescence is that point in life when, like some mythological creature, we are half one thing, half another. Teenagers think of themselves as adults; parents think of them as kids.

Which brings us to condoms.

Ah, condoms, this year's gnashing-of-teeth issue. Put the idea of teenagers and sex together, and you have two things: reality and controversy. The Chancellor proposes providing condoms to New York City high school students, and he is accused of promoting promiscuity and usurping the essential role of parents. I believe in the essential role. Parents should give their children accurate information about sex. They should discuss their own standards of morality, their ideas of right and wrong. They should let their kids know that they are always available to talk and, more important, to listen.

Adult authority often is missing.

It's just that they don't. Some great wall rises between parents and children on this issue, a wall that is only scaled by the stalwart. Partly this is because while parents are saying "no, no," adolescent hormones are saying "yes, yes." And partly it is that parents only want to listen to what they want to hear.

Teens are sexually active regardless.

The doctors at the clinic deal with what is: adolescents who need no permission from the Chancellor, the doctor or anyone else to begin sleeping together. The girl who got the notice that she was positive for the AIDS virus before she got her diploma. The girl who spent three weeks in the hospital being treated for kidney failure caused by secondary syphilis. AIDS has gotten most of the publicity in the condom debate. But one in four sexually active teenagers will get a sexually transmitted disease before high school graduation, and reducing that figure is one reason Dr. Cohall would like to dispense condoms to his patients.

Condoms reduce AIDS and STDs.

The staff at the clinic have lots of problems as compelling as this one. They have to keep in touch with the kids who are depressed and the ones with drug problems. They need to send pregnant young women to good prenatal care programs. They'd like to be able to prescribe contraceptives for those girls who want them, but for now they refer them to a hospital clinic and hope that they go. Despite abstinence counseling and family planning services, they have a hard time keeping pregnancy tests in stock.

The school clinic requires a parental consent form, and the form allows parents to cross out any services that they don't want their child to receive. Only about 5 percent of the parents do. Dr. Cohall says this is the refrain: "I wish my kid wasn't having sex, but . . ." — Teens have rights to their bodies.

His work is the "but." But keep him alive. Keep her from getting pregnant. Keep them all from getting sterile because of some disease. The staff at the clinic do what parents should do: They listen, and they inform, and they try to make the kids hear themselves, hear what they're really saying about how they feel. They deal with what is.

What is is that young men and women are getting sick, even dying, because of unprotected sex. And we can help prevent that. Abstinence, if you can sell it. A condom, if you cannot. To doom the young before they've even shed the chrysalis of adolescence because you disapprove of their behavior is the triumph of pride over charity and self-righteousness over sense. In this clinic, where the staff greet their patients with a hug, where the problems are so enormous, it seems both meanspirited and shortsighted. — The community is responsible for teens' bodies.

Body integrity is prior to moral integrity.

"Condom Sense." *Commonweal* 13 Sept. 1991: 499.

"You can play with them," reads a New York subway ad picturing teenagers gleefully playing volleyball with an inflated condom.

"Don't play around without them. Use a condom," it clinches its point. The clever word play delivers a message about preventing AIDS, but not the one that New York teenagers need to hear. Instead, the merry punsters at New York City's Health Department seem to encourage premature—and possibly lethal—sexual activity among the young while disinviting serious thinking about the dangers AIDS actually presents. The Health Department is not alone.

This past winter New York Schools Chancellor Joseph A. Fernandez pushed a condom distribution plan through the school board with the help of Mayor David Dinkins as part of a utilitarian approach to combating the spread of AIDS among sexually active adolescents. To insure the program's effectiveness, neither parental consent nor notification will be required. According to the experts, parents only scare students away. Nor will the schools require counseling as part of its condom distribution program. Presumably that too might scare students away. Condoms will be available in New York City high schools later this fall.

As the subway poster and the school board's decision demonstrate, something vital has been lost in the city's approach. That vital something is morality, and "moral" questions about sexual behavior. This is a policy that deethicizes sexual behavior precisely where sexual responsibility is most needed. What, after all, is the likely result of trying to modify sexual behavior without reference to concepts of moral responsibility? Volleyball seems to be the answer.

It's hard to believe the chancellor and his advisors have asked themselves how dispensing condoms along with textbooks can possibly shape the most intimate of human relations. Would they expect students to make themselves accountable if similar minimal expectations were applied to school work? Or to obtaining a driver's license? Could a high school field a sports team if students were simply issued uniforms and told to play the games as they saw fit? It is as if Mr. Fernandez reasons that survival during a drought depended on providing each individual with his or her own well-digging equipment. Survival in such desperate circumstances depends on more compelling forms of cooperation. Thus excluding parents from the school condom program has to be among the most self-defeating aspects of the policy. And there are others.

Mr. Fernandez argues that counseling or guidance is unnecessary: "People at any age have ready access to condoms at supermarkets and drugstores without the benefit of an educational or counseling component." (Let us leave aside the questions about why contraceptive services are being added to an overburdened school system if condoms are so readily available—as they are, and often for free.) More important, if someone is too thoughtless to buy condoms at a drugstore, what chance is there that he will bother to obtain a condom at school? Or that he or she would have the resolve to actually use a condom at the crucial moment? Indeed, the logic of Mr. Fernandez's argument suggests that the more responsible plan would have been to introduce supervised sex into the school system. If the children are going to have sex whether we think it proper or not, shouldn't we provide as safe an environment as possible? The city's unwillingness to go that far (we hope) demonstrates how the seemingly straightforward logic of the chancellor's argument conceals, rather than illuminates, the social and moral questions at stake.

The condom policy implicitly reduces sexual relations to a mechanical and nearly uncontrollable biological urge. It is this absence of a sense of human dignity—something adolescents, especially those who are poor, feel intensely in a society that already marginalizes them in countless ways—that lies at the root of this moral and sexual agnosticism. In an effort to make condom distribution matter-of-fact and therefore palatable, proponents present its case in a way that empties sex of meaning and moral consequence. Condoms and sexual information of all kinds are easily available, yet the tragic consequences of AIDS and other sexually transmitted diseases, of teen-age childbearing, and of sexual crime are increasingly with us, suggesting that sexual behavior is not so amenable to "common sense" and rationalized expectations as those with a penchant for social engineering would have us believe.

Condoms don't reduce AIDS and STDs.

But the problem goes still deeper. The condom plan's illusory practicality is symptomatic; a policy that medicalizes the social and moral question of adolescent sex is a way of avoiding more troubling realities. For example, it encourages us to continue to ignore the poverty and family breakdown that lie at the heart of destructive sexual behavior among many adolescents. AIDS is increasingly a disease of the urban poor, especially intravenous drug users and their sexual partners. Preventing the spread of AIDS among these adolescents is a question of influencing complex behavior and of understanding human motivation and the wellsprings of moral accountability. In subordinating sexual morality to the technology of contraception, the condom-distribution plan naively hopes to address human sexual life with the cause-and-effect logic of a vaccination procedure. Sex doesn't work that way. Indeed, in this context, the medicalization of sexual life dehumanizes it by removing it from the context of family life and the necessary ballast afforded the young by tradition and community values.

Teens are sexually active because adults do not teach moral behavior.

Authority figures can influence teens.

Protecting and promoting, rather than undermining, the authority of the family is essential in fostering the kind of moral responsibility that will keep young people alive in these circumstances. Adolescent sexual behavior is not a blind force

Parents are responsible for teens' bodies.

of nature. It is shaped and driven by many different cultural values—and at this time many of them are frankly exploitative. The school board's condom plan subtly absolves children of moral responsibility exactly where it should insist upon it. It establishes a premature adolescent autonomy and choice without examining what is being chosen. Self-reliance and self-discipline are essential qualities of maturity. Giving condoms to teen-agers because we have despaired of influencing their sexual decision making announces the board's enormous failure of moral and psychological imagination and tragically undermines the dignity of those it hopes to protect. Adolescents desperately want more, not less, expected of them.

Moral integrity is prior to bodily integrity.

"Clinic Visit" and "Condom Sense" agree about the facts: Many high school students are sexually active, and teenage AIDS cases rose at an alarming rate in the 1990s. From these facts, however, the articles move in different directions. The author of "Condom Sense" argues that providing condoms will aggravate the problem; the author of "Clinic Visit" argues that providing condoms will alleviate the problems.

The reason that the articles move in different directions is because the authors have different attitudes and different assumptions. These assumptions provide the links between evidence and claim. It takes some close analysis to identify these assumptions, but once they are laid out, it becomes clear how two very different positions can be constructed from the same evidence.

How Different Assumptions Produce Different Claims from the Same Evidence

Evidence: Many high school students are sexually active and at risk of contracting AIDS.

Claim 1: Providing condoms will help to alleviate the problem.

Claim 2: Providing condoms will make the problem worse.

First Assumption

Claim 1: Adult authority figures might not exist or might not have influence.

Claim 2: Authority figures do exist in teens' lives and can influence behavior.

(continued)

How Different Assumptions Produce Different Claims from the Same Evidence (continued)

Second Assumption

Claim 1: Teens are sexually active regardless.

Claim 2: Teens are sexually active because adults do not teach moral behavior.

Third Assumption

Claim 1: Using condoms reduces AIDS and STDs because they make sex safe.

Claim 2: Using condoms increases the risk of AIDS and STDs because they promote sexual activity and aren't 100 percent effective.

Fourth Assumption

Claim 1: Teens have the right to control their own bodies.

Claim 2: Parents have the right to control teens' bodies.

Fifth Assumption

Claim 1: The community is responsible for teens' bodies.

Claim 2: The parents or family are responsible for teens' bodies.

Sixth Assumption

Claim 1: Body integrity is prior to moral integrity.

Claim 2: Moral integrity is prior to bodily integrity.

Creating Your Readers

So far in this chapter on audience, you have been encouraged to think about your real audiences—the actual individuals who will read your arguments. But at the beginning of the chapter, you were also told that another kind of audience would be discussed before the chapter ends: the audience not *of* the argument but *in* the argument—the audience in the text.

What is the audience in the text? This is a rather difficult but important concept. First, consider an example—a short poem called "Spring and Fall: To a Young Child," written around 1880 by Gerard Manley Hopkins, a Jesuit priest who died in Dublin in 1889. The speaker in the poem is addressing a young child, "Margaret," who is crying in a sense of loss at the sight of "Goldengrove unleaving"—the sight of beautiful autumn leaves falling off the trees in front of her and turning into melancholy late November "leafmeal" (bits of leaves):

> Margaret, are you grieving
> Over Goldengrove unleaving?
> Leaves, like the things of man, you
> With your fresh thoughts care for, can you?
> Ah! As the heart grows older
> It will come to such sights colder
> By and by, nor spare a sigh
> Though worlds of wanwood leafmeal lie;
> And yet you weep and know why.
> Now no matter, child, the name:
> Sorrow's springs are the same.
> Nor mouth had, no nor mind, expressed
> What heart heard of, ghost guessed:
> It is the blight man was born for,
> It is Margaret you mourn for.

Who is the audience of this poem? Despite its title and the presence of "Margaret" in the poem, "Spring and Fall" wasn't really written for a young child at all. Children cannot understand poetry this complicated (indeed, it might be hard for you to understand parts of it). The theme of the poem— mutability (the idea that humans will all turn into leafmeal one day and had best remember that!)—isn't exactly an idea that young children are ready for. The real audience is adults who have grown older, adults whom Hopkins wants to remind that what is truly important in life is the certainty of death. "Margaret" serves as the **audience in the text**—a fictional character created by the author to aid him in making his rhetorical point. Think of it this way: Hopkins creates in his poem a sort of miniature drama, complete with characters (Margaret and the speaker) and action (the leaves falling, the tears, the speaker's sermon). The real readers eavesdrop on and observe this created drama for the author to achieve his rhetorical purpose: to remind readers, in a sort of sermon, about their ultimate end.

What does all this have to do with argument? All writing, believe it or not, can be seen as a sort of verbal drama akin to "Spring and Fall." It has fictional speakers just as this poem has a speaker; it has fictional listeners just as this poem has its Margaret; and it has verbal action. Sometimes the fictional listeners are overtly present, like young Margaret. An open letter that is published in a newspaper is one such example; the letter is addressed to a particular person but is really intended for all the readers of the paper. Martin Luther King, Jr.'s famous "Letter from Birmingham Jail" begins "To My Fellow Clergymen" and then seems to address those clergymen as "you" throughout the course of the letter. But the letter wasn't really addressed to the clergymen, or King would not have published it in several public places. The clergymen served as the audience in the text, but the real audience was the general public whose support King sought for the civil rights movement.

You can make these strategies work for you. When you write an argument, it's important first to think about what you want your readers to do. If you want to change their attitude, you will have to work hard to influence them with good reasons. But if you want them to take some action, you should give some thought to the kind of role you imply for your reader. You might want to say specifically to your readers that if they share your beliefs about a certain subject—for example, the importance of clean water in the streams and lakes of your city or town—then they should be willing to vote for strict zoning and pollution laws and to pay for the cost of enforcing them.

RICK REILLY

Bare in Mind

Rick Reilly (1958–) is a senior writer for Sports Illustrated. *His "Life of Reilly" column, which runs weekly on the last page of* SI, *both delights and infuriates many readers. The topics of his columns have ranged from following ice skater Katarina Witt behind the Iron Curtain to hanging out with actor Jack Nicholson in the front row of Los Angeles Lakers games to playing golf with Bill Clinton and with O.J. Simpson. He is the author of two novels,* Missing Links *and* Slo-Mo: My Untrue Story, *and a collection of his columns,* Life of Reilly, *and he is coauthor of biographies of Brian Bosworth, Wayne Gretzky, Charles Barkley, and Marv Albert.*

Jenny Thompson, winner of eight
Olympic gold medals.

*In "Bare in Mind," Reilly
writes in response to columns
and letters to the editor by
outraged readers of* Sports
Illustrated *that criticized the
publication of a partly nude
photo of Olympic swimmer
Jenny Thompson. The letters
and the controversial photo
are reproduced here. Typical of
his column, Reilly uses
provocative language, calling
critics of his magazine
"hypocrites" and "prudes." Why
do you think Reilly takes this
mocking tone? What responses
does he anticipate from the
readers of* Sports Illustrated?
*Ultimately, who do you agree
with, Reilly or one of the letter
writers—and why?*

Letters to the Editor, *Sports Illustrated*, September 4, 2000
Leave the toplessness in your swimsuit issue where the bimbos belong
and put Jenny Thompson in the same place of respect that you put other
top athletes.

Kim Baer, Broken Arrow, Okla.

After seeing the pose of Thompson, I turned every page of your magazine. Funny, the male athletes were fully clothed. Not one had his pants
off with his hands covering his anatomy.

Elizabeth Vidmar, Gobles, Mich.

1   **WOW**, Jenny Thompson has a nice pair, doesn't she? Massive. Firm.
Perfectly shaped.

2   Her thighs, I mean.

3   At least that's what blew *me* away when I saw the five-time Olympic
gold-medalist swimmer topless, hands over her breasts, in these pages re-

cently. Killer thighs that could crush anvils. Calves sharp enough to slice tomato. Biceps that ought to be on a box of baking soda.

4   So why do some women have their girdles all in a wad? Why is the Women's Sports Foundation (WSF) so upset? Why did former WSF president Donna de Varona say of Thompson and other women athletes who have posed nude, "I want them to keep their clothes on." Why did *USA Today* columnist Christine Brennan go all Aunt Bea, complaining that the Thompson picture "sends [girls] the insecure message that an old stereotype still lives and thrives. If you doubt this, look at the picture and notice where your eye goes first . . . right to her chest."

5   What a load of hypocrites. When Dennis Rodman posed nude on a motorcycle, I don't recall Brennan complaining about where women's eyes went. Lance Armstrong, Dan O'Brien and Ricky Williams have all posed nude, and I don't remember de Varona rushing around trying to get them to put on a towel.

6   "I don't get this," WSF executive director Donna Lopiano told *The Orlando Sentinel*. "When you've spent half your life looking down at the line at the bottom of the pool—and you've given up everything—it's incongruent to take that body you worked so hard to build and use it for sex."

7   I agree, Ms. Lopiano. You *don't* get it. Thompson took her clothes off *because* she spent her whole life looking at the bottom of swimming pools. If she had to miss a lifetime of proms and parties and triple fudge cake, at least she should be able to show the world what she was building in the gym six hours a day. "I'm proud of my body," Thompson says, "and the work it's taken to get it where it is."

8   Retired Olympic swimmer Anita Nall told ESPN's *Outside the Lines* that the picture gives young girls the message that "women achieve empowerment through sexuality." But I don't see sex in that picture. Thompson isn't half in heat. She's not pouring a pitcher of milk on herself. She's not biting her knuckles. She's just standing there, staring right at us, confident, strong, with a look that says, *C'mon, let's wrestle. You'll lose.*

9   I mean, *look* at that picture! That picture tells you more about the kind of dedication it takes to be an Olympian than could be said in an entire issue of *Women's Sports and Fitness*. Maybe that's why *Women's Sports and Fitness* just ran nude shots of Thompson along with sister swimmers Dara Torres, Amy Van Dyken and Angel Martino.

10   And it's not just them. The Australian women's soccer team and Katarina Witt and Brandi Chastain and 12 women U.S. track and field athletes, including middle-distance runner Nnenna Lynch and high jumpers Amy

Acuff and Tisha Waller, and plenty others have also posed in the buff. There's no old stereotype here. These women aren't hung up about getting liberated. They *are* liberated, were born that way. They're coming from a whole new place in feminism—rugged, gorgeous, prideful athleticism—free of the old butch, male-hater stereotype women jocks used to fight.

11   That's what's really insulting about this prude uproar. These aren't 18-year-old girls having to strip at the Baby Doll Club to pay their rent. These are intelligent, grown women. Thompson is heading for medical school. Lynch is a Rhodes scholar. Waller is a churchgoing former elementary school teacher. It's kind of like the Herminator holding up his Atomics or Richard Petty standing next to his Plymouth. *Hey, you wanna see under the hood?* Aren't these grumpy women pro choice?

12   Bad messages? Here are women with *real* bodies, *fit* bodies, *attainable* bodies—not bodies you can only get through the Lucky Gene Club or plastic surgery or throwing up your lunch every day. You want a bad message? Set up Elle Macpherson as the ideal feminine role model. Trying to be 5' 11", 103 pounds with a 22-inch waist and a 38-inch bust sends a bad message.

13   Thompson sends young girls a terrific message: Fit is sexy. Muscles are sexy. Sport is sexy. Give it a try sometime.

14   And will somebody please remind de Varona that ancient Olympians competed in the nude in the first place?

Ad for "Got Milk?" with Mark McGwire

Men's bodies, like women's bodies, are used to sell products. The "Got Milk?" series of ads display people with great bodies with the explicit claim that drinking milk helps to build those bodies. Bodies, however, convey multiple messages to audiences.

Mark McGwire's bulging biceps became controversial in 1998 when he set the major league home run record (later broken by Barry Bonds). McGwire admitted he used androstenedione, a legal steroid, which set off a debate about whether he was influencing teenage boys to believe that steroids are not harmful. McGwire also takes the dietary supplement creatine, which builds muscle mass and increases endurance. From the viewpoint of McGwire's critics, the "Got Milk?" ad that appeared in Sports Illustrated *in March 2000 may have been advertising more than milk.*

Going, going, gone.

Time for more milk. It's got stuff leading sports drinks don't—
like protein, potassium and calcium. That's why I always have
an ice-cold glass...as soon as I get home.

got milk?

Getting Started: Writing for Particular Audiences

1. Write a letter to the editor of your campus newspaper arguing that
   your college or university (A) should emphasize computer education
   OR (B) has placed too much emphasis on technology and should encourage more face-to-face education.

If you choose A, here are some points you might think about:

■ Technology will be increasingly involved in how we create, communicate, store, and use knowledge.

■ Computers offer access to vast amounts of information and to people around the world.

■ Nearly every occupation that requires a college education requires extensive use of computers.

If you choose B, here are some other points you might think about:

■ Technology is a means to an end, not an end in itself; therefore, emphasizing technology neglects what is at the heart of education.

■ Computers are expensive and divert money from other programs.

■ Occupations in the future will require people who can adapt quickly to change, not people who are trained in the use of specific technologies.

2. Rewrite your letter for junior high school students, persuading them that (A) gaining expertise in using computers will be essential for their later education OR (B) gaining a solid general education is more important than learning how to use computers.

3. Rewrite your letter for the governor of your state, urging him or her to take leadership. If you don't know your governor's views on education, assume for the moment that he or she is very much in favor of students going to school over the Internet and doesn't believe in building more campuses or hiring more faculty.

4. Analyze the changes you made when you rewrote the letters. Did you change any reasons? Did you provide different background? How did you adjust the style? What other changes did you make?

CHAPTER 4

The Rhetoric of Arguments

Facts Alone Do Not Persuade

Chapter 1 explains how *Silent Spring* became an influential book that shaped thinking about the environment in the United States. Rachel Carson was not the first person to warn against the excessive use of pesticides, nor was she the first to urge that people think of the environment as a unified system in which changing one part means affecting the others. But she engaged her readers as no scientific writer on the environment had done before. She had good reasons to support her claims, but the way she wrote also stirred her readers into action.

Part of the brilliance of *Silent Spring* is that Carson didn't let the facts speak for themselves. In the following two paragraphs, she makes a simple point that insect populations are held in check by nature. Notice how she illustrates this broad principle with a personal example:

No one knows how many species of insects inhabit the earth because there are so many yet to be identified. But more than 700,000 have already been described. This means that in terms of the number of species, 70 to 80 percent of the earth's creatures are insects. The vast majority of these insects are held in check by natural forces, without any intervention by man. If this were not so, it is doubtful that any conceivable volume of chemicals—or any other methods—could possibly keep down their population.

The trouble is that we are seldom aware of the protection afforded by natural enemies until it fails. Most of us walk unseeing through the world, unaware of its beauties, its wonders, and the strange and sometimes terrible intensity of the lives that are being lived about us. So it is that the activities of insect predators and parasites are known to few. Perhaps we many have noticed an oddly shaped insect of ferocious mien on a bush in the garden and been dimly aware that the praying mantis lives at the expense of other insects. But we see with understanding eye only if we have walked in the garden at night and here and there with a flashlight have glimpsed the mantis stealthily creeping upon her prey. Then we sense something of the drama of the hunter and the hunted. Then we begin to feel something of that relentlessly pressing force by which nature controls her own.

> **Your success in arguing depends on how you represent yourself and how you connect with your audience's values.**

Carson turned a dull point into a fascinating observation. She was keenly aware that the facts by themselves are not persuasive. She knew that she had to appeal to the heart as well as the mind. Her task wasn't simply to get people to feel sorry for animals that were killed by pesticides. She wanted people to think about nature differently. She wanted people to think of themselves as part of the natural world, and she wanted her readers to share her own great curiosity about nature. Convincing her readers that massive poisoning of insects meant also poisoning ourselves was a way to get people to think about ecology.

Let's take a look at a more recent book that also makes an argument that goes against the grain of popular thinking: *Eat Fat* by Richard Klein. Klein is a professor of comparative literature at Cornell University who grew tired of writing just for other professors and decided to write for a broad audience on a topic that was close to his heart: being overweight. *Eat Fat* became a brilliant success, enjoying rave reviews and selling many copies. Klein begins by observing that no nation is more obsessed with being thin than the United States. Consumers spend $33 billion a year on weight loss. But the results of all this money and self-denial are largely negative. People in the United States are the fattest people on the earth, at least among developed nations. Fashion models keep getting thinner to the point of looking like victims of starvation, but nearly half of U.S. women wear size 14 or larger, and about 32 percent wear size 16 or larger. Americans continue to gain weight at an astounding rate, adding 10 percent to their bulk on the average from 1984 to 1996, a time when health consciousness was never higher and when Americans dieted more and exercised more than they ever had in their history. But almost all their good efforts were doomed to failure. Out of 100 people who went on diets, 96 were even fatter three or four years later.

Richard Klein takes a position contrary to what most of us believe. He thinks that maybe the fact that Americans are getting fatter isn't really failure, that there may be good reasons why so many people are getting fatter. Furthermore, he argues that maybe this is a good thing rather than a bad thing. He begins by analyzing our hatred of fat. He says that there are three primary motives for people's desire to be thin. First, they believe that fat is ugly. Although this attitude is less than a hundred years old, it is constantly reinforced by the images of beautiful people that pervade the media. Second, people believe that fat is unhealthy. The medical, diet, and insurance industries have all promoted the idea that being thin is healthier and that thin people live longer. Third, people believe that fat weighs them down. Thinner people are seen as sexier, faster, and more agile—better suited for the fast-paced lifestyle of Western nations.

For each of these beliefs, Klein offers good reasons to think otherwise. Fat has not always seemed so disgusting to Americans. Indeed, a hundred years ago, fat signified health and well-being. People wanted to gain weight, and books were written telling them how to become plump. The turn of the century brought the so-called Banquet Years, marked by feasts on every occasion. One of the biggest eaters was President William H. Taft, who weighed over 300 pounds at his inauguration in 1908.

To question the attitude that fat is unhealthy, Klein notes that the spread of dieting has often led to less-healthy people, causing eating disorders in children as young as nine years of age, not to mention thousands of teenagers and adults. Furthermore, dieting has exactly the opposite effect of its purpose; it makes people fatter after a few years. Apparently, when the body is deprived of something it wants, it finds ingenious methods of satisfying those cravings. Evidence from research studies suggests that the human body has a certain level of fat that it tries to maintain. When someone cuts down on fat, the body may overreact and make fat more efficiently, thus causing the person to blow up rather than slim down. And contrary to the belief that thin people are sexier, Klein cites several studies showing that fat people are more sexually active.

Nevertheless, Klein is well aware that he is not going to convince many people with good reasons that appeal to the intellect. The problem (and opportunity) that Klein faces in defending fat is people's attitude toward it.

Nearly everyone in the United States believes down deep that being fat is bad. Klein writes, "It's easy in our society to love thin, but hard to achieve it. It's easy to be fat today, but hard to love it." Klein's task of arguing a position that people should not only accept fat but come to believe that fat is beautiful seems too ridiculous even to consider. After all, Americans have been taught all their lives to loathe fat.

So what do you do when you are in a very difficult rhetorical situation like the one into which Klein puts himself? Klein has an ingenious strategy, and he's honest about what he is attempting. He writes:

> My fundamental purpose, the whole aim of this book, summed up in its title, is not to convince but to charm you. By that I don't only mean to please you or seduce you into accepting my arguments, in the common sense of charm; I mean as well something more literal, more concrete: this book aims to work like a charm, to cast a spell by conjuring a spirit— a compelling voice, repetitive, monotonous, as if from another world, that says over and over EAT
>
> FAT.

Klein aims to persuade not through appealing to the reader's intellect but through the power of his voice. His voice makes the reader want to keep reading. And a reader who keeps reading at least grants the possibility that there are other attitudes toward fat besides the one that dominates in U.S. culture. Maybe the reader even admits that people in the United States would be a little happier if they weren't so obsessed with fat. If this happens, Klein has been successful.

In Chapter 1, we discuss how Aristotle recognized that good reasons that appeal to the intellect (logos) is only one strategy for effective arguments. He maintained that an audience has to view a speaker as trustworthy and reliable if they are to consider seriously the speaker's argument. Thus, an effective speaker has to seem credible to the audience through the effects of what Aristotle called ethos. Aristotle also recognized that appeals to emotions, values, and beliefs play important roles in effective arguments. He classified these appeals as pathos. Appeals to emotions, values, and beliefs often get downplayed in college writing courses, especially in the sciences and social sciences. But Rachel Carson knew that dry scientific argument would not move the government to ban DDT. And Richard Klein understood from the beginning that he would have to use alternative appeals; that is, he would have to win his readers by his witty style, his knowledge of history, and his shrewd observations about modern culture. Much can be learned from their tactics.

▨ Ethos: Creating an Effective Persona

You have probably noticed that many times in the course of reading, you get a very real sense of the kind of person who is doing the writing. Even if you have never read this person's writing before, even if you really know nothing about the actual person behind the message, you still often get a sense of the character and personality of the writer just by reading. How you respond to the message to some extent depends on how you respond to the person who delivers it. The term *ethos* refers to the persuasive value associated with this person that is created in the text. People sometimes use the term *persona* to distinguish the narrator—the voice in the text—from the real author. You have encountered a great number of created personas in your reading. Sometimes it is obvious that the narrator is not the author; for example, Huckleberry Finn is a created persona to be distinguished from the real author, Mark Twain. Mark Twain, the pen name used by Samuel Clemens, is also a kind of persona. Clemens did public lecture tours adopting the Mark Twain personality, performing the equivalent of today's stand-up comedy. But in fact, every piece of writing is delivered by a created character, a persona, who may or may not have much in common with the real author.

In March 1997, scientists at the Oregon Regional Primate Research Center held a press conference to announce that they had successfully cloned two rhesus monkeys from early stage embryos. They had taken a set of chromosomes from cells in a primitive monkey embryo and inserted them into egg cells from which the original DNA had been removed. These embryos were then implanted in the wombs of host mothers using in vitro fertilization techniques. The monkeys were born normally and were expected to live as long as twenty years. Donald Wolf, a senior scientist at the center, called the cloning a major breakthrough, since it would remove some of the uncertainties in animal research that might have been attributed to genetic differences among animals.

Other people were greatly alarmed by the cloning of the monkeys that followed closely the announcement of the successful cloning of sheep. President Bill Clinton called the research "troubling" and immediately banned any federal funding for experiments that might lead to the cloning of human beings. The U.S. Congress organized hearings that began in March 1997 to examine the implications of cloning research.

Following are two examples of letters sent to the House Science Subcommittee on Technology following the hearings. What persona did the writer of each of the following letters create?

Rep. Connie Morella, Chairperson
House Science Subcommittee on Technology
2319 Rayburn House Office Building
Washington, DC 20515

Dear Representative Morella:

I am pleased to see among members of Congress great concern that humans
should not be cloned. What perplexes me is the lack of protest against cloning
animals. "Repulsive," "repugnant," "offensive"—scientists and politicians alike
have used these words to describe human cloning experiments, but these adjec-
tives should also be invoked to describe cloning experiments on animals.

There are both ethical and scientific reasons to oppose the cloning of animals.
Animals are simply not commodities with whose genetic material we can tam-
per in pursuit of human ends. M. Susan Smith, director of the Oregon Primate
Research Center, where Rhesus monkeys were cloned from embryo cells, says
that we should be glad that scientists will now need to use "only" 3 or 4 animals
instead of 20 or 30. But Smith and other proponents of animal experimentation
really just don't get it. What about the 3 or 4 beings who will suffer and die in
experiments? We don't bargain with lives—3 or 40—it's their use in experiments
that's wrong.

Smith and other scientists justify their work by stating that genetically identical
monkeys will help research into AIDS, alcoholism, depression and other illnesses.
Scientists can clone a million monkeys, but they still won't be good models for
human disease. It is not genetic variability that limits the effectiveness of animal
experimentation—it's that the physiology of animal species differs. Animals are
not "little humans," and there's no way that researchers can clone themselves
around that reality.

At the recent Congressional hearings on the ethics of cloning, testimony was
heard from the following: the director of National Institutes of Health, the largest
funding agency of animal experimentation in the country; the head of Genzyme
Transgenics Corporation, a company that seeks to profit from genetically manipulated animals; a representative from the U.S. Department of Agriculture, which
is interested in the potential of cloning animals for food; Smith of Oregon Primate
Research Center; and an ethicist who declared (and numerous exposés of animal
experiments refute) that we do not permit research that is cruel to animals in our
society.

There was a voice missing from this panel biased in favor of animal cloning: someone to represent the animals, whose lives and interests are so readily dismissed.
We all need to speak up for them now and demand legislation to ban all cloning
experiments.

Sincerely,
Helen Barnes

Rep. Connie Morella, Chairperson
House Science Subcommittee on Technology
2319 Rayburn House Office Building
Washington, DC 20515

Dear Representative Morella:

I cannot believe you actually pretended to have a hearing on animal cloning and only invited people in favor of cloning. Why didn't you invite someone to speak for the animals? What a waste of our tax dollars! You should be passing laws against cloning instead of trying to justify it.

Don't you understand that the monkeys are being cloned to be killed? Thousands of monkeys have died in research on cancer and AIDS, and we're still no closer to finding cures. Don't you see that such research is useless? It's not that difficult to figure out. Monkeys are not people. It doesn't matter if they have identical genes or not.

We see what's happening. This is another example of government protecting big business over the interests of the people. The only people who will benefit from cloning animals are the big executives of the high-tech companies and a few scientists who will make big profits.

Haven't you read the polls and noticed that the great majority of Americans are opposed to cloning? You'll find out how we feel when you have to run for reelection!

                              Sincerely,
                              Ed Younger

Both letters contain the same major points, and both are passionate in demanding legislation to end cloning of animals. Both assert that cloning monkeys for research purposes is wrong because it lacks scientific and ethical justification. But they stand apart in the ethos of the writer.

The writer of the first letter, Helen Barnes, attempts to establish common ground by noting that nearly everybody is opposed to the cloning of humans. Barnes makes a bridge to her issue by noting that the terms used for human cloning—*repulsive, repugnant, offensive*—should also be used for the cloning of animals. She urges Representative Morella to look at monkeys as beings rather than genetic material for the use of researchers. She points out the absence of any voices opposed to the use of monkeys for experiments at the hearings on cloning. She takes a strong stand at the end, but she uses "we," inviting Representative Morella to join her.

The writer of the second letter, by contrast, is confrontational from the outset. Ed Younger accuses Representative Morella of stacking the deck by inviting only proponents of cloning to the hearing. He insinuates that she is stupid if she doesn't realize the cloned monkeys will be killed and that the use of animals for testing has not produced cures for diseases such as cancer and AIDS. He suggests that she is a dupe of high-tech companies by taking their side. He ends with a threat to vote her out of office. His persona is clearly that of angry citizen.

Representatives often receive more than a thousand letters, faxes, and emails each day, and they have to deal with letters from angry people all the time. Usually, staff members answer the mail and simply tally up who is for and against a particular issue. Often, the reply is a form letter thanking the writer for his or her concern and stating the representative's position. But sometimes, representatives personally write detailed answers to letters from their constituents. Imagine that you are Representative Morella and you have to answer these two letters. Ed Younger's persona makes it difficult to say more than "I appreciate hearing your opinion on this issue." Helen Barnes's persona leaves open the possibility of an exchange of ideas.

People make judgments about you that are based on how you represent yourself when you write. Sometimes the angry voice is the one to present if you believe that your readers need a wake-up call. However, most people don't like to be yelled at. Just as you can change your voice orally when the situation calls for it—just as you can speak in a friendly way, in an excited way, or in a stern way in different circumstances—so too you should be able to modulate your voice in writing, depending on what is called for. Some important factors are the following:

■ Your relationship with your audience (your voice can be less formal when you know someone well or when you are communicating with people in the same circumstances than when you are communicating with a relative stranger or with someone above or below you in an organization)

■ Your audience's personality (different people respond sympathetically to different voices)

■ Your argument (some arguments are more difficult to make than others)

■ Your purpose (you may take a more urgent tone if you want your readers to act immediately)

■ Your genre (arguments in formal proposals usually have a different voice from arguments in newspaper sports and opinion columns)

Argue Responsibly

In Washington, D.C., cars with diplomatic license plates often park illegally. Their drivers know they will not be towed or have to pay a ticket. For people who abuse the diplomatic privilege, the license plate says in effect, "I'm not playing by the rules."

In a similar way, you announce you are not playing by the rules when you begin an argument by saying "in my opinion." First, a reader assumes that if you make a claim in writing, you believe that claim. More important, it is rarely *only* your opinion. Most beliefs and assumptions are shared by many people. If it is only your opinion, it can be easily dismissed. But if your position is likely to be held by at least a few other members of your community, then a responsible reader must consider your position seriously.

Choosing an Appropriate Voice

Arguments that are totally predictable quickly lose their effectiveness. If you use the same strategy all the time—introduce your points, make your points, and summarize your points—you will get the job done, but you might not convince anyone who doesn't think the same way you do already. People who write about complex issues don't expect to convert everyone to their way of thinking with a few paragraphs. It's enough to both register a point of view and get their readers to think a little bit differently. Often they can have some fun along the way too.

In the September 24, 1987, issue of *Rolling Stone*, P. J. O'Rourke published "LSD: Let the Sixties Die" in response to a Sixties revival that was going on at the time. (A similar revival occurred in 1997–1998, and we'll no doubt see the Sixties return again in 2007–2008.) O'Rourke wasted no time letting his readers know how he felt about the revival:

> There's a stench of patchouli oil in the air. The overrated old Grateful Dead have a hit record. Hemlines are headed up. Beatle bangs are growing out. People are saddling their children with goofy names. The peace symbol—footprint of the American chicken—is giving the spray-paint industry a bad name again. Oh, God! The Sixties are coming back.
>
> Well, speaking strictly for this retired hippie and former pinko beatnik, if the Sixties head my way, they won't get past the porch steps. I've got a twelve-gauge, double-barreled duck gun chambered for three-inch Magnum shells. Any Sixties come around here, they'll be history. Which, for chrissakes, is what they're supposed to be.

O'Rourke goes on to make fun of the excesses of the Sixties, using the language of the Sixties. Slang that was popular in the Sixties—"can you dig it?," "the whole riff," "pick up on the heavy vibes," "if you know where I'm coming from"—now sounds silly. Other phrases, such as "Wow, man, which way to the bummer tent?" remind us that all wasn't peace and love at the big rock concerts.

Through the first half of his argument, O'Rourke uses satire to point out that many Sixties fads were ridiculous, much of its music was bad, and the acceptance of widespread drug use harmed many young people. But he didn't stop there. He next says, "Even if we wanted to, we couldn't recreate the Sixties now. We just don't have what it takes any more. First of all, there aren't any politicians left worth killing." The focus of his satire shifts subtly from the Sixties to the Eighties. Of young people, he writes, "And too many of today's college students are majoring in Comparative Greed and Advanced Studies in Real-Estate Arts." He also jabs his own generation, which used to shun possessions.

Near the end, O'Rourke gives his piece one more twist: "There was another bad thing about the Sixties, all those loopy beliefs—Karma, Krishna, Helter Skelter, participatory democracy, and all that." It's startling to find "participatory democracy" in that list of dismissed fads, but that's exactly O'Rourke's point. Thus, it's not until the end that O'Rourke chooses to make his implicit claim: that Sixties revivals are bad not just because they celebrate vacuous fads such as bell-bottom pants and psychedelic music but also because

they reduce what is worth recover-
ing from the Sixties to fad status.

Being aware of your options
in creating a voice when you
write is one of the secrets of arguing successfully. Before those options are described for a specific
argument, a little background for
the case in point will be useful. In
June 1989, the Supreme Court
ruled in *Texas* v. *Johnson* to uphold the First Amendment right
to burn the U.S. flag as symbolic
political speech. An outraged
Congress approved the Flag Protection Act of 1989, but the
Senate voted down an amendment to the Constitution. After
the Flag Protection Act became
law, there were many protests
against it. Some protesters were
arrested, but the courts ruled that
the Flag Protection Act was unconstitutional. Pressure built to
get a flag protection amendment

Demonstration in Washington, D.C.,
May 1970

into the Constitution, and legislation was introduced for such an amendment
in the 1995, 1997, 1999, and 2001 sessions of Congress.

Imagine that you have decided to write an argument arguing that flag
burning should be protected as free speech. You think that people could find
better ways to protest than by burning the flag, but nonetheless, they still
should have that right. When you start researching the issue and look at the
text of laws that have been passed against flag burning, you discover that
the laws are vague about defining what a flag is. You realize that people could
be arrested and put in prison for cutting a cake with an image of the flag in
the icing at a Fourth of July picnic.

You decide that examining definitions of the U.S. flag is a great way to
begin your paper because if the flag cannot be defined, then you have a good
argument that attempts to ban burning of the flag are doomed to failure.
Congress cannot pass an amendment against something that it cannot accurately define. You look up the U.S. Code about the flag that was federal law
from 1968 to 1989, when it was overturned in the Supreme Court case of
Texas v. *Johnson*. It reads:

Whoever knowingly casts contempt upon any flag of the United States by publicly mutilating, defacing, defiling, burning, or trampling upon it shall be fined not more than $1,000 or imprisoned for not more than one year, or both.

The term "flag of the United States" as used in this section, shall include any flag, standard colors, ensign, or any picture or representation of either, or of any part or parts of either, made of any substance or represented on any substance, of any size evidently purporting to be either of said flag, standard, color, or ensign of the United States of America, or a picture or a representation of either, upon which shall be shown the colors, the stars and the stripes, in any number of either thereof, or of any part or parts of either, by which the average person seeing the same without deliberation may believe the same to represent the flag, standards, colors, or ensign of the United States of America.

You think the definition in the second paragraph is ridiculous. It could apply to red and white striped pants or almost anything that has stars and is red, white, and blue. But the question is how to make the point effectively in your analysis. Here are three versions of an analysis paragraph that would come after you quote the above law:

Version 1 (Distant, balanced)
The language of the 1968 law, passed in the midst of the protest over the Vietnam War, demonstrates the futility of passing laws against flag burning. Congress realized that protesters could burn objects that resembled the American flag and evade prosecution so they extended the law to apply to anything "the average person" believed to represent the flag. The great irony was that the major violators of this law were the most patriotic people in America, who put flags on their cars and bought things with images of flags. When they threw away their flag napkins, they desecrated the flag and violated the law.

Version 2 (Involved, angry)
The 1968 law against flag burning is yet another example of why the Washington bureaucrats who love big government always get it wrong. They see on TV something they don't like—protesters burning a flag. So they say, "Let's pass a law against it." But for the law to have teeth, they realize that it has to be far reaching, including every imagined possibility. So they make the law as broad as possible so the police can bust the heads of anyone they want to. The attempt to ban flag burning shows how people with good intentions take away your liberties.

Version 3 (Comedic)
"Wait a second!" you're probably saying to yourself. "Any number of stars? Any part or parts of either? On any substance? Or a picture or representa-

tion?" You bet. Burning a photo of a drawing of a three-starred red, white, and blue four-striped flag would land you in jail for a year. I'm not making this up. Do you still trust them to define what a flag is? I don't.

You can hear the differences in voices of these paragraphs. The first is the modulated voice of a radio or television commentator, appearing to give a distanced and balanced perspective. The second is the voice of an angry libertarian, asserting that the government that governs best is the one that governs least. The third is the voice of Comedy Central or the alternative press, laughing at what government tries to do. Once again, the point is not which one is most effective, because each could be effective for different audiences. The point is to be aware that you can take on different voices when you write and to learn how to control these voices.

Strong Beginnings

Stephen Covey begins his international best-seller, *The Seven Habits of Highly Effective People,* with this sentence: "In more than 25 years of working with people in business, university, and marriage and family settings, I have come in contact with many individuals who have achieved an incredible degree of outward success, but have found themselves struggling with an inner hunger, a deep need for personal congruency and effectiveness and for healthy, growing relationships with other people." The first sentence tells you a great deal about why the book became a best-seller. In one sentence, Covey establishes his own credentials and sets out the central issues that the book addresses. He also accomplishes the two things you have to do before you can get anyone to consider your claims and good reasons. You first have to convince your readers that what you want to talk about is worth their time to read. Next, you have to convince them that you know enough to be worthy of their attention.

By starting out with "25 years of working with people in business, university, and marriage and family settings," Covey establishes his ethos as the voice of experience. In the main part of the sentence, Covey poses in a subtle way the problem the book addresses: "I have come in contact with many individuals who have achieved an incredible degree of outward success, but have found themselves struggling with an inner hunger." He could have said something like "Many people who are well off are still unhappy," but that's not quite his point. He sets out the problem as a

(continued)

Strong Beginnings *(continued)*

contrast: Many people who have achieved outward success struggle with an inner hunger. But what does *inner hunger* mean? Covey finishes the sentence by defining *inner hunger*—"a deep need for personal congruency and effectiveness and for healthy, growing relationships with other people"—in a grammatical construction called an **appositive.** You've heard appositives frequently on newscasts. Broadcasters use appositives to sum up or describe the significance of an event in sentences such as "Today, the prime ministers of India and Pakistan signed a treaty concerning disputed territory in Kashmir, an agreement that will help to ease building tensions between the two countries."

So far so good. But what exactly does Covey mean by "a deep need for personal congruency and effectiveness" and "healthy, growing relationships"? Those concepts are abstract, and if Covey is going to keep his potential readers, he must make those concepts relate to those readers. The primary readers for *The Seven Habits of Highly Effective People* presumably are people who already work for corporations and organizations. Therefore, Covey follows with a series of examples his clients have related to him:

> I've set and met my career goals and I'm having tremendous professional success. But it's cost me my personal and family life. I'm not even sure I know myself and what's really important to me. I've had to ask myself—is it worth it?
>
> I've started a new diet—for the fifth time this year. I know I'm overweight, and I really want to change. I read all the new information, I set goals, I get myself all psyched up with a positive mental attitude and tell myself I can do it. But I don't. After a few weeks, I fizzle. I just can't seem to keep a promise I make to myself.
>
> I'm busy—really busy. But sometimes I wonder if what I'm doing will make any difference in the long run. I'd really like to think there was meaning in my life, that somehow things were different because I was here.

Evidently readers recognized themselves in these examples. The sales of *The Seven Habits of Highly Effective People* remain strong years after it was first published.

Covey offers a lesson about strong beginnings. Even if you don't have twenty-five years of experience on a particular subject, you can still get off to a fast start. Establish your subject, your voice, and what's at stake for your readers right away, and there's a good chance your readers will stick with you.

Pathos: Appealing to Your Reader's Values

Chapter 3 on audience discusses how to take into account your audience's attitude toward you and your argument as you develop your content. *Pathos* also is audience-oriented and attitude-oriented; it refers to appeals to your audience's most basic, heartfelt attitudes and values.

Sometimes, pathos is defined (and dismissed) simply as an unsubtle appeal to your audience's barely controllable emotional side. You know that your reader fears something, loves something, or despises something, and you somehow tie your argument to those feelings. Critics of television advertising contend that advertisers depend on purely emotional arguments when they connect driving a particular automobile with achieving success or depict drinking a brand of beer as part of a happy social life. Because in Western culture the emotions are often associated with the instinctive and irrational and subconscious—with the so-called animal side of human beings—pathos seldom gets much respectful attention in argument. Most people in academic disciplines and the professions, especially the sciences and engineering, never want to be accused of making bald-faced emotional arguments like the ones you see on television. Therefore, it is not surprising that arguments in most academic writing are presented as sober and reasonable, avoiding overt appeals to an audience's subconscious instincts and emotions.

Then again, there is nothing necessarily irrational about the emotions. As many of the old *Star Trek* episodes with Mr. Spock show, emotions make people human just as much as reason does. There's nothing irrational or unreasonable about an argument that "Our city should attend to its solid waste problems because we want our children to live in safe, healthy, and attractive communities," even if there are emotional values latent in that argument. As that statement also illustrates, there is also probably no such thing as a purely emotional argument—an argument that totally bypasses reason. Even a beer ad on television that depicts men as beach bums and women as bikini-clad bodies has an implicit argument with a claim: "If you drink our beer, you'll have more fun."

Appealing to emotions is not necessarily a bad strategy, but pathos is a broader concept than simply appealing to emotions. The example claim, "Our city should attend to its solid waste problems because we want our children to live in safe, healthy, and attractive communities," illustrates that there is another way to think about pathos. Think of pathos as an appeal to the most basic values held by your audience. Pathos carries emotional values because it refers to the values that people hold so dearly that they don't think about them very much and don't question them very often—values such as the importance of safety and security, freedom and personal liberty, loyalty and friendship, equal opportunity and fairness. If your claim is "Interstate highways in urban areas should have concrete dividers placed in the median to prevent vehicles from skidding across the median into oncoming traffic," you have made a logical, matter-of-fact statement. But this argument carries pathetic overtones because safety is one of most basic values. Indeed, it might be a good strategy to begin with an example of a tragic head-on collision that might have been prevented if all urban interstate highways had concrete dividers on their median strips.

Pathos fails in argument when the linkage isn't clear. The linkage in TV ads is often absent. Many ads imply that the user of the product will be attractive to the opposite sex, younger, or happier, but how these changes are supposed to happen is never made clear. Using pathos is not a shortcut to making an effective argument.

Strong Endings

Endings are often the toughest part of a work to write. The easy way out is to repeat what you have said earlier. If you're writing a PhD dissertation, summarizing your conclusions is a good way to end. But if your argument is relatively short—the equivalent of three or four double-spaced pages— then you should hope that your readers have not forgotten your main points by the time they get to the end. Instead, think of a way to end that will be emphatic rather than sleep inducing. Here is how Anne Marie O'Keefe concluded an argument against the use of drug testing by employers ("The Case against Drug Testing," *Psychology Today* [June 1987]: 36–38):

> Civil libertarians claim that as long as employees do their work well, inquiries into their off-duty drug use are no more legitimate than inquiries into their sex lives. Then why has drug testing become so popular? Perhaps because it is simple and "objective"—a litmus test. It is not easily challenged because, like the use of lie detectors, it relies on technology that few understand. It is quicker and cheaper than serious and sustained efforts to reduce illegal drug use, such as the mass educational efforts that have successfully reduced cigarette smoking. And finally, while drug testing may do little to address the real problem of drug use in our society, it reinforces the employer's illusion of doing something.
>
> Apparently some employers would rather test their employees for drugs than build a relationship with them based on confidence and loyalty. Fortunately,

(continued)

Strong Endings *(continued)*

there are employers, such as Drexelbrook Engineering Company in Pennsylvania, who have decided against drug testing because of its human costs. As Drexelbrook's vice president put it, a relationship "doesn't just come from a pay-check. When you say to an employee, 'you're doing a great job; just the same, I want you to pee in this jar and I'm sending someone to watch you,' you've un-dermined that trust."

O'Keefe's next-to-last paragraph answers the question, If drug testing is so bad, then why do so many employers require it? Her last paragraph concludes her article with a positive example rather than restating what she has said before. An example, an additional point, a quotation, or a call to action is a good alternative to a bland summary in the final paragraph.

The Language of Arguments

So far, this chapter has focused on language as a means of creating a voice when you write, but voice is just one way to discuss style in arguments. Just as a personal style reflects all that a person does—the way she dresses, the way she talks, her personality—so too does style in argument. At the most fundamental level, style in argument begins with language—the words and sentences that the writer selects and assembles. Paying close attention to the words you use and how you put sentences together can pay big dividends for you as a writer.

Advertisers have long understood the critical role that words play in persuading people. The writers of advertising copy are well aware that the average American is exposed to over three thousand ads a day and that such oversaturation has made people cynical about ads. Advertisers have to be clever to get our attention, so ads often use the tactics of poets and comedians. Words in ads often use puns and metaphors to draw our attention to the products they promote. A watch ad runs with the banner "Every second counts." An ad for a coffeemaker asks, "Who better to handle his ugly mug in the morning?" A plastic wrap ad shows two chicken legs under the headline "Stop our legs from drying out." A used-car ad appears under the words "Born again."

But it is not just clever plays on words that do the work in the language of advertising. We often find words in ads that do not make much sense at first reading. For example, a Nikon camera ad displays in big bold letters, "It's a stealth bomber with fuzzy dice." Calling a camera a "stealth bomber with fuzzy dice" is an example of metaphor. **Metaphor** is a Greek term that means "carry over," which describes what happens when you encounter a metaphor. You carry over the meaning from one word to another. Metaphor is but one kind of **figurative language.** Also common in advertising are **synecdoche,** in which the part is used to represent the whole (a hood ornament represents a car), and **metonymy,** in which something stands for something else with which it is closely associated (using flowers to represent a product's fresh scent).

There are other kinds of figurative language, but all involve the transfer of meaning from one word or phrase to another. How this transfer works is more complicated. If we encounter an unfamiliar metaphor such as the stealth bomber example, we do our best to make sense of what the writer means. Most metaphors, however, are much more familiar and don't force us to put forth much mental effort. Think of all the clichés you hear daily: Clichés are the spice of life, the bread and butter of any conversation, the greatest things since sliced bread, the . . . well, you get the picture. Time flies when you're having fun, and we could keep writing clichés like there's no to-morrow, but there's no use flogging a dead horse. Clichés at some point in their past were original metaphors, but through repeated use, their attention-grabbing power has worn out.

Shakespeare used his knowledge of how figurative language works to great effect in his sonnets, in which, again and again, he sets up a cliché, such as comparing his love to a summer day in *Sonnet 18,* only to subvert that cliché by carrying over other meanings. He says that his love is more temper-ate and more lovely than a summer's day, but more important, a summer day is closely followed by autumn and winter: "A summer's lease hath all too short a date." If beauty lasts for only a day, then it's not desirable. Shakespeare turns the cliché of comparing one's lover to a summer's day inside out.

What meanings, then, is the reader supposed to carry over from "stealth bomber with fuzzy dice" to a Nikon camera? Cameras don't have wings, wheels, jet engines, or bomb bays, nor are they covered with fake fur. The ad-vertisers didn't want the reader to work too hard, so they put in fine print at the bottom their interpretation of the metaphor: "The technology of a seri-ous camera. The spontaneity of a point-and-shoot. Now you don't have to choose between the two."

Metaphors are but one way in which advertisers exploit the associations many words carry in addition to their literal meanings. Many ads are sexually suggestive. A moisturizing cream ad announces: "Shed your inhibitions." An ad for an online shopping service tells us to "Go naked to the mall." A whiskey ad in an outdoor magazine states: "Get in touch with your masculine side." Nowhere are the associative meanings of words more carefully consid-ered than in the discourse of politics. Politicians sprinkle their speeches with positive words referring to themselves and their party, words such as these:

change, opportunity, truth, moral, courage, reform, prosperity, crusade, children, family, debate, candid, humane, pristine, liberty, commitment, principle, unique, duty, precious, care, tough, listen, learn, help, lead, vision, success, empower(ment), citizen, activist, mobilize, dream, freedom, peace, rights, pioneer, proud/pride, building, preserve, flag, environment, reform, strength, choice/choose, fair, protect, confident, incentive, hard work, initiative, common sense, passionate

In referring to their opponents, they use words such as these:

decay, failure, crisis, destructive, destroy, sick, pathetic, lie, bureaucracy, betray, shallow, endanger, coercion, hypocrisy, radical, threaten, waste, corruption, incompetent, impose, self-serving, greed, ideological, insecure, pessimistic, excuses, intolerant, stagnation, corrupt, selfish, insensitive, status quo, shame, disgrace, punish, cynicism, cheat, steal, abuse of power

Saying good things about yourself and bad things about your opponents is characteristic of all politicians. The key to winning most elections is to get the positive associations linked to the candidate you are supporting and the negative associations linked to the opponent.

Some people denounce the language of advertising and politics as being corrupted with bias. Although it is unfortunate that much advertising and political discourse does involve outright deception, to expect such language to be completely objective and free of bias is unrealistic. With the exception of purely functional words such as *the, to,* and *for,* all words carry various meanings and associations that they have picked up in the larger culture and individual experience. The word "Mom," for example, brings associations of your own mother and how motherhood is understood in your culture.

Rhetorical Analysis

To the general public the term *rhetoric* most commonly seems to denote highly ornamental or deceptive or even manipulative speech or writing: "That politician is just using a bunch of rhetoric" or "the rhetoric of that advertisement is highly deceptive" you hear people say. But the term *rhetoric* is also commonly used as a synonym for speaking or writing in general or for any other kind of communication: "*Silent Spring* is one of the most influential pieces of environmental rhetoric ever written," someone might say. As a college subject, rhetoric is often associated with how to produce effective pieces of communication following Aristotle's classic definition of rhetoric as "the art of finding in any given case the available means of persuasion." But in recent years rhetoric has also taken on an interpretive function; it has come to be used not just as a means of producing effective communications but also as a way of understanding communication. In short, rhetoric can be understood as both a productive and interpretive enterprise: "the study of language—and the study of how to use it."

Aristotle's emphasis on persuasion has been influential in the history of rhetoric. And so it is now common to understand rhetoric as fundamentally involved in the study of persuasion. But "persuasion" as used here must be persuasion very broadly construed, because recently the realm of rhetoric has come to include a great deal of territory—written and oral language used to persuade, to be sure, but also a great many other kinds of communication that have general designs on people's values and actions, attitudes, and beliefs. Rhetorical analysis can be interpreted as *an effort to understand how people within specific social situations attempt to influence others through language.* But not just through language: Rhetoricians today attempt to understand every kind of important symbolic action—not only speeches and articles, but also architecture (isn't it clear that the U.S. Capitol building in Washington makes an argument?), movies and television shows (doesn't *Ally McBeal* offer an implicit argument about the appropriate conduct of young professional women? doesn't *Friends* have designs on viewers' values and attitudes?), memorials (don't the AIDS quilt and the Vietnam Veterans Memorial make arguments about AIDS and about our national understanding of the Vietnam War?), as well as visual art, Web sites, advertisements, photos and other images, dance, popular songs, and so forth.

Rhetorical analysis is applicable to all these persuasive uses of symbolic words and acts (in Part 3 we discuss visual rhetoric). Through rhetorical analysis, people strive to understand particular pieces of writing and other types of communication. Rhetorical analysis is a kind of critical reading, which we describe in Chapter 1 as opposed to ordinary reading. Today we study the words of Abraham Lincoln at Gettysburg or Martin Luther King's 1963 "I Have a Dream" speech or Abigail Adams's famous letters to her husband—rhetorical performances never intended for a twenty-first-century audience. As a rhetorical analyst your job is to understand them better, to appreciate the *rhetorical situation* (i.e., the circumstances of subject, audience, occasion, and purpose) that Lincoln, King, and Adams found themselves in and how they made choices to further their aims. Rhetorical analysis is an effort to read interpretively, with an eye toward understanding an act of communication from different perspectives and how that act is crafted to earn a particular response. All the chapters in this book give you tools for rhetorical analysis, and in the reading selection for this chapter, we show you a few ways they can be applied.

E. B. WHITE

Education

E. B. White (1899–1985) is best known today as the author of Charlotte's Web *(1952). He contributed many essays to* The New Yorker *and other publications over his long career. "Education" was published first in* Harper's *in 1939 and later collected in* One Man's Meat. *White wrote the essay over a half century ago, but you may find it interesting and readable still, in part at least because it concerns a perennial American question: What should our schools be like? Is education better carried out in large, fully equipped, but relatively impersonal settings, or in smaller but intensely personal, teacher-dominated schools? At first it might seem that the author takes no sides, that he simply wishes to describe objectively the two alternatives, to record his son's experiences in each circumstance, and to celebrate each as an expression of national values. He gives equal time to each school, he spends the same amount of space on concrete details about each, and he seems in firm control of his personal biases ("I have always rather favored public schools"). Through his light and comic tone White implies that all will be well for his son—and our children—in either circumstance, that the two schools each are to be neither favored nor feared by us. "All one can say is that the situation is different" (paragraph 4), not better, in the two places.*

Or is it? Perhaps "Education" is less an objective, neutral appraisal than it is a calculated argument that subtly favors the country school.

1   I have an increasing admiration for the teacher in the country school where we have a third-grade scholar in attendance. She not only undertakes to instruct her charges in all the subjects of the first three grades, but she manages to function quietly and effectively as a guardian of their health, their clothes, their habits, their mothers, and their snowball engagements. She has been doing this sort of Augean task for twenty years, and is both kind and wise. She cooks for the children on the stove that heats the room, and she can cool their passions or warm their soup with equal competence. She conceives their costumes, cleans up their messes, and shares their confidences. My boy already regards his

[margin note: The teacher who presides over the country school appeals to the reader's emotions as the "ideal mother" stereotype.]

[margin note: Cleaning the Augean stables was one of the labors of Hercules.]

teacher as his great friend, and I think tells her a great deal more than he tells us.

2   The shift from city school to country school was something we worried about quietly all last summer. I have always rather favored public school over private school, if only because in public school you meet a greater variety of children. This bias of mine, I suspect, is partly an attempt to justify my own past (I never knew anything but public schools) and partly an involuntary defense against getting kicked in the shins by a young ceramist on his way to the kiln. My wife was unacquainted with public schools, never having been exposed (in her early life) to anything more public than the washroom of Miss Winsor's. Regardless of our backgrounds, we both knew that the change in schools was something that concerned not us but the scholar himself. We hoped it would work out all right. In New York our son went to a medium-priced private institution with semi-progressive ideas of education, and modern plumbing. He learned fast, kept well, and we were satisfied. It was an electric, colorful, regimented existence with moments of pleasurable pause and giddy incident. The day the Christmas angel fainted and had to be carried out by one of the Wise Men was educational in the highest sense of the term. Our scholar gave imitations of it around the house for weeks afterward, and I doubt if it ever goes completely out of his mind.

3   His days were rich in formal experience. Wearing overalls and an old sweater (the accepted uniform of the private seminary), he sallied forth at morn accompanied by a nurse or a parent and walked (or was pulled) two blocks to a corner where the school bus made a flag stop. This flashy vehicle was as punctual as death: seeing us waiting at the cold curb, it would sweep to a halt, open its mouth, suck the boy in, and spring away with an angry growl. It was a good deal like a train picking up a bag of mail. At school the scholar was worked on

The country school is more personal and nurturing, and the teachers are more caring.

White establishes his ethos in this paragraph. By disclosing his bias and by poking gentle humor at just about everything— his son "the scholar"; his wife the prim graduate of Miss Winsor's private school; himself; and, of course, both schools—White makes himself seem enormously sympathetic and trustworthy: fair-minded and unflappable, balanced and detached.

White's son has to be "pulled" to the bus stop for the city school.

The metaphor for the school bus is a monster that sucks up children.

Students are not taught but "worked on" by a team of professionals.

for six or seven hours by half a dozen teachers and a nurse, and was revived on orange juice in mid-morning. In a cinder court he played games supervised by an athletic instructor, and in a cafeteria he ate lunch worked out by a dietitian. He soon learned to read with gratifying facility and discernment and to make Indian weapons of a semi-deadly nature. Whenever one of his classmates fell low of a fever the news was put on the wires and there were breathless phone calls to physicians, discussing periods of incubation and allied magic.

The experience of the city school makes children sick.

4   In the country all one can say is that the situation is different and somehow more casual. Dressed in corduroys, sweatshirt, and short rubber boots, and carrying a tin dinner pail, our scholar departs at the crack of dawn for the village school, two and a half miles down the road, next to the cemetery. When the road is open and the car will start, he makes the journey by motor, courtesy of his old man. When the snow is deep or the motor is dead or both, he makes it on the hoof. In the afternoons he walks or hitches all or part of the way home in fair weather, gets transported in foul. The schoolhouse is a two-room frame building, bungalow type, shingles stained a burnt brown with weather-resistant stain. It has a chemical toilet in the basement and two teachers above the stairs. One takes the first three grades, the other the fourth, fifth, and sixth. They have little or no time for individual instruction, and no time at all for the esoteric. They teach what they know themselves, just as fast and as hard as they can manage. The pupils sit still at their desks in class, and do their milling around outdoors during recess.

White's language describing the country school emphasizes activity as opposed to the regimentation of the city school.

The image of the one-room or two-room schoolhouse appeals to the American love of the frontier and small town (associated with values of self-reliance, decency, and innocence).

Facilities and staff are minimal at the country school.

Instruction in the country school is about the basics, but students learn fast and well.

5   There is no supervised play. They play cops and robbers (only they call it "Jail") and throw things at one another—snowballs in the winter, rose hips in fall. It seems to satisfy them. They also construct darts, pinwheels, and "pick-up-sticks" (jackstraws), and the school itself does a brisk

Play at the country school is organized by the students, not by the school staff. It is spontaneous and fresh.

trade in penny candy, which is for sale right in the classroom and which contains "surprises." The most highly prized surprise is a fake cigarette, made of cardboard, fiendishly lifelike.

6   The memory of how apprehensive we were at the beginning is still strong. The boy was nervous about the change too. The tension, on that first fair morning in September when we drove him to school, almost blew the windows out of the sedan. And when later we picked him up on the road, wandering along with his little blue lunch-pail, and got his laconic report "All right" in answer to our inquiry about how the day had gone, our relief was vast. Now, after almost a year of it, the only difference we can discover in the two school experiences is that in the country he sleeps better at night—and *that* probably is more the air than the education. When grilled on the subject of school-in-country vs. school-in-city, he replied that the chief difference is that the day seems to go so much quicker in the country. "Just like lightning," he reported.

White is quite subtle in his conclusion, but of course the bottom line is that his son likes to go to the country school. Although he never states his claim explicitly, clearly White finds a personalized, unstructured school environment superior to a structured, supervised curriculum.

The first and last paragraphs are the positions of emphasis. White gives both to the country school while placing the city school in a less prominent position in the middle.

Steps in Writing a Rhetorical Analysis

1. **Find an argument that you either strongly agree with or strongly disagree with.** You can find arguments on the editorial pages of newspapers; in opinion features in magazines such as *Time*, *Newsweek*, and *U.S. News and World Report*, in magazines that take political positions such as *National Review*, *Mother Jones*, *New Republic*, *Nation*, and the online journal *Slate*; and the Web sites of activist organizations (for a list of these organizations, see www.yahoo.com/Society_and_Culture/ Issues_and_Causes/). Letters to the editor and online newsgroup postings probably won't work for this assignment unless they are long and detailed.

2. **Analyze the structure of the argument.** First, number the paragraphs, then on a separate page write a sentence summarizing each of the paragraphs. Where is the main claim located? Underline it. What are the rea-

sons offered in support of the claim? Put stars beside those. Are any opposing positions considered? If so, put an "O" beside those.

3. **Analyze the language and style of the argument.** Make a list of the key words in the argument. Which are controversial? Are the key terms adequately defined? Are any metaphors or other figurative language used in the argument? Does the writer use "I" or "we" or does he or she speak from a distanced viewpoint? How would you characterize the writer's style? Is it formal or informal? Is it serious, humorous, or satirical?

4. **Analyze the ethos.** How does the writer represent himself or herself? Does the writer have any credentials to be an authority on the topic? Do you trust the writer? Why or why not?

5. **Analyze the logos.** Where do you find facts and evidence in the argument? What kinds of facts and evidence does the writer present: Direct observation? Statistics? Interviews? Surveys? Secondhand sources such as published research? Quotes from authorities?

6. **Analyze the pathos.** Who do you think the argument was written for? Are there any places where the writer attempts to invoke an emotional response? Where do you find appeals to shared values with the audience? You are a member of that audience, so what values do you hold in common with the writer? What values do you not hold in common?

7. **Write a draft.**

   Introduction:
   - Describe briefly the argument you are analyzing, including where it was published, how long it is, and who wrote it. If the argument is on an issue unfamiliar to your readers, you may have to supply some background.

   Body:
   - Analyze the language and structure of the argument, using steps 2 through 6. Remember that you don't want to present your analysis as a list. Instead you might wish to focus on a particular aspect. For example, if you are analyzing E. B. White's "Education," a possible thesis is "White builds his ethos in several ways in 'Education.'"

   Conclusion:
   - Do more than simply summarize what you have said. You might, for instance, end with an example that typifies the argument. You don't have to end by either agreeing or disagreeing with the writer. Your task in this assignment is to analyze the strategies the writer uses.

8. **Revise, revise, revise. See Chapter 11 for detailed instructions.**

   Stage 1. Read your analysis aloud.
   Do no more in this stage than put checks in the margins that you can return to later. Think in particular about these things:

- **Your claim.** When you finish reading, summarize in one sentence what you claim in your analysis.
- **Your representation of yourself.** Forget for a moment that you wrote what you are reading. What impression do you have of you, the writer?
- **Your consideration of your readers.** Do you give enough background if your readers are unfamiliar with the issue?

Stage 2. Analyze your argument in detail.

- **Examine your organization.** What are the topics of each paragraph? Is the relationship of one paragraph to another clearly signaled?
- **Examine your evidence.** Are your claims supported by evidence in your analysis?
- **Consider your title and introduction.** Be as specific as you can in your title and, if possible, suggest your stance. Does your introduction get off to a fast start and convince your reader to keep reading?
- **Consider your conclusion.** Think about whether there is a summarizing point you can make, an implication you can draw, or another example you can include that sums up your position.
- **Analyze the visual aspects of your text.** Do the font and layout you selected look attractive? Would headings and subheadings help to identify key sections of your argument? Would the addition of graphics augment key points?

Stage 3. Focus on your style and proofread carefully.

- **Check the connections between sentences.** Notice how your sentences are connected. If you need to signal the relationship from one sentence to the next, use a transitional word or phrase.
- **Check your sentences for emphasis.** Elements at the beginning and the end of sentences tend to stand out more than things in the middle.
- **Eliminate wordiness.** See how many words you can take out without losing the meaning.
- **Use active verbs.** Anytime you can use a verb besides a form of *be* (*is, are, was, were*), take advantage of the opportunity to make your style more lively.
- **Proofread your spelling carefully.** Your spelling checker will miss many mistakes.
- **Use your handbook to check items of mechanics and usage.** Look up any item you are unsure of.

PART 2

Putting Good Reasons into Action
Options for Arguments

Imagine that you bought a new car in June and you take some of your friends to your favorite lake over the Fourth of July weekend. You have a great time until, as you are heading home, a drunk driver—a repeat offender—swerves into your lane and totals your new car. You and your friends are lucky not to be hurt, but you're outraged because you believe that repeat offenders should be prevented from driving, even if that means putting them in jail. You also remember going to another state that had sobriety checkpoints on holiday weekends. If such a checkpoint had been at the lake, you would still be driving your new car. You live in a town that encourages citizens to contribute to the local newspaper, and you think you could get a guest editorial published. The question is, how do you want to write the editorial?

You could tell your story about how a repeat drunk driver endangered the lives of you and your friends. You could argue for a stricter definition of driving while intoxicated (DWI) and for standard testing procedures. You could compare the treatment of drunk drivers in your state with the treatment of drunk drivers in another state. You could cite statistics that drunk drivers killed 15,786 people in 1999, a figure that was down from previous years but still represented too many needless deaths. You could evaluate the present enforcement of drunk driving laws as unsuccessful or less than totally successful. You could propose taking vehicles away from repeat drunk drivers and forcing them to serve mandatory sentences. You could argue that your community should have sobriety checkpoints at times when drunk drivers are likely to be on the road.

You're not going to have much space in the newspaper, so you decide to argue for sobriety checkpoints. You know that they are controversial. One of your friends in the car with you said that they are unconstitutional because they involve search without cause. However, after doing some research to find out whether they are defined as legal or illegal, you learn that on June 14, 1990, the U.S. Supreme Court upheld the constitutionality of using checkpoints as a deterrent and enforcement tool against drunk drivers. But you still want to know whether most people would agree with your friend that sobriety checkpoints are an invasion of privacy. You find opinion polls and surveys going back to the 1980s that show 70 to 80 percent of those polled support sobriety checkpoints. You also realize that you can argue by analogy that security checkpoints for alcohol are similar in many ways to airport security checkpoints that protect the passengers. You decide you will finish by making an argument from consequence. If people who go to the lake with plans to drink a lot know in advance that there will be checkpoints, they will find a designated driver or some other means of safe transportation, and everyone else will also be a little safer.

The point of this example is that people very rarely set out to define something in an argument for the sake of definition, compare for the sake of comparison, or adopt any of the other ways of structuring an argument. Instead, they have a purpose in mind, and they use the kinds of arguments that are discussed in Part 2—most often in combination—as means to an end. Most arguments use multiple kinds of approaches and multiple sources of good reasons. Proposal arguments in particular often analyze a present situation with definition, causal, and evaluative arguments before advancing a course of future action. The advantage of thinking explicitly about the structure of arguments is that you often find other ways to argue. Sometimes you just need a way to get started writing about complex issues.

An even greater advantage of thinking explicitly about specific kinds of arguments is that they can often give you a sequence for constructing arguments. Take affirmative action policies for granting admission to college as an example. No issue has been more controversial on college campuses during the last ten years. But what exactly does *affirmative action* mean? You know that it is a policy that attempts to address the reality of contemporary inequality based on past injustice. But injustice to whom and by whom? Do all members of minorities, all women, and all people with disabilities have equal claims for redress of past injustices? If not, how do you distinguish among them? And what exactly does affirmative action entail? Do all students who are admitted by affirmative action criteria automatically receive scholarships? Clearly, you need to define affirmative action first before proposing any changes in the policy.

Since affirmative action policies have been around for a few years, next you might investigate how well they have worked. If you view affirmative action as a cause, then what have been its effects? You might find, for example, that the percentage of African Americans graduating from college dropped from 1991 through 2001 in many states. Furthermore, affirmative action policies have created a backlash attitude among many whites who believe, rightly or wrongly, that they are victims of reverse racism. But you might find that enrollment of minorities at your university has increased substantially since affirmative action policies were instituted. And you might come across a book by the then-presidents of Princeton and Harvard, William G. Bowen and Derek Bok, entitled *The Shape of the River: Long-Term Consequences of Considering Race in College and University Admissions*, which examines the effects of affirmative action policies at twenty-eight of the nation's most select universities. They found that African-American graduates of elite schools were more likely than their white counterparts to earn graduate degrees and to take on civic responsibilities after graduation.

With a definition established and evidence collected, you can move to evaluation. Is the goal of achieving diversity through affirmative action admissions policies a worthy one because white people enjoyed preferential treatment until the last few decades? Or are affirmative action admissions policies bad because they continue the historically bad practice of giving preference to people of certain races and because they cast into the role of victims the people they are trying to help? When you have a definition with evidence and have made an evaluation, you have the groundwork for making a recommendation in the form of a proposal. A proposal argues what "should" or "must" be done in the future.

Even though types of argument are distinguished in Part 2, they are closely linked parts of a whole. Though each type of argument can stand alone, they always involve multiple aspects. If you are clear in your purpose for your argument and have a good sense of the knowledge and attitudes of the people your argument is aimed toward, then the types of arguments you want to use will often be evident to you.

CHAPTER 5

Definition Arguments

In early 2000 Chrysler began selling its PT Cruiser, which quickly became one of its best-selling products. But what exactly is the PT Cruiser—a car or a truck? It is built on the chassis of a Dodge Neon, which is a car. The press referred to it as a station wagon. Chrysler, however, argued that the PT Cruiser is a truck because it has a flat cargo area when the rear seats are folded down. The definition of the PT Cruiser as a truck or as a car did not matter much to the people who bought the vehicle, but the definition mattered a great deal to Chrysler.

The National Highway Traffic and Safety Administration sets the standards for fuel economy for passenger cars and trucks, called Corporate Average Fuel Economy (CAFE). The CAFE standards for 2001 require that a manufacturer's cars average 27.5 miles per gallon and that its trucks average 20.7 miles per gallon. Chrysler had no difficulty meeting the car standard because it produces no cars with V-8 engines. Chrysler, however, sells many trucks and jeeps with V-8 and V-10 engines that get poor gas mileage, making it difficult to meet the CAFE standard for trucks. Exceeding the CAFE standard costs the manufacturer a huge chunk of money in penalties—$5.50 for each truck for each tenth of a mile over the limit. By lumping the PT Cruiser, which gets high gas

> **Definition arguments are the most powerful arguments.**

Chrysler's PT Cruiser

mileage, in with the trucks, Chrysler can sell many more V-8 and V-10 trucks and jeeps that would otherwise be assessed the penalty for poor gas mileage.

The PT Cruiser example illustrates why definitions often matter more than we might think at first. It also illustrates three very important principles that operate when definitions are used in arguments.

First, people make definitions that benefit their interests. You learned very early in life the importance of defining actions as "accidents." Windows can be broken from being careless, especially when you are tossing a ball against the side of the house, but if it's an accident, well, accidents just happen (and don't require punishment).

Second, most of the time when you are arguing a definition, your audience may either have a different definition in mind or be unsure of the definition. Your mother or father probably didn't think breaking the window was an accident, so you had to convince Mom or Dad that you were really being careful, but the ball just slipped out of your hand. It's your job to get them to accept your definition.

Third, if you can get your audience to accept your definition, then usually you succeed. For this reason definition arguments are the most powerful arguments.

Kinds of Definitions

Rarely do you get far into an argument without having to define something. Imagine that you are writing an argument about the United States's decades-old and largely ineffective "war on drugs." We all know that the war on drugs is being waged against drugs that are illegal, like cocaine and marijuana, and not against the legal drugs produced by the multibillion-dollar drug industry. Our society classifies drugs into two categories: "good" drugs, which are legal, and "bad" drugs, which are illegal.

How exactly does our society arrive at these definitions? Drugs would be relatively easy to define as good or bad if the difference could be defined at the molecular level. Bad drugs would contain certain molecules that define them as bad. The history of drug use in the United States, however, tells us that it is not so simple. In the last century alcohol was on the list of illegal drugs for over a decade, while opium was considered a good drug and distributed in many patent medicines by pharmaceutical companies. Similarly, LSD and MDMA (ecstasy) were developed by the pharmaceutical industry but later placed in the illegal category. In a few states marijuana is now crossing over to the legal category for medicinal use.

If drugs cannot be classified as good or bad by their molecular structure, then perhaps society classifies them by effects. In might be reasonable to assume that drugs that are addictive are illegal, but that's not the case. Nicotine is highly addictive and is a legal drug; so too are many prescription medicines. Neither are drugs taken for the purpose of offering pleasure necessarily illegal (think of alcohol and Viagra), nor are drugs that alter consciousness or change personality (Prozac).

How a drug is defined as legal or illegal apparently is determined by example. The nationwide effort in the United States to stop people from drinking alcohol during the first decades of the twentieth century led to the passage of the Eighteenth Amendment and the ban on sales of alcohol from 1920 to 1933, known as Prohibition. Those who argued for Prohibition used examples of drunkenness, especially among the poor, to show how alcohol broke up families and left mothers and children penniless in the street. Those who opposed Prohibition initially pointed to the consumption of beer and wine in many ethnic traditions. Later they raised examples of the bad effects of Prohibition—the rise of organized crime, the increase in alcohol abuse, and the general disregard for laws.

When you make a definitional argument, it's important to think about what kind of definition you will use.

FORMAL DEFINITIONS

Formal definitions typically categorize an item into the next higher classification and give distinguishing criteria from other items within that classification. Most dictionary definitions are formal definitions. For example, fish are cold-blooded aquatic vertebrates that have jaws, fins, and scales and are distinguished from other cold-blooded aquatic vertebrates (such as sea snakes) by the presence of gills. If you can construct a formal definition with specific criteria that your audience will accept, then likely you will have a strong argument. The key is to get your audience to agree to your criteria.

OPERATIONAL DEFINITIONS

Many concepts cannot be easily defined by formal definitions. Researchers in the natural and social sciences must construct operational definitions that they use for their research. For example, in the idea map in Chapter 1, we discuss a study of binge drinking among college students that defines a binge as five or more drinks in one sitting for a man, and four or more drinks for a woman. Some people think this standard is too low and should be raised to six to eight drinks to distinguish true problem drinkers from the general college population. No matter what the number, researchers must argue that the particular definition is one that suits the concept.

DEFINITIONS FROM EXAMPLE

Many human qualities such as honesty, courage, creativity, deceit, and love must be defined by examples that the audience accepts as representative of the concept. Few would not call the firemen who entered the World Trade Center on September 11, 2001, courageous. Most people would describe someone with a diagnosis of terminal cancer who refuses to feel self-pity as courageous. But what about a student who declines to go to a concert with her friends so she can study for an exam? Her behavior might be admirable, but most people would hesitate to call it courageous. The key to arguing a definition from examples is that the examples must strike the audience as in some way typical of the concept, even if the situation is unusual.

Building a Definitional Argument

Because definition arguments are the most powerful arguments, they are often at the center of the most important debates in American history. The major arguments of the civil rights movement were definition arguments, none more eloquent than Martin Luther King, Jr.'s "Letter from Birmingham Jail." From 1957 until his assassination in April 1968, King served as president of the Southern

Martin Luther King, Jr.

Christian Leadership Conference, an organization of primarily African-American clergymen dedicated to bringing about social change. King, who was a Baptist minister, tried to put into practice Mahatma Gandhi's principles of nonviolence in demonstrations, sit-ins, and marches throughout the South. During Holy Week in 1963, King led demonstrations and a boycott of downtown merchants in Birmingham, Alabama, to end racial segregation at lunch counters and discriminatory hiring practices.

On Wednesday, April 10, the city obtained an injunction directing the demonstrations to cease until their legality could be argued in court. But after meditation, King decided, against the advice of his associates, to defy the court order and proceed with the march planned for Good Friday morning. On Friday morning, April 12, King and fifty followers were arrested. King was held in solitary confinement until the end of the weekend, allowed neither to see his attorneys nor to call his wife. On the day of his arrest, King read in the newspaper a statement objecting to the demonstrations signed by eight white Birmingham clergymen of Protestant, Catholic, and Jewish faiths, urging that the protests stop and that grievances be settled in the courts.

On Saturday morning, King started writing an eloquent response that addresses the criticisms of the white clergymen, who are one primary audience of his response. But King intended his response to the ministers for widespread publication, and he clearly had in mind a larger readership. The clergymen gave him the occasion to address moderate white leaders in the South as well as religious and educated people across the nation and supporters of the civil rights movement. King begins "Letter from Birmingham Jail" by addressing the ministers as "My Dear Fellow Clergymen," adopting a conciliatory and tactful tone from the outset but at the same time offering strong arguments for the necessity of acting now rather than waiting for change. A critical part of King's argument is justifying not obeying certain laws. The eight white clergymen ask that laws be obeyed until they are changed. Here's how King responds:

> You express a great deal of anxiety over our willingness to break laws. This
> is certainly a legitimate concern. Since we so diligently urge people to obey

the Supreme Court's decision of 1954 outlawing segregation in the public schools, at first glance it may seem rather paradoxical for us consciously to break laws. One may well ask: "How can you advocate breaking some laws and obeying others?" The answer lies in the fact that there are two types of laws: just and unjust. I would be the first to advocate obeying just laws. One has not only a legal but a moral responsibility to obey just laws. Conversely, one has a moral responsibility to disobey unjust laws. I would agree with St. Augustine that "an unjust law is no law at all."

Now, what is the difference between the two? How does one determine whether a law is just or unjust? A just law is a man-made code that squares with the moral law or the law of God. An unjust law is a code that is out of harmony with the moral law. To put it in the terms of St. Thomas Aquinas: An unjust law is a human law that is not rooted in eternal law and natural law. Any law that uplifts human personality is just. Any law that degrades human personality is unjust. All segregation statutes are unjust because segregation distorts the soul and damages the personality. It gives the segregator a false sense of superiority and the segregated a false sense of inferiority. Segregation, to use the terminology of the Jewish philosopher Martin Buber, substitutes an "I-it" relationship and ends up relegating persons to the status of things. Hence segregation is not only politically, economically and sociologically unsound, it is morally wrong and sinful. Paul Tillich has said that sin is separation. Is not segregation an existential expression of man's tragic separation, his awful estrangement, his terrible sinfulness? Thus it is that I can urge men to obey the 1954 decision of the Supreme Court, for it is morally right; and I can urge them to disobey segregation ordinances, for they are morally wrong.

Martin Luther King's analysis of just and unjust laws is a classic definitional argument. Definitional arguments take this form: *X is a Y if X possesses certain criteria that differentiate it from other similar things in its general class.* According to King, a **just law** possesses the criteria of being consistent with moral law and uplifting human personality. Just as important, King sets out the criteria of **unjust law,** when X is not a Y. Unjust laws have the criteria of being out of harmony with moral law and damaging human personality. The criteria are set out in because clauses: *X is a Y because it has criteria A and B.* The criteria provide the link between X and Y:

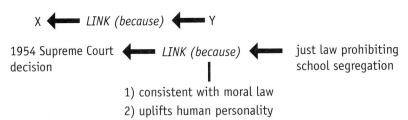

The negative can be argued in the same way:

Segregation laws ⟵ *LINK (because)* ⟵ unjust law

1) inconsistent with moral law
2) degrades human personality

An extended definition like King's is a two-step process. First you have to determine the criteria of Y. Then you have to argue that X has these criteria. If you want to argue that housing prisoners in unheated and non-air-conditioned tents is cruel and unusual punishment, then you have to make exposing prisoners to hot and cold extremes one of the criteria of cruel and unusual punishment. The keys to a definitional argument are getting your audience to accept your criteria and getting your audience to accept that the case in point meets those criteria. King's primary audience was the eight white clergymen; therefore, he used religious criteria and cited Protestant, Catholic, and Jewish theologians as his authority. His second criterion about just laws uplifting the human personality was a less familiar concept than the idea of moral law. King therefore offered a more detailed explanation drawing on the work of Martin Buber.

But King was smart enough to know that not all of his potential readers would put quite so much stock in religious authorities. Therefore, he follows the religious criteria with two other criteria that appeal to definitions of democracy:

> Let us consider a more concrete example of just and unjust laws. An unjust law is a code that a numerical or power majority group compels a minority group to obey but does not make binding on itself. This is *difference* made legal. By the same token, a just law is a code that a majority compels a minority to follow and that it is willing to follow itself. This is *sameness* made legal.
>
> Let me give another explanation. A law is unjust if it is inflicted on the minority that, as a result of being denied the right to vote, has no part in enacting or devising the law. Who can say that the legislature of Alabama which set up that state's segregation laws was democratically elected? Throughout Alabama all sorts of devious methods are used to prevent Negroes from becoming registered voters, and there are some counties in which, even though Negroes constitute a majority of the population, not a single Negro is registered. Can any law enacted under such circumstances be considered democratically structured?

King expands his criteria for just and unjust laws to include four major criteria, and he defines both by classifying and by giving examples.

Segregation laws ⬅━ *LINK (because)* ⬅━ unjust law

1) inconsistent with moral law
2) damages human personality
3) applies to minority group but not
   majority group that made the law
4) made by a body that was not
   democratically elected

King's "Letter from Birmingham Jail" draws much of its rhetorical power from its reliance on a variety of arguments that are suited for different readers. An atheist could reject the notion of laws made by God but could still be convinced by the criteria that segregation laws are undemocratic and therefore unjust.

To make definitional arguments work, often you must put much effort into identifying and explaining your criteria. You must convince your readers that your criteria are the best ones for what you are defining and that they apply to the case your are arguing. King backs up his assertion that Alabama's segregation laws in 1963 were unjust because the Alabama legislature was not democratically elected by pointing to counties that had African-American majorities but no African-American voters.

SCOTT MCCLOUD

Setting the Record Straight

Scott McCloud is the pseudonym of Scott Willard McLeod, who was born in Boston in 1960 and graduated from Syracuse University in 1982. After a short stint in the production department at DC Comics, he quickly became a highly regarded writer and illustrator of comics. His works include the ten-issue series Zot! *(1984–1985),* Destroy!! *(1986), and the nonfiction* Understanding Comics: The Invisible Art *(Northampton, MA: Tundra, 1993), from which this selection is taken.*

Understanding Comics is a brilliant explanation of how comics combine words and pictures to achieve effects that neither words nor pictures can do alone. At the beginning of the book, McCloud finds it necessary to define what comics are and are not before he can begin to analyze the magic of comics. Notice how he has to refine his criteria several times before he has an adequate definition.

Understanding Comics © *Copyright 1993 Scott McCloud. Published by Kitchen Sink Press Inc.*
Reprinted with the permission of HarperCollins Publishers, Inc.

IN LESS THAN A *YEAR*, I BECAME *TOTALLY* **OBSESSED** WITH COMICS! I DECIDED TO BECOME A *COMICS ARTIST* IN *10th* GRADE AND BEGAN TO *PRACTICE, PRACTICE,* **PRACTICE!**

I FELT THAT THERE WAS SOMETHING *LURKING* IN COMICS... SOMETHING THAT HAD *NEVER BEEN DONE.*

SOME KIND OF *HIDDEN* **POWER!**

BUT WHENEVER I TRIED TO *EXPLAIN* MY FEELING, I FAILED *MISERABLY.*

COMIC BOOKS?! HA! HA! HA!

BUT IT-- BUT IT'S-- BUH...

SURE, I REALIZED THAT COMIC BOOKS WERE USUALLY *CRUDE, POORLY-DRAWN, SEMILITERATE, CHEAP, DISPOSABLE KIDDIE FARE--*

--BUT--

THEY DON'T *HAVE* TO BE!

THE *PROBLEM* WAS THAT FOR *MOST PEOPLE,* THAT WAS WHAT *"COMIC BOOK"* **MEANT!**

DON'T GIMME THAT *COMIC BOOK* TALK, BARNEY!

IF PEOPLE FAILED TO *UNDERSTAND* COMICS, IT WAS BECAUSE THEY DEFINED WHAT COMICS COULD BE *TOO* **NARROWLY!**

A *PROPER DEFINITION,* IF WE COULD *FIND* ONE, MIGHT GIVE *LIE* TO THE STEREOTYPES--

--AND SHOW THAT THE *POTENTIAL* OF COMICS IS *LIMITLESS* AND *EXCITING!*

THIS IS WHERE OUR JOURNEY *BEGINS.*

[Scott McCloud observes that the problem is finding a definition that is broad enough to cover the many different kinds of comics but not so broad as to include anything that is not comics. A comic book is a physical object, but what exactly is comics*?]*

THE ARTFORM--THE *MEDIUM*--KNOWN AS COMICS IS A *VESSEL* WHICH CAN HOLD ANY *NUMBER* OF *IDEAS* AND *IMAGES*.

THE *"CONTENT"* OF THOSE IMAGES AND IDEAS IS, OF COURSE, UP TO *CREATORS,* AND WE ALL HAVE DIFFERENT *TASTES*.

≈GLUG≈
≈GLUG≈

PTUI!!!

≈GAAK≈
≈WHEEEEZ≈
≈KAF! KAF!≈
GLUGH·GGH...

≈ahem≈
THE *TRICK* IS TO NEVER MISTAKE THE *MESSAGE*--

--FOR THE *MESSENGER*.

COMICS

AT ONE TIME OR ANOTHER VIRTUALLY *ALL* THE GREAT MEDIA HAVE RECEIVED *CRITICAL EXAMINATION,* IN AND OF *THEMSELVES*.

WRITTEN WORD   MUSIC   VIDEO

THEATRE   VISUAL ART   FILM

BUT FOR *COMICS,* THIS ATTENTION HAS BEEN *RARE.* *

LET'S SEE IF WE CAN HELP *RECTIFY* THE SITUATION.

*EISNER'S OWN *COMICS AND SEQUENTIAL ART* BEING A HAPPY EXCEPTION.

*JUXTAPOSED= ADJACENT, SIDE-BY-SIDE.
GREAT ART SCHOOL WORD.

MEGHANN O'CONNOR

Cheerleading Is a Competitive Sport

Meghann O'Connor cheered for four years on both the varsity basketball squad and the competitive squad at Lewisburg (Pennsylvania) Area High School. Her letter is addressed to the Lewisburg Athletic Director, Jim Cotner, who is in charge of funding and practice times and spaces for the sports teams.

November 11, 1998

Dear Mr. Cotner,

1   Imagine individuals propelling their bodies to flip, twist, and turn in ways one did not know was humanly possible. Picture these individuals being hurled into the air, reaching unfathomable heights, and then being safely caught by their own teammates. Feel the excitement in your own being as you watch strength and skill come together to create an awesome display of athleticism. Realize that these individuals are cheerleaders; their sport, cheerleading.

2   Sport? Cheerleading? Many feel that these two words have no business being grouped in the same sentence together. It is a popular stereotype to consider cheerleaders to be a group of screaming girls in short skirts. Because there is no equipment involved, and there are not any playoffs for the cheerleading squads, many support the opinion that cheerleading is far from a competitive sport. However, in the following paragraphs I will explain why cheerleading should be weighed as a competitive sport and be granted the same rights and respect that other athletic teams receive.

3   There is a myriad of rationale as to why cheerleading should be defined as a competitive sport instead of only an activity. One of the most important reasons is because of the fact that cheerleaders do, in fact, compete. The New Merriam Webster Dictionary defines competition as a **contest, match;** *also*: **one's competitors.** Cheerleaders from all over the world compete at various levels in many different kinds of competitions. Who do they compete against? They oppose their competitors, of course. How is it, then, that both schools and organizations claim that cheerleading is not a competitive sport? There are local, state, regional, and national competitions for cheerleading squads of all different levels including, Midget, Junior High, Jayvee, Varsity, Coed, All-Star, and Collegiate. A qualified panel of judges

rate the cheerleading squads based on a point system and that determines the winners of these competitions. The squad that finishes with the highest total of points will then be declared the winner. There are many different areas that the judges focus on, including the levels of difficulty, creativity, and athletic ability. This type of judging is similar to the panels of judges found in the Olympic Games, such as figure skating and gymnastics. Both of these activities are viewed as competitive sports, so why can cheerleading not be viewed in the same way? When dealing with the issue of pragmatics, it is only sensible to agree with the fact that cheerleading is a competitive sport. To say that competition is not a huge aspect of cheerleading would be incorrect and inaccurate.

4   Just as other sporting teams practice and prepare for upcoming contests, so do cheerleaders. Football teams sweat on the field. Basketball players run up and down the court. Swimmers race in the pool. Each of these teams practice day in and day out, making sure that their skills are where they should be and that they are prepared for their upcoming competition. Cheerleaders do the same! They practice, sweat, and strive to be the best they can be, just as other teams do. It would be unfair to discredit the time and energy cheerleaders spend preparing for their upcoming contest. Ethically, it is unjust and discriminatory to not give cheerleaders credit where credit is due. Ultimately, they put an equal amount of time into practicing and getting ready for their "games" as the other sporting teams do.

5   Cheerleaders are talented athletes who work hard. If one has ever taken the time to pause on ESPN long enough to watch a National Cheerleading Competition, one would see the great acts of athleticism that are displayed by squads from all different areas and of all different age groups. Coordination and timing are crucial in synchronizing motions and dance movements. Strength is required for the amazing stunts that are built within the routine. Power and grace are necessities in tumbling from one end of the floor to the other. If these aspects are not considered characteristics of an athlete, then what are the components that make up this type of individual? All athletes compete; therefore, since cheerleaders accomplish athletic feats, it is only evenhanded to consider them competitors.

6   Schools who falter in considering cheerleading a competitive game will lag behind what the rest of society is doing. By failing to label cheerleading as a competitive sport, an example of regressiveness is being exhibited. For instance, many high schools, colleges, and universities around the country already group cheerleading in the same category as all other sports. The University of Michigan and Ohio State University provide scholarships for the

cheerleaders that attend their universities. If these prestigious institutions of higher education are able to view cheerleading as the competitive sport it truly is, then why cannot all school districts and colleges do the same? Just because it has traditionally been thought that cheerleading is not a sport doesn't mean that this line of thinking has to continue. It will one day be out of date and against the norm to not classify cheerleading as a competitive sport, so it is imperative to make the crucial change now.

7   Several arguments have been made against cheerleading as a competitive sport. One of them is the fact that in cheerleading, a team can not win anything such as a district championship. This argument is entirely false because cheerleaders are always up for awards in their competitions. Not only can they win first, second, or third place, at many different levels, but also they can place in other categories as well such as jumping ability, tumbling ability, and how difficult their stunting is.

8   Another unsupported claim against the sport of cheerleading is the statement made by Dr. Shaft, who claims that, "Real athletes don't wear skirts." This assertion is absolutely ridiculous. It should not matter at all what the uniforms of the athletes look like. That is a frivolous and unnecessary aspect of competition and should have nothing to do with the subject at hand. The fact that Dr. Shaft is drawing attention to the cheerleaders' skirts could also be grounds for sexual discrimination. A skirt is a form of clothing for women, and when Dr. Shaft proclaims cheerleading an invalid sport due to the fact that a skirt is worn, it seems as though he is discrediting women's sports in general.

9   Another justification Dr. Shaft has of why cheerleading should not be a sport is because he feels that there are no coaches involved. This is entirely inaccurate. At every level of cheerleading there are coaches who put in just as much time, effort and energy as any other coach of any other sport. These coaches are paid for their hard work and deserve the respect the coaches of other sporting teams receive.

10   My support of the idea that cheerleading should be a competitive sport remains even after hearing the points made by those who oppose me. Cheerleaders compete and spend just as much time practicing as any other team, they display great feats of athletic talent, and by not considering cheerleading a competitive sport, one is ultimately primitive and tardy in their beliefs, due to the increasing number of organizations that are in accordance with my thoughts. How would one feel if he or she spent endless hours planning and preparing for upcoming competitions to only then be told that they do not even participate in a "real" sport? This individual may become extremely discouraged and confused, which are the last emotions

any school wants for its active students. By acknowledging the cheerleading squad as competitors, a great deal of self-esteem could rise from each individual member. This cheerleader would feel that they are equal with the other athletes in their school and feel as if they were finally treated on the same level. This "happiness" could become contagious. First, it may spread throughout the squad, causing them to have a sense of belonging to their school. Their renewed spirit would radiate at matches, games, and competitions, which would benefit those who the cheerleaders were supporting. The added confidence felt when the squad performs would not only be beneficial to them but to their organization and all of its members as well. On the subject of aesthetics, their renewed sense of ease and comfort would shine through during practices and competitions, bringing nothing but positive consequences to considering cheerleaders competitive athletes.

11   Our society has made a great deal of progress when dealing with the issues of equality and fairness. To continue on with this tradition, it would only be fair to view cheerleading as a competitive sport.

Steps in Writing a Definition Argument

If your instructor asks for a topic proposal, use steps 1–4 to guide you in writing the proposal.

1. **Make a definitional claim on a controversial issue that focuses on a key term.** Use this formula: X *is (or is not) a* Y *because it has (or does not have) features A, B, and C (or more)*.

   Examples:
   - Hate speech (or pornography, literature, films, and so on) is (or is not) free speech protected by the First Amendment because it has (does not have) these features.
   - Hunting (or using animals for cosmetics testing, keeping animals in zoos, wearing furs, and so on) is (or is not) cruelty to animals because it has (or does not have) these features.
   - Doctors should be (should not be) allowed to assist patients to die if they are terminally ill and suffering.
   - Displaying pinup calendars (or jokes, innuendo, rap lyrics, and so on) is (is not) an example of sexual harrassment.

2. **What's at stake in your claim?** If nearly everybody would agree with you, then your claim probably isn't interesting or important. If you can

think of people who would disagree, then something is at stake. Who argues the opposite of your claim? Why do they benefit from a different definition?

3. **Make your list of criteria.** Write as many criteria as you can think of. Which criteria are necessary for X to be a Y? Which are not necessary? Which are the most important? Does your case in point meet all the criteria?

4. **Analyze your potential readers.** Who are your readers? How does the definitional claim you are making affect them? How familiar will they be with the issue, concept, or controversy that you're writing about? What are they likely to know and not know? Which criteria are they most likely to accept with little explanation and which will they disagree with? Which criteria will you have to argue for?

5. **Write a draft.**

Introduction:
- Set out the issue, concept, or controversy.
- Explain why the definition is important.
- Give the background that your intended readers will need.

Body:
- Set out your criteria and argue for the appropriateness of the criteria.
- Determine whether the criteria apply to the case in point.
- Anticipate where readers might question either your criteria or how they apply to your subject.
- Address opposing points of view by acknowledging how their definitions might differ and by showing why your definition is better.

Conclusion:
- Do more than simply summarize what you have said. You can, for example, go into more detail about what is at stake or the implications of your definition.

6. **Revise, revise, revise. See Chapter 11 for detailed instructions.**

Stage 1. Read your argument aloud.
Do no more in this stage than put checks in the margins that you can return to later. Think in particular about these things:
- **Your claim.** When you finish reading, summarize in one sentence what you are arguing. What's at stake in your claim?
- **Your criteria.** How many criteria do you offer? Where are they located? Are they clearly connected to your claim?
- **Your representation of yourself.** Forget for a moment that you wrote what you are reading. What impression do you have of you, the writer?

▪ **Your consideration of your readers.** Do you give enough background if your readers are unfamiliar with the issue? Do you acknowledge opposing views that they might have? Do you appeal to common values that you share with them?

Stage 2. Analyze your argument in detail.

▪ **Examine your organization.** What are the topics of each of the paragraphs? Is the relationship of one paragraph to another clearly signaled? If any paragraphs appear out of order, think of another way to arrange them.

▪ **Examine your evidence.** If you noted places where you could use more evidence when you read through the first time, now is the time to determine what kinds of additional evidence you need.

▪ **Consider your title and introduction.** Be as specific as you can in your title, and if possible, suggest your stance. Does your introduction get off to a fast start and convince your reader to keep reading?

▪ **Consider your conclusion.** Think about whether there is a summarizing point you can make, an implication you can draw, or another example you can include that sums up your position.

▪ **Analyze the visual aspects of your text.** Do the font and layout you selected look attractive? Would headings and subheadings help to identify key sections of your argument? Would the addition of graphics augment key points?

Stage 3. Focus on your style and proofread carefully.

▪ **Check the connections between sentences.** Notice how your sentences are connected. If you need to signal the relationship from one sentence to the next, use a transitional word or phrase.

▪ **Check your sentences for emphasis.** Elements at the beginning and the end of sentences tend to stand out more than things in the middle.

▪ **Eliminate wordiness.** See how many words you can take out without losing the meaning.

▪ **Use active verbs.** Anytime you can use a verb besides a form of *be* (*is, are, was, were*), take advantage of the opportunity to make your style more lively.

▪ **Proofread your spelling carefully.** Your spelling checker will miss many mistakes.

▪ **Use your handbook to check items of mechanics and usage.** Look up any item you are unsure of.

CHAPTER 6

Causal Arguments

Why has binge drinking greatly increased among college students over the last fifteen years while the overall percentage of students who drink has remained about the same? Why do some countries have long histories of people of different religious and ethnic backgrounds living together in peace while in other countries

> **Effective causal arguments move beyond the obvious to get at underlying causes.**

people regularly kill each other because of religious and ethnic differences? Why do owners of professional sports teams complain about losing money and then offer multimillion-dollar salaries not only to stars but even to mediocre players? Why is the United States the only major industrialized country not to have a system of national health care? Why do universities in the United States have general education requirements while universities in most of the rest of the world do not, allowing students to take courses only in their major and minor fields? Why have the death rates for some kinds of cancer gone way up in this country (for example, deaths from lung cancer in women increased 438 percent from 1962 to 1992) while the rates for other kinds of cancer went down (deaths from cancer of the cervix dropped 67 percent during the same period)? If meteorologists now have massive amounts of satellite data and supercomputers to crunch the numbers for long-range weather forecasting, why haven't they become much more reliable than the *Farmer's Almanac*?

Besides big questions like the ones above, you also are confronted with little questions of causation in your everyday life. Why did the driver who passed you on a blind curve risk his life to get one car ahead at the next traffic light? Why is it hard to recognize people you know when you run into them unexpectedly in an unfamiliar setting? Why do nearly all kids want the same toy each Christmas, forcing their parents to stand in line for hours to buy them? Why does your mother or father spend an extra hour plus the extra gas driving to a grocery store across town just to save a few pennies on one or two items on sale? Why do some people get upset about animals that are killed for medical research but still eat meat and wear leather clothing? Why do some of your friends keep going to horror films when they can hardly sit through them and have nightmares afterward?

Life is full of big and little mysteries, and people spend a lot of time speculating about the causes. Most of the time, however, they don't take the time to analyze in depth what causes a controversial trend, event, or phenomenon. But before and after you graduate, you likely will have to write causal arguments that require in-depth analysis. In a professional career you will have to make many detailed causal analyses: Why did a retail business fail when it seemed to have an ideal location? What causes cost overruns in the development of a new product? What causes people in some circumstances to prefer public transportation over driving? What causes unnecessary slowdowns in a local computer network? Answering any of these questions requires making a causal argument, which takes a classic form: X *causes (or does not cause)* Y. The causal claim is at the center of a causal argument. Therefore, to get started on a causal argument, you need to propose one or more causes.

■ Methods of Finding Causes

The big problem with causal arguments is that any topic worth writing about is likely to be complex. Identifying causes usually isn't easy. The philosopher John Stuart Mill recognized this problem long ago and devised four methods for finding causes:

1. ***The Common Factor Method.*** When the cause-and-effect relationship occurs more than once, look for something in common in the events and circumstances of each effect; any common factor could be the cause. Scientists

have used this method to explain how seemingly different phenomena are associated. There were a variety of explanations of fire until, in the 1700s, Joseph Priestley in England and Antoine Lavoisier in France discovered that oxygen was a separate element and that burning was caused by oxidation.

2. **The Single Difference Method.** This method works only when there are at least two similar situations, one that leads to an effect and one that does not. Look for something that was missing in one case and present in another— the single difference. The writer assumes that if everything is substantially alike in both cases, then the single difference is the (or a) cause. At the Battle of Midway in 1942, the major naval battle of World War II in the Pacific, the Japanese Navy had a four-to-one advantage over the U.S. Navy. Both fleets were commanded by competent, experienced leaders. But the U.S. commander, Admiral Nimitz, had a superior advantage in intelligence, which proved to be decisive.

3. **Concomitant Variation.** This tongue twister is another favorite method of scientists. If an investigator finds that a possible cause and a possible effect have a similar pattern of variation, then one can suspect that a relationship exists. For example, scientists noticed that peaks in the eleven-year sunspot cycle have predictable effects on high-frequency radio transmission on the earth.

4. **Process of Elimination.** Many possible causes can be proposed for most trends and events. If you are a careful investigator, you have to consider all that you can think of and eliminate the ones that cannot be causes.

For an example of how these methods might work for you, suppose you want to research the causes of the increase in legalized lotteries in the United States. You might discover that lotteries go back to colonial times. Harvard and Yale have been longtime rivals in football, but the schools' rivalry goes back much further. Both ran lotteries before the Revolutionary War! In 1747, the Connecticut legislature voted to allow Yale to conduct a lottery to raise money to build dormitories, and in 1765, the Massachusetts legislature gave Harvard permission for a lottery. Lotteries were common before and after the American Revolution, but they eventually ran into trouble because they were run by private companies that occasionally took off with the money without paying off the winners. After 1840, laws against lotteries were passed, but they came back after the Civil War in the South. The defeated states of the Confederacy needed money to rebuild the bridges, buildings, and schools that had been destroyed in the Civil War, and they turned to selling lottery tickets throughout the nation, tickets which, perhaps ironically, were very popular in the North. Once again, the lotteries were run by private companies, and scandals eventually led to their banning.

In 1964, the voters in New Hampshire approved a lottery as a means of funding education in preference to an income tax or sales tax. Soon other northeastern states followed this lead, establishing lotteries with the reasoning that if people are going to gamble, the money should remain at home. During the 1980s, other states approved not only lotteries but also other forms of state-run gambling such as keno and video poker. By 1993, only Hawaii and Utah had no legalized gambling of any kind.

If you are analyzing the causes of the spread of legalized gambling, you might use the **common factor method** to investigate what current lotteries have in common with earlier lotteries. That factor is easy to identify: It's economic. The early colonies and later the states have turned again and again to lotteries as a way of raising money that avoids unpopular tax increases. But why have lotteries spread so quickly and seemingly become so permanent since 1964, when before that, they were used only sporadically and were eventually banned? The **single difference method** points us to the major difference between the lotteries of today and those of previous eras: Lotteries in the past were run by private companies, and inevitably someone took off with the money instead of paying it out. Today's lotteries are owned and operated by state agencies or else contracted under state control, and while they are not immune to scandals, they are much more closely monitored than lotteries were in the past.

The controversies over legal gambling now focus on casinos. In 1988, Congress passed the Indian Gaming Regulatory Act, which started a new era of casino gambling in the United States. The Foxwoods Casino in Connecticut, owned by the Mashantucket Pequot Tribe, became a huge moneymaker—with over $1 billion wagered in 2000—and its revenues exceeded those of the Connecticut lottery. Other tribes and other states were quick to cash in on casino gambling. Iowa legalized riverboat gambling in 1989, followed shortly by Louisiana, Illinois, Indiana, Mississippi, and Missouri. As with lotteries, the primary justification for approving casino gambling has been economic. States have been forced to fund various programs that the federal government used to pay for. Especially in states where lottery revenues had begun to sag, legislatures and voters turned to casinos to make up the difference.

Casinos, however, have been harder to sell to voters than lotteries. For many voters, casinos are a NIMBY ("not in my back yard") issue. They may believe that people should have the right to gamble, but they don't want a casino in their town. Casino proponents have tried to overcome these objections by arguing that casinos bring added tourist dollars, benefiting the community as a whole. Opponents argue the opposite: that people who go to casinos spend their money on gambling and not on tourist attractions. The cause-and-effect benefit of casinos to community businesses can be examined by **concomitant variation.** Casino supporters argue that people who come to gamble spend a lot of money elsewhere. Opponents of casinos claim that people who come for gambling don't want to spend money elsewhere. Furthermore, they point out that gambling represents another entertainment option for people within easy driving distance and can hurt area businesses such as restaurants, amusement parks, and bowling alleys. So far, the record has been mixed, some businesses being helped and others being hurt when casinos are built nearby.

Many trends don't have causes as obvious as the spread of legalized gambling. One such trend is the redistribution of wealth in the United States since 1973. From 1950 to 1973, businesses in the United States grew by 90 percent, and the resulting wealth benefited all income classes. Since 1973, however, almost all the growth in wealth has gone to people at the top of the economic ladder. During the 1980s, the incomes of the richest 1 percent of the population grew by 62.9 percent, and the incomes of the bottom 60 percent actually declined. According to *U.S. News & World Report*, in 1996, the richest 1 percent of Americans, with minimum assets of $2.3 million per family, hold 42 percent of all marketable assets, exerting unprecedented influence on the economy. Often-cited statistics are those for the pay of top executives. *Business Week* reports that the average CEO of a major corporation made 42 times the average hourly worker's pay in 1980, 85 times in 1990, and an incredible 531 times in 2000.

The increasing divide between the rich and the rest of the people in the United States is well documented, but economists don't agree about the reasons why the U.S. middle class has been increasingly divided into those who are very well off and those who are struggling to keep their heads above water. The explanations that have been given include the tax cuts of 1986, the decline of labor unions, the downsizing of corporations, the increase in corporate mergers, automation, competition from low-wage nations, and simple greed. Although each of these may be a contributing cause, there must be other causes too.

The **process of elimination** method can be a useful tool when several possible causes are involved. The shift in income to the wealthy started before the tax cuts of 1986, so the tax cuts cannot be the only cause. Low-wage nations now produce cheap exports, but the sectors of the U.S. economy that compete directly with low-wage nations make up a small slice of the total pie (about 2 percent). And it's hard to explain why people might be greedier now than in earlier decades; greed has always been a human trait.

In a book published in 1995 entitled *The Winner-Take-All Society*, Robert H. Frank and Phillip J. Cook argue that changes in attitudes help to account for the shifts in wealth since 1973. In an article summarizing their book, published in *Across the Board* (33:5 [May 1996]: 4), they describe what they mean by the winner-take-all society:

Our claim is that growing income inequality stems from the growing importance of what we call "winner-take-all markets"—markets in which small differences in performance give rise to enormous differences in economic reward. Long familiar in entertainment, sports, and the arts, these markets have increasingly permeated law, journalism, consulting, medicine, investment banking, corporate management, publishing, design, fashion, even the hallowed halls of academe.

An economist under the influence of the human-capital metaphor might ask: Why not save money by hiring two mediocre people to fill an important position instead of paying the exorbitant salary required to attract the best? Although that sort of substitution might work with physical capital, it does not necessarily work with human capital. Two average surgeons or CEOs or novelists or quarterbacks are often a poor substitute for a single gifted one.

The result is that for positions for which additional talent has great value to the employer or the marketplace, there is no reason to expect that the market will compensate individuals in proportion to their human capital. For these positions—ones that confer the greatest leverage or "amplification" of human talent—small increments of talent have great value and may be greatly rewarded as a result of the normal competitive market process. This insight lies at the core of our alternative explanation of growing inequality.

A winner-take-all market is one in which reward depends on relative, not absolute, performance. Whereas a farmer's pay depends on the absolute amount of wheat he produces and not on how that compares with the amounts produced by other farmers, a software developer's pay depends largely on her performance ranking. In the market for personal income-tax software, for instance, the market reaches quick consensus on which among the scores or even hundreds of competing programs is the most comprehensive and user-friendly. And although the best program may be only slightly better than its nearest rival, their developers' incomes may differ a thousandfold.

Frank and Cook find that technology has accelerated the trend toward heaping rewards on those who are judged best in a particular arena. In the 1800s, for example, a top tenor in a major city such as London might have commanded a salary many times above that of other singers, but the impact of the tenor was limited by the fact that only those who could hear him live could appreciate his talent. Today, every tenor in the world competes with Luciano Pavarotti because opera fans everywhere can buy Pavarotti's CDs. This worldwide fan base translates into big money. In another example, it might not surprise you that in 1992, Michael Jordan reportedly received $20 million for promoting Nike shoes, an amount that was greater than the combined annual payrolls for all six factories in Indonesia that made the shoes.

What is new is how other professions have become more like sports and entertainment.

The Winner-Take-All Society is a model of causal analysis that uses the **process of elimination** method. The authors

- Describe and document a trend

- Set out the causes that have been previously offered and show why together they are inadequate to explain the trend, and then

- Present a new cause, explaining how the new cause works in concert with those that have been identified

But it's not enough just to identify causes. They must be connected to effects. For trends in progress, such as the growing divide between the rich and the rest in the United States, the effects must be carefully explored to learn about what might lie ahead. Frank and Cook believe that the winner-take-all attitude is detrimental for the nation's future because, like high school basketball players who expect to become the next Michael Jordan, many people entering college or graduate school grossly overestimate their prospects for huge success and select their future careers accordingly:

> The lure of the top prizes in winner-take-all markets has also steered many of our most able graduates toward career choices that make little sense for them as individuals and still less sense for the nation as a whole. In increasing numbers, our best and brightest graduates pursue top positions in law, finance, consulting, and other overcrowded arenas, in the process forsaking careers in engineering, manufacturing, civil service, teaching, and other occupations in which an infusion of additional talent would yield greater benefit to society.
>
> One study estimated, for example, that whereas a doubling of enrollments in engineering would cause the growth rate of the GDP to rise by half a percentage point, a doubling of enrollments in law would actually cause a decline of three-tenths of a point. Yet the number of new lawyers admitted to the bar each year more than doubled between 1970 and 1990, a period during which the average standardized test scores of new public-school teachers fell dramatically.
>
> One might hope that such imbalances would fade as wages are bid up in underserved markets and driven down in overcrowded ones, and indeed there have been recent indications of a decline in the number of law-school applicants. For two reasons, however, such adjustments are destined to fall short.
>
> The first is an informational problem. An intelligent decision about whether to pit one's own skills against a largely unknown field of adversaries obviously requires a well-informed estimate of the odds of

winning. Yet people's assessments about these odds are notoriously inaccurate. Survey evidence shows, for example, that some 80 percent of us think we are better-than-average drivers and that more than 90 percent of workers consider themselves more productive than their average colleague. Psychologists call this the "Lake Wobegon Effect," and its importance for present purposes is that it leads people to overestimate their odds of landing a superstar position. Indeed, overconfidence is likely to be especially strong in the realm of career choice, because the biggest winners are so conspicuous. The seven-figure NBA stars appear on television several times each week, whereas the many thousands who fail to make the league attract little notice.

The second reason for persistent overcrowding in winner-take-all markets is a structural problem that economists call "the tragedy of the commons." This same problem helps explain why we see too many prospectors for gold. In the initial stages of exploiting a newly discovered field of gold, the presence of additional prospectors may significantly increase the total amount of gold that is found. Beyond some point, however, additional prospectors contribute very little. Thus, the gold found by a newcomer to a crowded gold field is largely gold that would have been found by others.

This short example illustrates why causal arguments for any significant trend that involves people almost necessarily have to be complex. Most people don't quit their day job expecting to hit it big in the movies, the record business, or professional athletics, yet people do select fields such as law that have become in many ways like entertainment, with a few big winners and the rest just getting by. Frank and Cook point to the "Lake Wobegon Effect" (named for Garrison Keillor's fictional town where "all children are above average") to give an explanation of why people are realistic about their chances in some situations and not in others.

BUILDING A CAUSAL ARGUMENT

Effective causal arguments move beyond the obvious to get at underlying causes. The immediate cause of the growing income inequality in the United States is that people at the top make a lot more now than they did thirty years ago while people in the middle make the same and people at the bottom make less. Those causes are obvious to anyone who has looked at the numbers. What isn't obvious is why those changes occurred.

Insightful causal analyses of major trends and events avoid oversimplification by not relying on only one direct cause but instead showing how that cause arises from another cause or works in combination with other causes. Indeed, Frank and Cook have been criticized for placing too much emphasis on the winner-take-all hypothesis.

The great causal mystery today is global warming. Scientists generally agree that the average surface temperature on earth has gone up by 0.3 to 0.6 degrees Celsius over the last hundred years and that the amount of carbon dioxide has increased by 25 percent. But the causes of those facts are much disputed. Some people believe that the rise in temperature is a naturally occurring climate variation and that the increase in carbon dioxide is only minimally the cause or not related at all. Others argue that the burning of fossil fuels and the cutting of tropical forests have led to the increase in carbon dioxide, which in turn traps heat, thus increasing the temperature of the earth. The major problem for all participants in the global warming debate is that the causation is not a simple, direct one.

Scientists use powerful computer models to understand the causes and effects of climate change. These models predict that global warming will affect arctic and subarctic regions more dramatically than elsewhere. In Iceland, average summer temperatures have risen by 0.5 to 1.0 degrees Celsius since the early 1980s. All of Iceland's glaciers except a few that surge and ebb independent of weather are now in rapid retreat, a pattern observed throughout regions in the far north. Arctic sea ice shrank by 6 percent from 1978 to 1998, and Greenland's massive ice sheet has been thinning by more than three feet a year. Environmentalists today point to the melting of the glaciers and sea ice as proof that human-caused global warming is taking place.

Scientists, however, are not so certain. Their difficulty is to sort human causes from naturally recurring climate cycles. Much of the detailed data about the Great Melt in the north goes back only to the early 1990s—not long enough to rule out short-term climate cycles. If we are in a

Glaciers in retreat

regular, short-term warming cycle, then the question becomes how does greenhouse warming interact with that cycle? Computer models suggest there is a very low probability that such rapid change could occur naturally. But the definitive answers to the causes of the Great Melt are probably still a long way off.

Another pitfall common in causal arguments using statistics is mistaking correlation for causation. For example, the FBI reported that criminal victimization rates in the United States in 1995 dropped 13 percent for personal crimes and 12.4 percent for property crimes, the largest decreases ever. During that same year, the nation's prison and jail populations reached a record high of 1,085,000 and 507,000 inmates, respectively. The easy inference is that putting more people behind bars lowers the crime rate, but there are plenty of examples to the contrary. The drop in crime rates in the 1990s remains quite difficult to explain. Others have argued that the decline in SAT verbal scores during the late 1960s and 1970s reflected a decline in literacy caused by an increase in television viewing. But the fact that the number of people who took the SAT during the 1970s greatly increased suggests that there was not an actual decline in literacy, only a great expansion in the population who wanted to go to college.

EDWARD R. TUFTE

The Cholera Epidemic in London, 1854

Edward R. Tufte (1942–) is a leading thinker on the construction and presentation of visual information. Tufte's ideas on visual design are set out in three influential books: The Visual Display of Quantitative Information *(1983),* Envisioning Information *(1990), and* Visual Explanations: Images and Quantities, Evidence and Narrative *(1997). He urges that visual information be presented truthfully, with a minimum of unnecessary noise and with full respect for the complexity of what is being represented. Educated at Stanford and Yale Universities, Tufte has been a professor of political economy and graphic design at Yale since 1977.*

In "The Cholera Epidemic in London, 1854," taken from Envisioning Information, *Tufte demonstrates his belief that effective graphics can extend our powers of reasoning. He also shows how the presentation of data is critical in reaching conclusions based on visual evidence.*

The Cholera Epidemic in London, 1854

In a classic of medical detective work, *On the Mode of Communication of Cholera,*[1] John Snow described—with an eloquent and precise language of evidence, number, comparison—the severe epidemic:

> The most terrible outbreak of cholera which ever occurred in this kingdom, is probably that which took place in Broad Street, Golden Square, and adjoining streets, a few weeks ago. Within two hundred and fifty years of the spot where Cambridge Street joins Broad Street, there were upwards of five hundred fatal attacks of cholera in ten days. The mortality in this limited area probably equals any that was ever caused in this country, even by the plague; and it was much more sudden, as the greater number of cases terminated in a few hours. The mortality would undoubtedly have been much greater had it not been for the flight of the population. Persons in furnished lodgings left first, then other lodgers went away, leaving their furniture to be sent for. . . . Many houses were closed altogether owing to the death of the proprietors; and, in a great number of instances, the tradesmen who remained had sent away their families; so that in less than six days from the commencement of the outbreak, the most afflicted streets were deserted by more than three-quarters of their inhabitants.[2]

Cholera broke out in the Broad Street area of central London on the evening of August 31, 1854. John Snow, who had investigated earlier epidemics, suspected that the water from a community pump-well at Broad and Cambridge Streets was contaminated. Testing the water from the well on the evening of September 3, Snow saw no suspicious impurities, and thus he hesitated to come to a conclusion. This absence of evidence, however, was not evidence of absence:

> Further inquiry . . . showed me that there was no other circumstance or agent common to the circumscribed locality in which this sudden increase of cholera occurred, and not extending

---

[1] John Snow, *On the Mode of Communication of Cholera* (London, 1855). An acute disease of the small intestine, with severe watery diarrhea, vomiting, and rapid dehydration, cholera has a fatality rate of 50 percent or more when untreated. With the rehydration therapy developed in the 1960s, mortality can be reduced to less than 1 percent. Epidemics still occur in poor countries, as the bacterium *Vibrio cholerae* is distributed mainly by water and food contaminated with sewage.

[2] Snow, *Cholera*, p. 38.

beyond it, except the water of the above mentioned pump. I found, moreover, that the water varied, during the next two days, in the amount of organic impurity, visible to the naked eye, on close inspection, in the form of small white, flocculent [loosely clustered] particles. . . .[3]

From the General Register Office, Snow obtained a list of 83 deaths from cholera. When plotted on a map, these data showed a close link between cholera and the Broad Street pump. Persistent house-by-house, case-by-case detective work had yielded quite detailed evidence about a possible cause-effect relationship, as Snow made a kind of streetcorner correlation:

> On proceeding to the spot, I found that nearly all of the deaths had taken place within a short distance of the pump. There were only ten deaths in houses situated decidedly nearer to another street pump. In five of these cases the families of the deceased persons informed me that they always sent to the pump in Broad Street, as they preferred the water to that of the pump which was nearer. In three other cases, the deceased were children who went to school near the pump in Broad Street. Two of them were known to drink the water; and the parents of the third think it probable that it did so. The other two deaths, beyond the district which this pump supplies, represent only the amount of mortality from cholera that was occurring before the irruption took place.
>
> With regard to the deaths occurring in the locality belonging to the pump, there were sixty-one instances in which I was informed that the deceased persons used to drink the pump-water from Broad Street, either constantly or occasionally. In six instances I could get no information, owing to the death or departure of every one connected with the deceased individuals; and in six cases I was informed that the deceased persons did not drink the pump-water before their illness.[4]

Thus the theory implicating the particular pump was confirmed by the observed covariation: in this area of London, there were few occurrences of cholera exceeding the normal low level, except among those people who drank water from the Broad Street pump. It was now time to act; after all, the reason we seek causal explanations is in order to *intervene*, to govern

[3]Snow, *Cholera*, p. 39.
[4]Snow, *Cholera*, pp. 39–40.

the cause so as to govern the effect: "Policy-thinking is and must be causality-thinking."[5] Snow described his findings to the authorities responsible for the community water supply, the Board of Guardians of St. James's Parish, on the evening of September 7, 1854. The Board ordered that the pump-handle on the Broad Street well be removed immediately. The epidemic soon ended.

Moreover, the result of this intervention (a before/after experiment of sorts) was consistent with the idea that cholera was transmitted by impure water. Snow's explanation replaced previously held beliefs that cholera spread through the air or by some other means. In those times many years before the discovery of bacteria, one fantastic theory speculated that cholera vaporously rose out of the burying grounds of plague victims from two centuries earlier.[6] In 1886 the discovery of the bacterium *Vibrio cholerae* confirmed Snow's theory. He is still celebrated for establishing the mode of cholera transmission *and* consequently the method of prevention: keep drinking water, food, and hands clear of infected sewage. Today at the old site of the Broad Street pump there stands a public house (a bar) named after John Snow, where one can presumably drink more safely than 140 years ago.

Why was the centuries-old mystery of cholera finally solved? Most importantly, Snow had a *good idea*—a causal theory about how the disease spread—that guided the gathering and assessment of evidence. This theory developed from medical analysis and empirical observation; by mapping earlier epidemics, Snow detected a link between different water supplies and varying rates of cholera (to the consternation of private water companies who anonymously denounced Snow's work). By the 1854 epidemic, then, the intellectual framework was in place, and the problem of how cholera spread was ripe for solution.

Along with a good idea and a timely problem, there was a *good method*. Snow's scientific detective work exhibits a shrewd intelligence about evidence, a clear logic of data display and analysis:

1. *Placing the data in an appropriate context for assessing cause and effect.* The original data listed the victims' names and described their circumstances, all in order by date of death. Such a stack of death certificates naturally lends itself to time-series displays, chronologies of the epidemic (see Figures 6.1 and 6.2). *But descriptive narration is not*

[5]Robert A. Dahl, "Cause and Effect in the Study of Politics," in Daniel Lerner, ed., *Cause and Effect* (New York, 1965), p. 88.
[6]H. Harold Scott, *Some Notable Epidemics* (London, 1934), pp. 3–4.

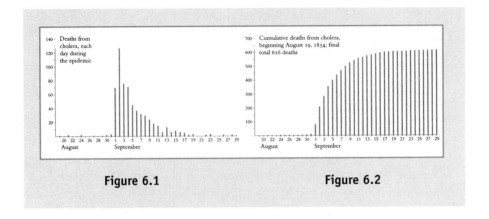

Figure 6.1   **Figure 6.2**

causal explanation; the passage of time is a poor explanatory variable, practically useless in discovering a strategy of how to intervene and stop the epidemic.

Instead of plotting a time-series, which would simply report each day's bad news, Snow constructed a graphical display that provided direct and powerful testimony about a possible cause-effect relationship. Recasting the original data from their one-dimensional temporal ordering into a two-dimensional spatial comparison, Snow marked deaths from cholera (Figure 6.3) on this map, along with locations of the area's 11 community water pump-wells (•). The notorious well is located amid an intense cluster of deaths, near the D in BROAD STREET. This map reveals a strong association between cholera and proximity to the Broad Street pump, in a context of simultaneous comparison with other local water sources and the surrounding neighborhoods without cholera.

2. *Making quantitative comparisons.* The deep, fundamental question in statistical analysis is *Compared with what?* Therefore, investigating the experiences of the victims of cholera is only part of the search for credible evidence; to understand fully the cause of the epidemic also requires an analysis of those who *escaped* the disease. With great clarity, the map presented several intriguing clues for comparisons between the living and the dead, clues strikingly visible at a brewery and a workhouse. Snow wrote in his report:

> There is a brewery in Broad Street, near to the pump, and on perceiving that no brewer's men were registered as having died of cholera, I called on Mr. Huggins, the proprietor. He informed me that there were above seventy workmen

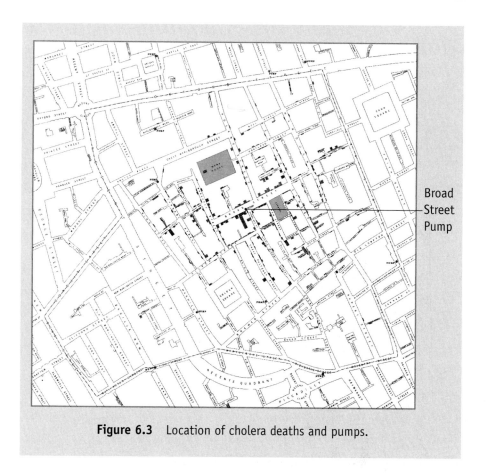

Broad Street Pump

Figure 6.3 Location of cholera deaths and pumps.

employed in the brewery, and that none of them had suffered from cholera—at least in severe form—only two having been indisposed, and that not seriously, at the time the disease prevailed. The men are allowed a certain quantity of malt liquor, and Mr. Huggins believes they do not drink water at all; and he is quite certain that the workmen never obtained water from the pump in the street. There is a deep well in the brewery, in addition to the New River water. (p. 42)

Saved by the beer! And at a nearby workhouse, the circumstances of non-victims of the epidemic provided important and credible evidence about the cause of the disease, as well as a quantitative calculation of an expected rate of cholera compared with the actual observed rate:

> The Workhouse in Poland Street is more than three-fourths surrounded by houses in which deaths from cholera occurred, yet out of five-hundred-thirty-five inmates only five died of cholera, the other deaths which took place being those of persons admitted after they were attacked. The workhouse has a pump-well on the premises, in addition to the supply from the Grand Junction Water Works, and the inmates never sent to Broad Street for water. If the mortality in the workhouse had been equal to that in the streets immediately surrounding it on three sides, upwards of one hundred persons would have died. (p. 42)

3. *Considering alternative explanations and contrary cases.* Sometimes it can be difficult for researchers—who both report *and* advocate their findings—to face up to threats to their conclusions, such as alternative explanations and contrary cases. Nonetheless, the credibility of a report is enhanced by a careful assessment of *all* relevant evidence, not just the evidence overtly consistent with explanations advanced by the report. The point is to get it right, not to win the case, not to sweep under the rug all the assorted puzzles and inconsistencies that frequently occur in collections of data.

    Both Snow's map and the time-sequence of deaths show several apparently contradictory instances, a number of deaths from cholera with no obvious link to the Broad Street pump. And yet . . .

> In some of the instances, where the deaths are scattered a little further from the rest on the map, the malady was probably contracted at a nearer point to the pump. A cabinet-maker who resided on Noel Street [some distance from Broad Street] worked in Broad Street. . . . A little girl, who died in Ham Yard, and another who died in Angel Court, Great Windmill Street, went to the school in Dufour's Place, Broad Street, and were in the habit of drinking the pump-water. . . .[7]

In a particularly unfortunate episode, one London resident made a special effort to obtain Broad Street well-water, a delicacy of taste with a side-effect that unwittingly cost two lives. Snow's report is one of careful description and precise logic:

---

[7]Snow, *Cholera*, p. 47.

Dr. Fraser also first called my attention to the following circumstances, which are perhaps the most conclusive of all in proving the connexion between the Broad Street pump and the outbreak of cholera. In the 'Weekly Return of Births and Deaths' of September 9th, the following death is recorded: 'At West End, on 2nd September, the widow of a percussion-cap maker, aged 59 years, diarrhea two hours, *cholera epidemica* sixteen hours.' I was informed by this lady's son that she had not been in the neighbourhood of Broad Street for many months. A cart went from Broad Street to West End every day, and it was the custom to take out a large bottle of the water from the pump in Broad Street, as she preferred it. The water was taken on Thursday, 31st August, and she drank of it in the evening, and also on Friday. She was seized with cholera on the evening of the latter day, and died on Saturday. . . . A niece, who was on a visit to this lady, also drank of the water; she returned to her residence, in a high and healthy part of Islington, was attacked with cholera, and died also. There was no cholera at the time, either at West End or in the neighbourhood where the niece died.[8]

Although at first glance these deaths appear unrelated to the Broad Street pump, they are, upon examination, strong evidence pointing to that well. There is here a clarity and undeniability to the link between cholera and the Broad Street pump; only such a link can account for what would otherwise be a mystery, this seemingly random and unusual occurrence of cholera. And the saintly Snow, unlike some researchers, gives full credit to the person, Dr. Fraser, who actually found this crucial case.

Ironically, the most famous aspect of Snow's work is also the most uncertain part of his evidence: it is not at all clear that the removal of the handle of the Broad Street pump had much to do with ending the epidemic. As shown by this time-series (see Figure 6.4), the epidemic was already in rapid decline by the time the handle was removed. Yet, in many retellings of the story of the epidemic, the pump-handle removal is *the* decisive event, the unmistakable symbol of Snow's contribution. Here is the dramatic account of Benjamin Ward Richardson:

On the evening of Thursday, September 7th, the vestrymen of St. James's were sitting in solemn consultation on the

---

[8]Snow, *Cholera*, pp. 44–45.

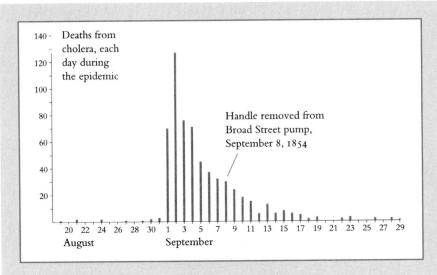

Figure 6.4 Plotted from the table in Snow, *Cholera,* p. 49.

causes of the [cholera epidemic]. They might well be solemn,
for such a panic possibly never existed in London since the
days of the great plague. People fled from their homes as
from instant death, leaving behind them, in their haste, all
the mere matter which before they valued most. While,
then, the vestrymen were in solemn deliberation, they were
called to consider a new suggestion. A stranger had asked,
in modest speech, for a brief hearing. Dr. Snow, the stranger
in question, was admitted and in few words explained his
view of the 'head and front of the offending.' He had fixed
his attention on the Broad Street pump as the source and
center of the calamity. He advised removal of the pump-
handle as the grand prescription. The vestry was incredulous,
but had the good sense to carry out the advice. The pump-
handle was removed, and the plague was stayed.[9]

Note the final sentence, a declaration of cause and effect. Modern epi-
demiologists, however, are distinctly skeptical about the evidence that
links this intervention to the epidemic's end:

---

[9]Benjamin W. Richardson, "The Life of John Snow, M.D.," foreword to John Snow, *On Chloroform
and Other Anaesthetics: Their Action and Administration* (London, 1858), pp. XX–XXI.

John Snow, in the seminal act of modern public health epidemiology, performed an intervention that was non-randomized, that was appraised with historical controls, and that had major ambiguities in the equivocal time relation-ship between his removal of the handle of the Broad Street pump and the end of the associated epidemic of cholera—but he correctly demonstrated that the disease was trans-mitted through water, not air.[10]

At a minimum, removing the pump-handle prevented a recur-rence of cholera. Snow recognized several difficulties in evaluating the effect of his intervention; since most people living in central London had fled, the disease ran out of possible victims—which happened simultaneously with shutting down the infected water supply. The case against the Broad Street pump, however, was based on a diversity of ad-ditional evidence: the cholera map, studies of unusual instances, com-parisons of the living and dead with their consumption of well-water, and an idea about a mechanism of contamination (a nearby under-ground sewer had probably leaked into the infected well). Also, the finding that cholera was carried by water—a life-saving scientific dis-covery that showed how to intervene and prevent the spread of cholera—derived not only from study of the Broad Street epidemic but also from Snow's mappings of several other cholera outbreaks in rela-tion to the purity of community water supplies.

4. *Assessment of possible errors in the numbers reported in graphics.* Snow's analysis attends to the sources and consequences of errors in gathering the data. In particular, the credibility of the cholera map grows out of supplemental details in the text—as image, word, and number combine to present the evidence and make the argument. De-tailed comments on possible errors annotate both the map and the table, reassuring readers about the care and integrity of the statistical detective work that produced the data graphics:

The deaths which occurred during this fatal outbreak of cholera are indicated in the accompanying map, as far as I could ascertain them. There are necessarily some deficien-cies, for in a few of the instances of persons who died in the hospitals after their removal from the neighbourhood of

[10]Alvan R. Feinstein, *Clinical Epidemiology: The Architecture of Clinical Research* (Philadelphia, 1985), pp. 409–410.

Broad Street, the number of the house from which they had been removed was not registered. The address of those who died after their removal to St. James's Workhouse was not registered; and I was only able to obtain it, in a part of the cases, on application at the Master's Office, for many of the persons were too ill, when admitted, to give any account of themselves. In the case also of some of the workpeople and others who contracted the cholera in this neighbourhood, and died in different parts of London, the precise house from which they had removed is not stated in the return of deaths. I have heard of some persons who died in the country shortly after removing from the neighbourhood of Broad Street; and there must, no doubt, be several cases of this kind that I have not heard of. Indeed, the full extent of the calamity will probably never be known. The deficiencies I have mentioned, however, probably do not detract from the correctness of the map as a diagram of the topography of the outbreak; for, if the locality of the few additional cases could be ascertained, they would probably be distributed over the district of the outbreak in the same proportion as the large number which are known.[11]

The deaths in the above table [the time-series of daily deaths] are compiled from the sources mentioned above in describing the map; but some deaths which were omitted from the map on account of the number of the house not being known, are included in the table. . . .[12]

Snow drew a *dot map*, marking each individual death. This design has statistical costs and benefits: death *rates* are not shown, and such maps may become cluttered with excessive detail; on the other hand, the sometimes deceptive effects of aggregation are avoided. And of course dot maps aid in the identification and analysis of individual cases, evidence essential to Snow's argument.

The big problem is that dot maps fail to take into account the number of people living in an area and at risk to get a disease: "an area of the map may be free of cases merely because it is not populated."[13]

[11]Snow, *Cholera*, pp. 45–46.
[12]Snow, *Cholera*, p. 50.
[13]Brian MacMahon and Thomas F. Pugh, *Epidemiology: Principles and Methods* (Boston, 1970), p. 150.

Snow's map does not fully answer the question *Compared with what?* For example, if the population as a whole in central London had been distributed just as the deaths were, then the cholera map would have merely repeated the unimportant fact that more people lived near the Broad Street pump than elsewhere. This was not the case; the entire area shown on the map—with and without cholera—was thickly populated. Still, Snow's dot map does not assess varying densities of population in the area around the pump. Ideally, the cholera data should be displayed on both a dot and a rate map, with population-based rates calculated for rather small and homogeneous geographic units. In the text of his report, however, Snow did present rates for a few different areas surrounding the pump.

Even in the face of issues raised by a modern statistical critique, it remains wonderfully true that John Snow did, after all, show exactly how cholera was transmitted and therefore prevented. In 1955, the *Proceedings of the Royal Society of Medicine* commemorated Snow's discovery. A renowned epidemiologist, Bradford Hill, wrote: "For close upon 100 years we have been free in this country from epidemic cholera, and it is a freedom which, basically, we owe to the logical thinking, acute observations and simple sums of Dr. John Snow."[14]

 Steps in Writing a Causal Argument

If your instructor asks for a topic proposal, use steps 1–4 to guide you in writing the proposal.

1. **Make a causal claim on a controversial trend, event, or phenomenon.** Use this formula: *X causes (or does not cause) Y or X causes Y, which in turn causes Z.*

   Examples:
   - One-parent families (or television violence, bad diet, and so on) is (or is not) the cause of emotional and behavioral problems in children.

---

[14]A. Bradford Hill, "Snow—An Appreciation," *Proceedings of the Royal Society of Medicine,* 48 (1955), p. 1012

- Firearms control laws (or right-to-carry-handgun laws) reduce (or increase) violent crimes.
- The trend toward home schooling (or private schools) is (or is not) improving the quality of education.
- The length of U.S. presidential campaigns forces candidates to become too much influenced by big-dollar contributors (or prepares them for the constant media scrutiny that they will endure as president).
- Putting grade school children into competitive sports teaches them how to succeed in later life (or puts undue emphasis on winning and teaches many who are slower to mature to have a negative self-image).

2. **What's at stake in your claim?** If the cause is obvious to everyone, then it probably isn't worth writing about. Sex is the cause of STDs among college students, of course, but why do some students engage in unprotected sex when they know they are at risk?

3. **Make a diagram of causes.** Write as many causes as you can think of. Then make a fishbone diagram in which you show the causes.

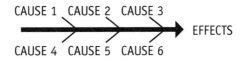

Which are the immediate causes? Which are the background causes? Which are the hidden causes? Which are the causes that most people have not recognized?

4. **Analyze your potential readers.** Who are your readers? How familiar are they with the trend, event, or phenomenon that you're writing about? What are they likely to know and not know? How does it affect them? How likely are they to accept your causal explanation? What alternative explanation might they argue for?

5. **Write a draft.**

Introduction:
- Describe the controversial trend, event, or phenomenon.
- Give the background necessary for your intended readers.

Body:
- For a trend, event, or phenomenon that is unfamiliar to your readers, you can explain the cause or chain of causation. Remember that providing facts is not the same thing as estab-

lishing causes, although facts can help to support your causal analysis.

■ Another way of organizing the body is to set out the causes that have been offered and reject them one by one. Then you can present the cause that you think is most important.

■ A third way is to treat a series of causes one by one, analyzing the importance of each.

Conclusion:

■ Do more than simply summarize what you have said. You might consider additional effects beyond those that have been previously noted.

6. **Revise, revise, revise. See Chapter 11 for detailed instructions.**

Stage 1. Read your argument aloud.

Do no more in this stage than put checks in the margins that you can return to later. Think in particular about these things:

■ **Your claim.** When you finish reading, summarize in one sentence what you are arguing. What's at stake in your claim?

■ **Your good reasons.** What are the good reasons for your claim? Would a reader have any trouble identifying them?

■ **Your representation of yourself.** Forget for a moment that you wrote what you are reading. What impression do you have of you, the writer?

■ **Your consideration of your readers.** Do you give enough background if your readers are unfamiliar with the issue? Do you acknowledge opposing views that they might have? Do you appeal to common values that you share with them?

Stage 2. Analyze your argument in detail.

■ **Examine your organization.** What are the topics of each of the paragraphs? Is the relationship of one paragraph to another clearly signaled? If any paragraphs appear out of order, think of another way to arrange them.

■ **Examine your evidence.** If you noted places where you could use more evidence when you read through the first time, now is the time to determine what kinds of additional evidence you need.

■ **Consider your title and introduction.** Be as specific as you can in your title, and if possible, suggest your stance. Does your introduction get off to a fast start and convince your reader to keep reading?

- **Consider your conclusion.** Think about whether there is a summarizing point you can make, an implication you can draw, or another example you can include that sums up your position.
- **Analyze the visual aspects of your text.** Do the font and layout you selected look attractive? Would headings and subheadings help to identify key sections of your argument? Would the addition of graphics augment key points?

Stage 3. Focus on your style and proofread carefully.

- **Check the connections between sentences.** Notice how your sentences are connected. If you need to signal the relationship from one sentence to the next, use a transitional word or phrase.
- **Check your sentences for emphasis.** Elements at the beginning and the end of sentences tend to stand out more than things in the middle.
- **Eliminate wordiness.** See how many words you can take out without losing the meaning.
- **Use active verbs.** Anytime you can use a verb besides a form of *be* (*is, are, was, were*), take advantage of the opportunity to make your style more lively.
- **Proofread your spelling carefully.** Your spelling checker will miss many mistakes.
- **Use your handbook to check items of mechanics and usage.** Look up any item you are unsure of.

CHAPTER 7

Evaluation Arguments

People make evaluations all the time. Newspapers and magazines have picked up on this love of evaluation by running "best of" polls. They ask their readers what's the best Mexican, Italian, or

> **Evaluation arguments depend on the criteria you select.**

Chinese restaurant; the best pizza; the best local band; the best coffeehouse; the best dance club; the best neighborhood park; the best swimming hole; the best bike ride (scenic and challenging); the best volleyball court; the best place to get married; and so on. If you ask one of your friends who voted in a "best" poll why she picked a particular restaurant as the best of its kind, she might respond by saying simply, "I like it." But if you ask her why she likes it, she might start offering good reasons such as these: The food is good, the service prompt, the prices fair, and the atmosphere comfortable. It's really not a mystery why these polls are often quite predictable and why the same restaurants tend to win year after year. Many people think that evaluations are matters of personal taste, but when we begin probing the reasons, we often discover that the criteria that different people use to make evaluations have a lot in common.

If you simply want to announce that you like or don't like something, then all you have to do is say so, but if you want to convince other people that your judgment is sound, then you have to appeal to criteria that they will agree with and, if necessary, argue for the validity of additional criteria that you think your readers should also consider. Once you have established the criteria you will use for your evaluation, then you can apply those criteria to whatever you are evaluating to see how well it measures up. You make judgments of good or bad, best or worst, on the basis of the match with the criteria. For some items the criteria are relatively easy to establish, and the judgment is easy to make. If you accidentally knock your clock radio off your nightstand, break it, and have to replace it, you might do a little comparison shopping. Setting the alarm on your old clock was more difficult than it should have been, so you want an alarm that is easy to set. You need to see the clock at night, so you want a luminous display. You sometimes listen to the radio while you're waking up, so the radio needs to sound good enough to get your day off to a pleasant start. And you don't want to pay much. So you decide to test several brands that all cost about $20, and you buy the one that is easiest to use with the best sound and display.

Kinds of Evaluations

Arguments of evaluation are structured much like arguments of definition. Recall that the criteria in arguments of definition are set out in because clauses: X *is a Y because it has criteria A and B*. In arguments of evaluation the claim takes the form X *is a good (bad, the best, the worst) Y if measured by criteria A, B, and C*.

X ⟵ *LINK (because)* ⟵ good (bad, best, worst) Y

X is ⟵ *LINK (because)* ⟵ the best clock radio for under $20

A) it has the best display
B) it has the best sounding radio
C) it is easy to use

The key move in writing most evaluative arguments is first deciding what kind of criteria to use and then finding appropriate criteria.

Imagine that the oldest commercial building in your city is about to be torn down. Your goal is to get the old store converted to a museum, which is a proposal argument. First you will need to make an evaluative argument that will form the basis of your proposal. You might argue that the stonework in the building is of excellent quality and deserves preservation. You might argue that a downtown museum would be much better than more office space because it would draw more visitors. Or you might argue that it is only fair that the oldest commercial building be preserved because the oldest house and other historic buildings have been saved.

Each of these arguments uses different criteria. An argument that the old building is beautiful and that beautiful things should be preserved uses **aesthetic** criteria. An argument that a museum is better than an office building because it would bring more visitors to the downtown area is based on **practical** criteria. An argument that the oldest store building deserves the same treatment as the oldest house is based on fairness, a concept that relies on **moral** criteria.

Building an Evaluation Argument

Most people have a lot of practice making consumer evaluations, and when they have enough time to do their homework, they usually make an informed decision. But sometimes, criteria for evaluations are not so obvious, and evaluations are much more difficult to make. Sometimes, one set of criteria favors one choice while another set of criteria favors another. You might have encountered this problem when you chose a college. If you were able to leave home to go to school, you had a potential choice of over 1,400 accredited colleges and universities. Until twenty years ago, there wasn't much information about choosing a college other than what colleges said about themselves. You could find out the price of tuition and what courses were offered, but it was hard to compare one college with another.

In 1983, the magazine *U.S. News & World Report* began ranking U.S. colleges and universities from a consumer's perspective. Those rankings have remained highly controversial ever since. Many college officials have attacked the criteria that *U.S. News* uses to make its evaluations. In an August 1998 *U.S. News* article, Gerhard Casper, the president of Stanford University (which is consistently near the top of the rankings), says, "Much about these rankings—particularly their specious formulas and spurious precision—is utterly misleading." Casper argues that using graduation rates as a criterion of quality rewards easy schools. Other college presidents have called for a national boycott of the *U.S. News* rankings (without much success).

U.S. News replies in its defense that colleges and universities themselves do a lot of ranking, beginning with ranking students for admissions, using their SAT or ACT scores, high school GPA, ranking in high school class, quality of high school, and other factors, and then grading the students and ranking them against each other when they are enrolled in college. Furthermore, schools also evaluate faculty members and take great interest in the national ranking of their departments. They care very much about where they stand in relation to each other. Why, then, *U.S. News* argues, shouldn't people be able to evaluate colleges and universities, since colleges and universities are so much in the business of evaluating people?

Arguing for the right to evaluate colleges and universities is one thing; actually doing comprehensive and reliable evaluations is quite another. *U.S. News* uses a formula in which 25 percent of a school's ranking is based on a survey of reputation in which the president, provost, and dean of admissions at each college rate the quality of schools in the same category, and the remaining 75 percent is based on statistical criteria of quality. These statistical criteria fall into six major categories: retention of students, faculty resources, student selectivity, financial resources, alumni giving, and (for national universities and liberal arts colleges only) "graduation rate performance," the difference between the proportion of students who are expected to graduate and the proportion that actually do. These major categories are made up of factors that are weighted for their importance. For example, the faculty resources category is determined by the size of classes (the proportion of classes with fewer than twenty students and the proportion of classes with fifty or more students), the average faculty pay weighted by the cost of living in different regions of the country, the percentage of professors with the highest degree in their field, the overall student-faculty ratio, and the percentage of faculty who are full time.

Those who have challenged the *U.S. News* rankings argue that the magazine should use different criteria or weight the criteria differently. *U.S. News* answers those charges on its Web site (http://www.usnews.com/usnews/edu/college/corank.htm) by claiming that it has followed a trend toward emphasizing outcomes such as graduation rates. If you are curious about where your school ranks, take a look at the *U.S. News* Web site.

Reviews are a common type of evaluative argument that uses aesthetic criteria. When you read movie reviews, concert reviews, or other reviews, notice how the writer identifies criteria. Sometimes, these criteria are not obvious, and you will notice that the writer makes an argument about what criteria make a truly excellent horror film or a superior rock concert. You might have to argue for your criteria too. For example, suppose you want to argue that the 1955 film *Rebel without a Cause*, starring James Dean, Natalie Wood, and Sal Mineo, is a classic of teen drama films. The obvious definitional criteria are that *Rebel without a Cause* is a film, is a drama, and is about teens. But if you want to argue that *Rebel without a Cause* is exemplary of the genre and has qualities that make it timeless, then you have to define qualities that make a film a classic in this genre.

You mention your idea to your roommate, and she says, "That's total nonsense. Have you seen it recently? The dialog is awful, and the plot is even worse with that sappy ending. If James Dean hadn't gotten killed in a car wreck at age twenty-four, believe me, nobody would ever watch it now." You realize that she has a point about the tragic deaths of the main characters. Not only did James Dean die in the most famous car crash in history before Princess Diana, but also Natalie Wood later drowned mysteriously in a boating accident off Catalina, and Sal Mineo was murdered near his West Hollywood apartment. And she's right that the dialog hasn't aged well and that the ending, in which the James Dean character reconciles with his father, doesn't fit with the rest of the film. But there's still something about *Rebel without a Cause* that makes it a classic, and that's what you want to convince her of.

James Dean

First, you realize that even though there have been a lot of bad films about teens since *Rebel without a Cause*, there really were none before it. So you argue that *Rebel without a Cause* is a classic because it pioneered much of what was to come later. It was the first film to portray teens in a somewhat realistic fashion (though the stars did overact). The main character, Jim Stark (played by James Dean), is both vulnerable and defiant. His friend Plato (the Sal Mineo character) is about as gay as a film character could be in the 1950s, when direct portrayal of homosexuality was banned by the censors. Jim's eventual girlfriend, Judy (Natalie Wood), who snubs him at the beginning, is confused and rejected by her parents. And the parents in the film are totally ineffectual. Jim has a weak father (played by Jim Backus, the voice of Mr. Magoo) who won't stand up against his domineering wife. Judy also lacks parental support, and Plato's parents have abandoned him. So even if *Rebel without a Cause* is a little cheesy, it's honest about teen problems.

You decide to argue that another criterion that makes *Rebel without a Cause* a classic is its implicit critique of U.S. culture. It was released in 1955 at the peak of U.S. self-confidence and at the high-water mark of what later came to be called family values. These were supposed to be the years of the family ideal—of *Father Knows Best, Leave It to Beaver*, and *Donna Reed*—yet the film depicted an entire generation of young men and women who were struggling to find an identity. The film was the first to ask why U.S. teenagers were so troubled if everything was supposed to be so good. It exposed a big flaw in the portrait of the United States as the ideal society and accused the parents of being responsible for the alienation of the teenagers.

Finally, you won't concede that the fame of the film is strictly because of James Dean's early death. It's no accident, you argue, that boys in the 1950s spent hours trying to comb their hair into pompadours to look like James Dean. He has a terrific screen presence, and he conveys many conflicting emotions. But above all, he's always lonely, always groping for love from a family and society he finds unresponsive. Dean's role is the blueprint for the alienated teen. He's still a rebel after all these years.

ERIC GABLE AND RICHARD HANDLER

In Colonial Williamsburg, the New History Meets the Old

Eric Gable is an assistant professor of sociology and anthropology at Mary Washington College. Richard Handler is a professor of anthropology at the University of Virginia. They are the authors of The New History in an Old Museum: Creating the Past at Colonial Williamsburg *(Duke University Press, 1997).*

Some evaluations are obviously evaluations from the moment you glance at them. Reviews fall into this category. But other evaluations can be more subtle. "In Colonial Williamsburg, the New History Meets the Old," originally published in the Chronicle of Higher Education, *takes a long time giving background before the authors begin to make evaluative judgments. Notice how they define the criteria for a good museum. Do you agree with these criteria?*

1   **IN** recent years, the way in which museums and other public displays have presented history often has generated vituperative debate among scholars

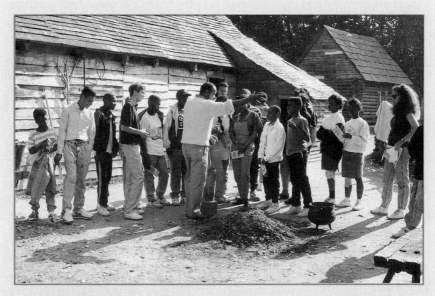

An interpreter explains eighteeth-century life at the reconstructed slave quarters of Colonial Williamsburg.

and the public at large. The popular media have portrayed public history as an ideological struggle—left-wing professors shattering (desecrating) popular assumptions. In the most common media treatment, "tenured radicals" view the previous generation's scholarly work as little more than ruling-class propaganda papering over the negative aspects of American history. In reaction, today's historians promulgate a more pessimistic version of America's past— one that destroys Americans' grounds for taking pride in their country.

2   We stepped into the middle of these often contentious appraisals of public history a few years ago, when we conducted an ethnographic study of Colonial Williamsburg, arguably America's premier public-history site. Colonial Williamsburg is a replica of the capital of Revolutionary-era Virginia. The reconstruction of this entire town, begun in 1926, was initially underwritten by John D. Rockefeller's largesse, but it is now financed by public donations, ticket sales, hotel and restaurant revenues, the marketing of Colonial-era reproductions, and revenue from an endowment established by Rockefeller.

3   For much of its history, the replica was widely criticized by historians and knowledgeable laypeople as little more than an airbrushed, consumer-oriented, patriotic shrine celebrating an upscale idyll loosely based on the life styles of Virginia's Colonial elite. But beginning in the 1970s, a new group of

historians was hired as researchers and curators to refashion the site. They were trained in the "new social history," which emerged out of the social turmoil of the 1960s and which focused on groups and individuals neglected by older, traditional scholars. The top administrators prompted this change in part to keep Colonial Williamsburg at the cutting edge of scholarship, and in part because historians have argued convincingly that a new version of the past will be more popular, accurate, and inclusive than the entrenched story.

4   As a result of this shift, we wanted to see how public history was being made "on the ground." We focused on the way it was managed, as historians attempted to use the materials at this particular site to create their vision of the past; as middle-level managers trained front-line staff members (dressed in reproduction costumes as craftworkers, farmers, and other residents of the town) to deliver historical stories to the public; as these front-line employees resisted or opposed new interpretations; and as visitors digested what they heard and saw.

5   We found that, during the past decade, Colonial Williamsburg has changed in significant ways the history that it presents to the public. Most notable is the greater prominence of African Americans—those the museum calls "the other half"—in its narrative of nationhood. A small but active unit devoted to African-American history has created dozens of special programs and tours to illuminate the lives of slaves and free black people in colonial Virginia. For example, you can now tour a reconstructed slave quarter and meet a costumed African-American guide who will tell you about the daily life of the enslaved. Or you can stroll Williamsburg's back alleys with such characters as the entrepreneurial Chicken Hattie, who sells eggs to the town's white inhabitants.

6   Some programs do not dodge the horror of slavery: an enactment of a slave auction, a video about a runaway slave, a tour with graphic discussions of the Middle Passage on slave ships, and discussions of the breakup of African-American families.

7   Yet the more widely disseminated story still is an upbeat one, in which slaves, like other immigrants, establish themselves in a new land and work hard to improve their lot. Moreover, black history remains secondary at Williamsburg. It is still easy for visitors to tour the entire site without hearing anything about African Americans other than how much they cost their owners, and how many lived and worked in a particular white person's residence.

8   At Colonial Williamsburg, then, the influence of social historians has apparently been less than media depictions of "tenured radicals" might lead one to expect. There has been no all-out ideological struggle, and the bulk of the history told here is not so different from that told 30 years ago. We asked ourselves why.

9   It seems to us that Colonial Williamsburg and sites like it remain stages for the retelling of such conventional American narratives as the Horatio Alger story. In this scenario, individuals or ethnic groups are depicted as pulling themselves up by their bootstraps. This narrative is applied as readily to African slaves such as Chicken Hattie as to a European-immigrant-turned-entrepreneurial-businessman such as Mr. Benjamin Powell, whose house you can visit. What this narrative does not do is challenge visitors to rethink their notions of America's past, or its present.

10   Like many other museums, Colonial Williamsburg is a tourist attraction as well as an educational institution, and the ideas of hospitality and courtesy are deeply ingrained in its corporate culture. Management repeats ceaselessly that visitors—customers—will not return unless they enjoy their visits. The assumption is that stories depicting the harshness of slavery—and, more generally, histories critical of America's shortcomings—will pain, embarrass, and ultimately turn away tourists.

11   Moreover, on the front line, where employees meet visitors—and behind the scenes, where managers of competing programs at the site wage institutional turf wars—facts are weapons more readily wielded than are the complicated arguments that social historians favor about the ideological underpinnings of history. Thus, for example, at one point we observed African-American guides and white guides at a particular re-created house debate how to discuss miscegenation: The general issue of the entanglement of sexual practices and racial politics was displaced by an unresolvable factual dispute: whether a particular slaveholder had fathered a particular child by a particular slave.

12   Time and again, we watched as seemingly productive debates deteriorated into narrowly construed arguments about fact. Even staff historians were prone to lose sight of the big picture as they chased after stray details. This "just the facts, please" tendency was exacerbated because the market niche of history museums depends on their claim to possess "real" history, embodied in their buildings and objects, in contrast to what the museums see as the "fakery" of their major competitors—theme parks such as those of Disney.

13   Thus, despite some changes, the new social history has not transformed this particular old museum and its decades-old culture of patriotic realism. The Fife and Drum Corps continues to play patriotic songs as it marches down the main street—the high point of a tourist's day. More significantly, the corps continues to be the central icon in the photographs, brochures, and commercials that the museum produces to attract visitors and convince people that donating to the site's continuing work is an act of patriotism. Other such icons are the coach and coachmen (usually black) in

livery. Visitors continue to pay extra for the privilege of a short coach ride through town, perhaps to identify themselves with the masters.

14   Because of the efforts of historians who have worked at Williamsburg, the site is now demographically more diverse than it used to be. It has more African-American employees in positions other than menial ones, and African Americans are often included in the stories that guides tell about America's Revolutionary past. But, by and large, these changes are just additional pieces in a narrative framework that continues to celebrate America while playing down inequalities.

15   In the end, then, Colonial Williamsburg continues to be a patriotic shrine that fosters tourists' fantasies. Despite media portrayals of ideological revolutions in the nation's museums, the new social historians at this site have not subverted the old story. It is not so much that they have been muzzled—or have backed down—as that their efforts have not overcome a wider cultural tendency, in which older cultural images persist and continue to frame the site as a whole. Williamsburg thus provides a fractured puzzle of the past—and continues to play down historic and current inequalities.

NATASCHA POCEK

The Diet Zone: A Dangerous Place

In 1997 Natascha Pocek wrote the following essay as a response to an assignment in her first-year writing course at Penn State.

1   DIET Coke, diet Pepsi, diet Cherry Coke, diet pills, diet shakes, no-fat diet, vegetable diet, carbohydrate diet, diet, diet, diet—enough! We are assaulted by the word "diet" every time we go into a supermarket, turn on the television, listen to the radio, or read an advertisement. We are not only surrounded by the word "diet" everywhere we look and listen, but we as "Americans" are also linked with "diet" in general; Americans are automatically associated with the stereotypical image of either extreme thinness or obesity. We have so easily been lured by the promise and potential of diet products, which include everything from pills to foods, that we have stopped thinking about what diet products are doing to us. Diet products, in fact, promote the "easy way out," a most elemental form of deception. It is imperative that we realize that diet products adversely affect not only our

weight, but also our values of dedication and persistence. We are paying for products that harm us, physically and psychologically. Therefore, we must stop purchasing diet products without recognizing the harm we are doing to ourselves. We must realize that in purchasing diet products we are effectively purchasing physical problems and psychological decay in a commercial package. The time has come for us to accept the fact that solutions don't come in bottles or from miracle no-calorie chemicals; solutions come from the mind, and diet products are promoting the wrong solution.

2   As a teenager, I learned the hard way that losing weight with diet products as an aid only results in a vicious cycle of failure. Statistically overweight from the age of 15 to 18, I was unhappy and sought a solution, a way to lose the extra pounds that I carried around on my frame. No bottle, pill, powder, or shake took off my excess weight; I earned the body that I now live in by watching what I ate. Period. As a typical teenager, I admit, I tried many fad diets. I attempted an advertised vegetable diet which reduced me to the meal plan of a rabbit, and a drink-as-much-water-as-you-can-so-you're-not-hungry diet. I also tried to lose weight by using diet pills and diet food products. The diet pills were, without a doubt, one of my biggest mistakes. The pills were only a temporary solution because while taking the pills my eating habits didn't change. I had not learned how to eat healthily and moderately. I had learned how to quickly lose a few pounds with no effort. The pills shifted my focus from the most important aspect, the food, and placed it on watching the clock to see when I needed to swallow the next pill. The pills circumvented the real issue of my unhealthy eating habits; I didn't even consider my eating habits since I had not taken any foods out of my daily food intake. Consequently, as soon as I stopped popping the miracle pills, the few pounds I had lost returned, along with a few more unexpected ones. Success had obviously eluded me.

3   The consumption of "diet-food" products was *the* single biggest mistake that I made in attempting to lose weight. I allowed myself to fall into a very relaxed mind set in which I did not really have to think about what I ate; my brain was dormant while my stomach was active. The diet foods and drinks that I consumed became my excuse for the chocolate cake at dinner, the extra helping of pasta, and the late-night cup of hot chocolate. It was acceptable to allow myself these treats because I had "saved calories" elsewhere. Needless to say, although I lost weight, it didn't stay off for long. Once again, I had not trained myself to acquire a taste for healthier foods. My eating habits stayed bad from the first Diet Coke I drank, to the last Low-Fat Granola Bar I ate. Diet foods, just like the diet pills, had been a huge failure which resulted from my lack of thought.

4 The mistake that I—and countless other Americans—made in using diet products carries much greater significance than not losing weight for the long run: diet products significantly weaken us psychologically. On one level, we are not allowing our brains to acknowledge that our weight problems lie not in actually losing the weight, but in controlling the consumption of fatty, high-caloric, unhealthy foods. Diet products allow us to skip the thinking stage completely and instead go straight for the scale. Dr. James Ferguson, a nationally prominent clinician who specializes in treating eating disorders and teaching weight control, says that "self-observation [is the] prime method of assessing eating behaviors" (65). Precisely. Diet products only allow us to ignore the crucial issue of eating habits altogether: They bypass the real problem. In reality, we aren't the ones contributing to the loss of our pounds; the diet products are responsible for shedding the pounds from our bodies. All we have to be able to do is swallow or recognize the word "diet" in food labels. The effort we put into losing weight is zero, no effort, non-existent. Consequently, when we stop consuming diet products, our bodies lose the dictators that worked to control the unruly pounds and our eating habits fall into chaos again.

5 On another level, the psychological effects of diet products have much greater ramifications. Every time we swallow a pill or drink a zero-calorie beverage, we are unconsciously telling ourselves that we don't have to work to get results, that we can select the "easy way out," the quick way out. I see Americans eating sweet foods endlessly because they are pacified by the low-fat label; they don't just eat the cakes and candies and cookies, they inhale them in huge amounts, and their excuse is that "they're low-fat, so it's okay." Diet products are subconsciously instilling in Americans the idea that gain comes without pain, that life can be devoid of resistance and struggle. The diet industry is not only making it easy to ignore the principle of not always getting what you want—it is, in fact, promoting its disappearance. People *can* eat whatever they want because most "bad foods" are now diet, light, or reduced fat. The diet pills and potions become important at the end of the vicious diet cycle when we say, "Oops, I ate twice as many cookies because they were low-fat and I gained weight." The diet pills become the dust pan and brush that clean up the mess we made with the diet products. The cycle of diet products is a virus that affects us psychologically and doesn't enforce any values of determination, perseverance, hard work, or self-discipline.

6 The danger of diet products lies not only in the psychological effects they have on us, but also in the immediate physical danger that they present. Death is unfortunately a possible side-effect of using diet products. In 1994, the drug Ephedrine, which is found in diet pills, was "linked to the

deaths of two people and severe reactions in several others" (Rosencrans). Cellulose fiber diet pills were identified as a "cause of esophageal obstruction" (Jones) and in 1992, 26 cases were reported to the Food and Drug Administration in which diet pills were the cause of "esophageal and small bowel obstruction" (Lewis 1424). Clearly, diet pills pose health threats. Diet foods become dangerous when used in place of other foods because they contain a minimal amount of nutrients. The next time you go to the supermarket and have the urge to buy a diet beverage, read the label. For example, the nutrition label of a Crystal Light bottle reads: Total Fat, 0 grams; Total Carb, 0 grams; Protein, 0 grams; Calories, 5. Wouldn't it be more appropriate to name the label the "malnutrition" label? When we drink a Crystal Light, we are swallowing a lot of precisely what, if there are 0 grams of everything in it? The answer is nothing—besides chemicals. As you continue reading the label on the bottle, you will come to the ingredient list, which includes sodium benzoate, artificial flavor, potassium sorbate, potassium citrate (controls acidity), BHA (preserves freshness) and so on. The ingredient and nutrition label illustrates the fact that diet foods can indirectly harm our bodies because consuming them instead of healthy foods means we are depriving our bodies of essential nutrients. Beyond an indirect harm, diet products can actually cause direct harm as well. Packets of Sweet n' Low and Care-Free gum carry warning labels which read, the "use of this product may be hazardous to your health. This product contains saccharin, which has been determined to cause cancer in laboratory animals." Would you like to take the chance that saccharin might give *you* cancer? The point is that diet foods and diet pills are only zero-caloric because the diet industry has created chemicals that can be manipulated to produce these miracle products. There is no insurance that a diet product is nutritional, and the chemicals that go into diet products are potentially dangerous.

7   As we walk down the aisle of the supermarket tomorrow, we will once again be bombarded by "diet" food labels that call to us from left and right. We will also see all the promising diet pills that make losing weight seem so easy. After demonstrating the harmful physical and psychological effects that diet products have on us, our instinct should be to turn and walk away. Now that we are more knowledgeable on the subject of diet products and can no longer claim ignorance about the harms that diet products have, it is time to seriously contemplate our purchase of diet products. Losing weight lies in the power of our minds, not in the power of chemicals. Once we realize this, we will be much better able to resist diet products, and thereby resist the psychological deterioration and physical deprivation that comes from using diet products.

Works Cited

Ferguson, James M. *Habits Not Diets: The Secret to Lifetime Weight Control.* Palo Alto, CA: Bull Publishing, 1988.

Jones, K. R. "Cellulose Fiber Diet Pills, A New Cause of Esophageal Obstruction." *Archives of Otolaryngology—Head and Neck Surgery* 116 (1990): 1091.

Lewis, J. H. "Esophageal and Small Bowel Obstruction from Guar Gum-Containing 'Diet Pills.'" *American Journal of Gastroenterology* 87 (1992): 1424–28.

Rosencrans, Kendra. "Diet Pills Suspected in Deaths." *Healthy Weight Journal* 8:4 (1994): 68.

Steps in Writing an Evaluation Argument

If your instructor asks for a topic proposal, use steps 1–4 to guide you in writing the proposal.

1. **Make an evaluative claim based on criteria.** Use this formula: *X is a good (bad, the best, the worst) Y if measured by certain criteria (aesthetic, practical, or moral).*

   Examples:
   - Write a book review or a movie review.
   - Write a defense of a particular kind of music or art.
   - Evaluate a controversial aspect of sports (e.g., the current system of determining who is champion in Division I college football by a system of bowls and polls) or evaluate a sports event (e.g., this year's WNBA playoffs) or a team.
   - Evaluate the effectiveness of an educational program (such as your high school honors program or your college's core curriculum requirement) or some other aspect of your campus.
   - Evaluate the effectiveness of a social policy or law such as legislating 21 as the legal drinking age, current gun control laws, or environmental regulation.

2. **What's at stake in your claim?** If nearly everybody would agree with you, then your evaluative claim probably isn't interesting or important. If you can think of people who would disagree, then something is at stake. Who argues the opposite of your claim? Why do they make a different evaluation?

3. **Make a list of criteria (aesthetic, practical, moral).** Which criteria make something a good Y? Which are the most important?

Which are fairly obvious and which will you have to argue for? Or what are all the effects of what you are evaluating? Which are the most important? Which are fairly obvious and which will you have to argue for?

4. **Analyze your potential readers.** Who are your primary and secondary readers? How familiar will they be with the person, group, institution, event, or thing that you are evaluating? What are they likely to know and not know? Which criteria are most important to them?

5. **Write a draft.**

Introduction:
- Introduce the person, group, institution, event, or object that you are going to evaluate. You might want to announce your stance at this point or wait until the concluding section.
- Give the background necessary for your intended readers.
- If there are opposing views, briefly describe them.

Body:
- If you are making an evaluation by criteria, describe each criterion and then analyze how well what you are evaluating meets that criterion.
- If you are making an evaluation according to the effects someone or something produces, describe each effect in detail.

Conclusion:
- If you have not yet announced your stance, then you can conclude that, on the basis of the criteria you set out or the effects you have analyzed, X is a good (bad, best, worst) Y. If you have made your stance clear from the beginning, then you can end with a compelling example or analogy.

6. **Revise, revise, revise. See Chapter 11 for detailed instructions.**

Stage 1. Read your argument aloud.
Do no more in this stage than put checks in the margins that you can return to later. Think in particular about these things:

- **Your claim.** When you finish reading, summarize in one sentence what you are arguing. What's at stake in your claim?
- **Your criteria.** How many criteria do you offer? Where are they located? Are they clearly connected to your claim?
- **Your representation of yourself.** Forget for a moment that you wrote what you are reading. What impression do you have of you, the writer?

- **Your consideration of your readers.** Do you give enough background, if your readers are unfamiliar with the issue? Do you acknowledge opposing views that they might have? Do you appeal to common values that you share with them?

Stage 2. Analyze your argument in detail.

- **Examine your organization.** What are the topics of each of the paragraphs? Is the relationship of one paragraph to another clearly signaled? If any paragraphs appear out of order, think of another way to arrange them.
- **Examine your evidence.** If you noted places where you could use more evidence when you read through the first time, now is the time to determine what kinds of additional evidence you need.
- **Consider your title and introduction.** Be as specific as you can in your title, and if possible, suggest your stance. Does your introduction get off to a fast start and convince your reader to keep reading?
- **Consider your conclusion.** Think about whether there is a summarizing point you can make, an implication you can draw, or another example you can include that sums up your position.
- **Analyze the visual aspects of your text.** Do the font and layout you selected look attractive? Would headings and subheadings help to identify key sections of your argument? Would the addition of graphics augment key points?

Stage 3. Focus on your style and proofread carefully.

- **Check the connections between sentences.** Notice how your sentences are connected. If you need to signal the relationship from one sentence to the next, use a transitional word or phrase.
- **Check your sentences for emphasis.** Elements at the beginning and the end of sentences tend to stand out more than things in the middle.
- **Eliminate wordiness.** See how many words you can take out without losing the meaning.
- **Use active verbs.** Anytime you can use a verb besides a form of *be* (*is, are, was, were*), take advantage of the opportunity to make your style more lively.
- **Proofread your spelling carefully.** Your spelling checker will miss many mistakes.
- **Use your handbook to check items of mechanics and usage.** Look up any item you are unsure of.

CHAPTER 8

Narrative Arguments

In 1980, 53,172 people were killed in traffic accidents in the United States, and over half the deaths involved alcohol. Americans had become accustomed to losing around 25,000 to 30,000 people every year to drunk drivers. But it was the tragic death in 1980 of Cari Lightner, a thirteen-year-old California girl who was killed by a hit-and-run drunk driver while walking along a city street, that made people start asking whether this carnage could be prevented. The driver had been out on bail only two days for another hit-and-run drunk driving crash, and he had three previous drunk driving arrests. He was allowed to plea bargain for killing Cari and avoided going to prison. Cari's mother, Candy Lightner, was outraged that so little was being done to prevent needless deaths and injuries. She and a small group of other women founded Mothers Against Drunk Driving (MADD) with the goals of getting tougher laws against drunk driving, stiffer penalties for those who kill and injure while driving drunk, and greater public awareness of the seriousness of driving drunk.

Cari Lightner's story aroused to action other people who had been injured

> **Narrative arguments often do not make a specific claim but rely on the reader to infer the writer's position.**

themselves or lost loved ones to drunk drivers. Chapters of MADD spread quickly across the country, and it has become one of the most effective citizen groups ever formed, succeeding in getting much new legislation against drunk driving on the books. These laws and changing attitudes about drunk driving have had a significant impact. The National Highway Traffic Safety Administration reported that in 2000, 16,653 people were killed in alcohol-related traffic accidents in the United States compared to 24,045 in 1986, a 30 percent reduction.

The success of MADD points to why arguing by narrating succeeds sometimes when other kinds of arguments have little effect. The story of Cari Lightner appealed to shared community values in ways that statistics did not. The story vividly illustrated that something was very wrong with the criminal justice system if a repeat drunk driver was allowed to run down and kill a child on a sidewalk only two days after committing a similar crime.

Martin Luther King, Jr., was another master of using narratives to make his points. In "Letter from Birmingham Jail," he relates in one sentence the disappointment of his six-year-old daughter when he had to explain to her why, because of the color of her skin, she could not go to an amusement park in Atlanta advertised on television. This tiny story vividly illustrates the pettiness of segregation laws and their effect on children.

Kinds of Narrative Arguments

Using narratives for advocating change is nothing new. As far back as we have records, we find people telling stories and singing songs about their own lives that argue for change. Folk songs have always given voice to political protest and have celebrated marginalized people. When workers in the United States began to organize in the 1880s, they adapted melodies that soldiers had sung in the Civil War. In the 1930s, performers and songwriters such as Paul Robeson, Woody Guthrie, Huddie Ledbetter (Leadbelly), and Aunt Molly Jackson relied on traditions of hymns, folk songs, and African-American blues to protest social conditions. In the midst of the politically quiet 1950s, folk songs told stories that critiqued social conformity and the dangers of nuclear war. In the 1960s, the civil rights movement and the movement against the Vietnam War brought a strong resurgence of folk music. The history of folk music is a continuous recycling of old tunes, verses, and narratives to engage new political situations. What can be said for folk songs is also true for any popular narrative genre, be it the short story, novel, drama, movies, or even rap music.

Folk singer/songwriter Shawn Colvin is one of many contemporary folk and blues singers who continue the tradition of making narrative arguments in their songs.

Narrative arguments work in a different way from those that spell out their criteria and argue for explicit links. A narrative argument succeeds if the experience being described invokes the life experiences of the readers. Anyone who has ever been around children knows that most kids love amusement parks. Martin Luther King, Jr., did not have to explain to his readers why going to an amusement park advertised on television was so important for his daughter. Likewise, the story of Cari Lightner was effective because even if you have not known someone who was killed by a drunk driver, most people have known someone who died tragically and perhaps needlessly. Furthermore, you often read about and see on television many people who die in traffic accidents. Narrative arguments allow readers to fill in the conclusion. In the cases of King's arguments against segregation laws and MADD's campaign against drunk drivers, that's exactly what happened. Public outcry led to changes in laws and public opinion.

Narrative arguments can be representative anecdotes, as we have seen with the examples from MADD and Martin Luther King, Jr., or they can be longer accounts of particular events that express larger ideas. One such story is George Orwell's account of a hanging in Burma (the country that is now known as Myanmar) while he was a colonial administrator in the late 1920s. In "A Hanging," first published in 1931, Orwell narrates an execution of a nameless prisoner who was convicted of a nameless crime. Everyone quietly and dispassionately performs their jobs—the prison guards, the hangman, the superintendent, and even the prisoner, who offers no resistance when he is bound and led to the gallows. All is totally routine until a very small incident makes Orwell aware of what is happening:

> It was about forty yards to the gallows. I watched the bare brown back of
> the prisoner marching in front of me. He walked clumsily with his bound
> arms, but quite steadily, with that bobbing gait of the Indian who never

straightens his knees. At each step his muscles slid neatly into place, the lock of hair on his scalp danced up and down, his feet printed themselves on the wet gravel. And once, in spite of the men who gripped him by each shoulder, he stepped lightly aside to avoid a puddle on the path.

It is curious; but till that moment I had never realized what it means to destroy a healthy, conscious man. When I saw the prisoner step aside to avoid the puddle, I saw the mystery, the unspeakable wrongness, of cutting a life short when it is in full tide. This man was not dying, he was alive just as we are alive. All the organs of his body were working— bowels digesting food, skin renewing itself, nails growing, tissues form- ing—all toiling away in solemn foolery. His nails would still be growing when he stood on the drop, when he was falling through the air with a tenth-of-a-second to live. His eyes saw the yellow gravel and gray walls, and his brain still remembered, foresaw, reasoned—even about puddles. He and we were a party of men walking together, seeing, hearing, feeling, understanding the same world; and in two minutes, with a sudden snap, one of us would be gone—one mind less, one world less.

Orwell's narrative leads a dramatic moment of recognition, which gives this story its lasting power.

Building a Narrative Argument

The biggest problem with narrative arguments is that anyone can tell a story. On the one hand, there are compelling stories that argue against capital punishment. For example, a mentally retarded man who was executed in Arkansas had refused a piece of pie at his last meal, telling the guards that he wanted to save the pie for later. On the other hand, there are also many sto- ries about the victims of murder and other crimes. Many families have Web sites on which they call for killing those responsible for murdering their loved ones. They too have compelling stories to tell.

Violent deaths of all kinds make for especially vivid narrative argu- ments. In the late 1990s, there were several incidents in which schoolchild- ren used guns taken from the family home to kill other students. Stories of these tragedies provided strong arguments for gun control. Gun rights organi- zations, including the National Rifle Association (NRA), attempted to counter these stories by claiming that they are not truly representative. The NRA claims that between sixty million and sixty-five million Americans own guns and thirty million to thirty-five million own handguns. They argue that more than 99.8 percent of all guns and 99.6 percent of handguns will not be used to commit crimes in any given year. Thus, the NRA argues that narratives of tragic gun deaths are either not representative or the result of allowing too many criminals to avoid prison or execution.

There are two keys to making effective narrative arguments: establishing credibility and establishing representativeness. It's easy enough to make up stories that suit the point you want to make. Writing from personal experience can give you a great deal of impact, but that impact vanishes if your readers doubt that you are telling the truth. Second, the story you tell may be true enough, but the question remains how representative the incident is. We don't ban bananas because someone once slipped on a banana peel. Narratives are often useful for illustrating how people are affected by particular issues or events, but narrative arguments are more effective if you have more evidence than just one incident. The death of Cari Lightner was a tragedy, but the deaths of over 25,000 people a year caused by drunk drivers made Cari Lightner's death representative of a national tragedy, a slaughter that could be prevented. Cari Lightner's tragic story had power because people understood it to be representative of a much larger problem.

LESLIE MARMON SILKO

The Border Patrol State

Leslie Marmon Silko (1948–) was born in Albuquerque and graduated from the University of New Mexico. She now teaches at the University of Arizona. She has received much critical acclaim for her writings about Native Americans. Her first novel, Ceremony *(1977), describes the struggles of a veteran returning home after World War II to civilian life on a New Mexico reservation. Her incorporation of Indian storytelling techniques in* Ceremony *drew strong praise. One critic called her "the most accomplished Indian writer of her generation." She has since published two more novels,* Almanac of the Dead *(1991) and* Gardens in the Dunes *(1999); a collection of essays,* Yellow Woman and a Beauty of the Spirit: Essays on Native American Life Today *(1996); two volumes of poems and stories; and many shorter works. Silko's talents as a storyteller are evident in this essay, which first appeared in the magazine* Nation *in 1994.*

1   I used to travel the highways of New Mexico and Arizona with a wonderful sensation of absolute freedom as I cruised down the open road and across the vast desert plateaus. On the Laguna Pueblo reservation, where I

was raised, the people were patriotic despite the way the U.S. government had treated Native Americans. As proud citizens, we grew up believing the freedom to travel was our inalienable right, a right that some Native Americans had been denied in the early twentieth century. Our cousin, old Bill Pratt, used to ride his horse 300 miles overland from Laguna, New Mexico, to Prescott, Arizona, every summer to work as a fire lookout.

2   In school in the 1950s, we were taught that our right to travel from state to state without special papers or threat of detainment was a right that citizens under communist and totalitarian governments did not possess. That wide open highway told us we were U.S. citizens; we were free. . . .

3   Not so long ago, my companion Gus and I were driving south from Albuquerque, returning to Tucson after a book promotion for the paperback edition of my novel *Almanac of the Dead*. I had settled back and gone to sleep while Gus drove, but I was awakened when I felt the car slowing to a stop. It was nearly midnight on New Mexico State Road 26, a dark, lonely stretch of two-lane highway between Hatch and Deming. When I sat up, I saw the headlights and emergency flashers of six vehicles—Border Patrol cars and a van were blocking both lanes of the highway. Gus stopped the car and rolled down the window to ask what was wrong. But the closest Border Patrolman and his companion did not reply; instead, the first agent ordered us to "step out of the car." Gus asked why, but his question seemed to set them off. Two more Border Patrol agents immediately approached our car, and one of them snapped, "Are you looking for trouble?" as if he would relish it.

4   I will never forget that night beside the highway. There was an awful feeling of menace and violence straining to break loose. It was clear that the uniformed men would be only too happy to drag us out of the car if we did not speedily comply with their request (asking a question is tantamount to resistance, it seems). So we stepped out of the car and they motioned for us to stand on the shoulder of the road. The night was very dark, and no other traffic had come down the road since we had been stopped. All I could think about was a book I had read—*Nunca Mas*—the official report of a human rights commission that investigated and certified more than 12,000 "disappearances" during Argentina's "dirty war" in the late 1970s.

5   The weird anger of these Border Patrolmen made me think about descriptions in the report of Argentine police and military officers who became addicted to interrogation, torture and the murder that followed. When the military and police ran out of political suspects to torture and kill, they resorted to the random abduction of citizens off the streets. I thought how easy it would be for the Border Patrol to shoot us and leave our bodies and

car beside the highway, like so many bodies found in these parts and ascribed to "drug runners."

6   Two other Border Patrolmen stood by the white van. The one who had asked if we were looking for trouble ordered his partner to "get the dog," and from the back of the van another patrolman brought a small female German shepherd on a leash. The dog apparently did not heel well enough to suit him, and the handler jerked the leash. They opened the doors of our car and pulled the dog's head into it, but I saw immediately from the expression in her eyes that the dog hated them, and that she would not serve them. When she showed no interest in the inside of the car, they brought her around back to the trunk, near where we were standing. They half-dragged her up into the trunk, but still she did not indicate any stowed-away human beings or illegal drugs.

7   The mood got uglier; the officers seemed outraged that the dog could not find any contraband, and they dragged her over to us and commanded her to sniff our legs and feet. To my relief, the strange violence the Border Patrol agents had focused on us now seemed shifted to the dog. I no longer felt so strongly that we would be murdered. We exchanged looks—the dog and I. She was afraid of what they might do, just as I was. The dog's handler jerked the leash sharply as she sniffed us, as if to make her perform better, but the dog refused to accuse us: She had an innate dignity that did not permit her to serve the murderous impulses of those men. I can't forget the expression in the dog's eyes; it was as if she were embarrassed to be associated with them. I had a small amount of medicinal marijuana in my purse that night, but she refused to expose me. I am not partial to dogs, but I will always remember the small German shepherd that night.

8   Unfortunately, what happened to me is an everyday occurrence here now. Since the 1980s, on top of greatly expanding border checkpoints, the Immigration and Naturalization Service and the Border Patrol have implemented policies that interfere with the rights of U.S. citizens to travel freely within our borders. I.N.S. agents now patrol all interstate highways and roads that lead to or from the U.S.-Mexico border in Texas, New Mexico, Arizona and California. Now, when you drive east from Tucson on Interstate 10 toward El Paso, you encounter an I.N.S. check station outside Las Cruces, New Mexico. When you drive north from Las Cruces up Interstate 25, two miles north of the town of Truth or Consequences, the highway is blocked with orange emergency barriers, and all traffic is diverted into a two-lane Border Patrol checkpoint—ninety-five miles north of the U.S.-Mexico border.

9   I was detained once at Truth or Consequences, despite my and my companion's Arizona driver's licenses. Two men, both Chicanos, were detained at

the same time, despite the fact that they too presented ID and spoke English without the thick Texas accents of the Border Patrol agents. While we were stopped, we watched as other vehicles—whose occupants were white—were waved through the checkpoint. White people traveling with brown people, however, can expect to be stopped on suspicion they work with the sanctuary movement, which shelters refugees. White people who appear to be clergy, those who wear ethnic clothing or jewelry and women with very long hair or very short hair (they could be nuns) are also frequently detained; white men with beards or men with long hair are likely to be detained, too, because Border Patrol agents have "profiles" of "those sorts" of white people who may help political refugees. (Most of the political refugees from Guatemala and El Salvador are Native American or mestizo because the indigenous people of the Americas have continued to resist efforts by invaders to displace them from their ancestral lands.) Alleged increases in illegal immigration by people of Asian ancestry mean that the Border Patrol now routinely detains anyone who appears to be Asian or part Asian, as well.

10   Once your car is diverted from the Interstate Highway into the checkpoint area, you are under the control of the Border Patrol, which in practical terms exercises a power that no highway patrol or city patrolman possesses: They are willing to detain anyone, for no apparent reason. Other law-enforcement officers need a shred of probable cause in order to detain someone. On the books, so does the Border Patrol; but on the road, it's another matter. They'll order you to stop your car and step out; then they'll ask you to open the trunk. If you ask why or request a search warrant, you'll be told that they'll have to have a dog sniff the car before they can request a search warrant, and the dog might not get there for two or three hours. The search warrant might require an hour or two past that. They make it clear that if you force them to obtain a search warrant for the car, they will make you submit to a strip search as well.

11   Traveling in the open, though, the sense of violation can be even worse. Never mind high-profile cases like that of former Border Patrol agent Michael Elmer, acquitted of murder by claiming self-defense, despite admitting that as an officer he shot an "illegal" immigrant in the back and then hid the body, which remained undiscovered until another Border Patrolman reported the event. (Last month, Elmer was convicted of reckless endangerment in a separate incident, for shooting at least ten rounds from his M-16 too close to a group of immigrants as they were crossing illegally into Nogales in March 1992.) Or that in El Paso a high school football coach driving a vanload of players in full uniform was pulled over on the freeway and a

Border Patrol agent put a cocked revolver to his head. (The football coach was Mexican-American, as were most of the players in his van; the incident eventually caused a federal judge to issue a restraining order against the Border Patrol.) We've a mountain of personal experiences like that which never make the newspapers. A history professor at U.C.L.A. told me she had been traveling by train from Los Angeles to Albuquerque twice a month doing research. On each of her trips, she had noticed that the Border Patrol agents were at the station in Albuquerque scrutinizing the passengers. Since she is six feet tall and of Irish and German ancestry, she was not particularly concerned. Then one day when she stepped off the train in Albuquerque, two Border Patrolmen accosted her, wanting to know what she was doing, and why she was traveling between Los Angeles and Albuquerque twice a month. She presented identification and an explanation deemed "suitable" by the agents, and was allowed to go about her business.

12   Just the other day, I mentioned to a friend that I was writing this article and he told me about his 73-year-old father, who is half Chinese and who had set out alone by car from Tucson to Albuquerque the week before. His father had become confused by road construction and missed a turnoff from Interstate 10 to Interstate 25; when he turned around and circled back, he missed the turnoff a second time. But when he looped back for yet another try, Border Patrol agents stopped him and forced him to open his trunk. After they satisfied themselves that he was not smuggling Chinese immigrants, they sent him on his way. He was so rattled by the event that he had to be driven home by his daughter.

13   This is the police state that has developed in the southwestern United States since the 1980s. No person, no citizen, is free to travel without the scrutiny of the Border Patrol. In the city of South Tucson, where 80 percent of the respondents were Chicano or Mexicano, a joint research project by the University of Wisconsin and the University of Arizona recently concluded that one out of every five people there had been detained, mistreated verbally or nonverbally, or questioned by I.N.S. agents in the past two years.

14   Manifest Destiny may lack its old grandeur of theft and blood—"lock the door" is what it means now, with racism a trump card to be played again and again, shamelessly, by both major political parties. "Immigration," like "street crime" and "welfare fraud," is a political euphemism that refers to people of color. Politicians and media people talk about "illegal aliens" to dehumanize and demonize undocumented immigrants, who are for the most part people of color. Even in the days of Spanish and Mexican rule, no attempts were made to interfere with the flow of people and goods from south to north and north

to south. It is the U.S. government that has continually attempted to sever contact between the tribal people north of the border and those to the south.[1]

15   Now that the "Iron Curtain" is gone, it is ironic that the U.S. government and its Border Patrol are constructing a steel wall ten feet high to span sections of the border with Mexico. While politicians and multinational corporations extol the virtues of NAFTA and "free trade" (in goods, not flesh), the ominous curtain is already up in a six-mile section at the border crossing at Mexicali; two miles are being erected but are not yet finished at Naco; and at Nogales, sixty miles south of Tucson, the steel wall has been all rubber-stamped and awaits construction likely to begin in March. Like the pathetic multimillion-dollar "antidrug" border surveillance balloons that were continually deflated by high winds and made only a couple of meager interceptions before they blew away, the fence along the border is a theatrical prop, a bit of pork for contractors. Border entrepreneurs have already used blowtorches to cut passageways through the fence to collect "tolls," and are doing a brisk business. Back in Washington, the I.N.S. announces a $300 million computer contract to modernize its record-keeping and Congress passes a crime bill that shunts $255 million to the I.N.S. for 1995, $181 million earmarked for border control, which is to include 700 new partners for the men who stopped Gus and me in our travels, and the history professor, and my friend's father, and as many as they could from South Tucson.

16   It is no use; borders haven't worked, and they won't work, not now, as the indigenous people of the Americas reassert their kinship and solidarity with one another. A mass migration is already under way; its roots are not simply economic. The Uto-Aztecan languages are spoken as far north as Taos Pueblo near the Colorado border, all the way south to Mexico City. Before the arrival of the Europeans, the indigenous communities throughout this region not only conducted commerce, the people shared cosmologies, and oral narratives about the Maize Mothers, the Twin Brothers and their Grandmother, Spider Woman, as well as Quetzalcoatl the benevolent snake. The great human migration within the Americas cannot be stopped; human beings are natural forces of the Earth, just as rivers and winds are natural forces.

17   Deep down the issue is simple: The so-called "Indian Wars" from the days of Sitting Bull and Red Cloud have never really ended in the Americas.

---

[1]The Treaty of Guadalupe Hidalgo, signed in 1848, recognizes the right of Tohano O'Odom (Papago) people to move freely across the U.S.-Mexico border without documents. A treaty with Canada guarantees similar rights to those of the Iroquois nation in traversing the U.S.-Canada border. [Author's note]

The Indian people of southern Mexico, of Guatemala and those left in El Salvador, too, are still fighting for their lives and for their land against the "cavalry" patrols sent out by the governments of those lands. The Americas are Indian country, and the "Indian problem" is not about to go away.

18   One evening at sundown, we were stopped in traffic at a railroad crossing in downtown Tucson while a freight train passed us, slowly gaining speed as it headed north to Phoenix. In the twilight I saw the most amazing sight: Dozens of human beings, mostly young men, were riding the train; everywhere, on flat cars, inside open boxcars, perched on top of boxcars, hanging off ladders on tank cars and between boxcars. I couldn't count fast enough, but I saw fifty or sixty people headed north. They were dark young men, Indian and mestizo; they were smiling and a few of them waved at us in our cars. I was reminded of the ancient story of Aztlán, told by the Aztecs but known in other Uto-Aztecan communities as well. Aztlán is the beautiful land to the north, the origin place of the Aztec people. I don't remember how or why the people left Aztlán to journey farther south, but the old story says that one day, they will return.

Steps in Writing a Narrative Argument

If your instructor asks for a topic proposal, use steps 1–4 to guide you in writing the proposal.

1.   **Identify an experience that you had that makes an implicit argument.** Think about experiences that made you realize that something is wrong or that things need to be changed. The experience does not have to be one that leads to a moral lesson at the end, but it should be one that makes your readers think.

   Examples:

   ■ Being arrested and hauled to jail for carrying a glass soft drink bottle in a glass-free zone made you realize how inefficiently your police force is being used.

   ■ After going through a complicated system of getting referrals for a serious medical condition and then having the treatment your physician recommends denied by your HMO, you want to tell your story to show just how flawed the HMO system really is.

- When you moved from a well-financed suburban school to a much poorer rural school, you came to realize what huge differences exist among school systems in your state.

- If you have ever experienced being stereotyped in any way, narrate that experience and describe how it affected you.

2. **List all the details you can remember about the experience.** When did it happen? How old were you? Why were you there? Who else was there? Where did it happen? If the place is important, describe what it looked like. Then go through your list of details and put a check beside the ones that are important to your story.

3. **Examine the significance of the event for you.** Take a few minutes to write about how you felt about the experience at the time. How did it affect you then? What was your immediate reaction? Next, take a few minutes to write about how you feel about the experience now. How do you see it differently now?

4. **Analyze your potential readers.** How much would your readers know about the background of the experience you are describing? Are they familiar with the place where it happened? Would anything similar ever likely have happened to them? How likely are they to agree with your feelings about the experience?

5. **Write a draft.**
   - You might need to give some background first, but if you have a compelling story, often it's best to launch right in.
   - You might want to tell the story as it happened (chronological order) or you might want to begin with a striking incident and then go back to tell how it happened (flashback).
   - You might want to reflect on your experience at the end, but you want your story to do most of the work. Your readers should share your feelings if you tell your story well.

6. **Revise, revise, revise. See Chapter 11 for detailed instructions.**
   Stage 1. Read your argument aloud.
      Do no more in this stage than put checks in the margins that you can return to later. Think in particular about these things:
   - **Your story.** Narratives must be well told to be effective. Note any places where a break or rough spot occurs.

- **Your representation of yourself.** Forget for a moment that you wrote what you are reading. What impression do you have of you, the writer?
- **Your consideration of your readers.** Do you give enough background if your readers are unfamiliar with what you describe? How are they likely to judge what you describe?

Stage 2. Analyze your argument in detail.

- **Examine your organization.** Many narratives do not follow strict chronological order. Look at the sequence of events you set out and ask yourself whether that sequence works best.
- **Check for details.** Key details often make a narrative come alive. Look for places where you might add details that contribute to your reader's understanding.
- **Consider your title and introduction.** Be as specific as you can in your title and, if possible, suggest your stance. In the introduction, get off to a fast start and convince your reader to keep reading.
- **Consider your conclusion.** Sometimes you may announce what you consider to be the significance of your narrative, but in many cases, you want a more subtle conclusion. Leave your reader thinking about what you have written.

Stage 3. Focus on your style and proofread carefully.

- **Check the connections between sentences.** Notice how your sentences are connected. If you need to signal the relationship from one sentence to the next, use a transitional word or phrase.
- **Check your sentences for emphasis.** Elements at the beginning and the end of sentences tend to stand out more than things in the middle.
- **Eliminate wordiness.** See how many words you can take out without losing the meaning.
- **Use active verbs.** Anytime you can use a verb besides a form of *be* (*is, are, was, were*), take advantage of the opportunity to make your style more lively.
- **Proofread your spelling carefully.** Your spelling checker will miss many mistakes.
- **Use your handbook to check items of mechanics and usage.** Look up any item you are unsure of.

CHAPTER 9

Rebuttal Arguments

When you hear the word **rebuttal,** you might think of a debate team or the part of a trial when the attorney for the defense answers the plaintiff's accusations. Although **rebuttal** has those definitions, arguments of rebuttal can be thought of in much larger terms. Indeed, much of what people know about the world today is the result of centuries of arguments of rebuttal.

In high school and college, you no doubt have taken many courses that required the memorization of knowledge and evidence, which you demonstrated by repeating these facts on tests. You probably didn't think much about how the knowledge came about. Once in a while, though, something happens that makes people think consciously about a piece of knowledge that they have learned. For example, in elementary school, you learned that the earth rotates on its axis once a day. Maybe you didn't think about it much at the time, but once, years later, you were out on a clear night and noticed the Big Dipper in one part of the sky, and then you looked for it later and found it in another part of the sky. Perhaps you became interested enough that you watched the stars for a few hours. If you've ever spent a clear night out stargazing, you

> **Effective rebuttal arguments depend on critical thinking.**

have observed that the North Star, called Polaris, stays in the same place. The stars near Polaris appear to move in a circle around Polaris, and the stars farther away move from east to west until they disappear below the horizon.

If you are lucky enough to live in a place where the night sky is often clear, you can see the same pattern repeated night after night. And if you stop to think about why you see the stars circling around Polaris, you remember what you were taught long ago—that you live on a rotating ball, so the stars appear to move across the sky, but in fact, stars are so distant from the earth that their actual movement is not visible to humans over a short term.

An alternative explanation for these facts not only is possible but is the one that people believed from ancient times until about five hundred years ago. People assumed that their position on the earth was fixed and that the entire sky rotated on an axis connecting Polaris and the earth. The flaw in this theory for people in ancient times is the movement of the planets. If you watch the path of Mars over several nights, you will observe that it also moves across the sky from east to west, but it makes an anomalous backward movement during its journey and then goes forward again. The other planets also seem to wander back and forth as they cross the night sky. The ancient Greeks developed an explanation of the strange wanderings of the planets by theorizing that the planets move in small circles imposed on larger orbits. By graphing little circles on top of circles, the course of planets could be plotted and predicted. This theory culminated in the work of Ptolemy, who lived in Alexandria in the second century A.D. Ptolemy proposed displaced centers for the small circles called *epicycles*, which gave a better fit for predicting the path of planets.

Because Ptolemy's model of the universe was numerically accurate in its predictions, educated people for centuries assumed its validity, even though there was evidence to the contrary. For example, Aristarchus of Samos, who lived in the fourth century B.C.E., used the size of the earth's shadow cast on the moon during a lunar eclipse to compute the sizes of the moon and sun and their distances from the earth. Even though his calculations were inaccurate, Aristarchus recognized that the sun is much bigger than the earth, and he advanced the heliocentric hypothesis: that the earth orbits the sun.

Many centuries passed, however, before educated people believed that the sun, not the earth, was the center of the solar system. In the early sixteenth century, the Polish astronomer Nicolaus Copernicus recognized that Ptolemy's model could be greatly simplified if the sun was at the center of the solar system. He kept his theory a secret for much of his life and saw the published account of his work only a few hours before his death in 1543. Even though Copernicus made a major breakthrough, he was not able to take full advantage of the heliocentric hypothesis because he followed the tradition that orbits are perfect circles; thus, he still needed circles on top of circles to explain the motion of the planets but far fewer than did Ptolemy.

The definitive rebuttal of Ptolemy came a century later with the work of the German astronomer Johannes Kepler. Kepler performed many tedious calculations, which were complicated by the fact that he had to first assume an orbit for the earth before he could compute orbits for the planets. Finally he made a stunning discovery: All the orbits of the planets could be described as an ellipse with the sun at the center. The dominance of the Ptolemaic model of the universe was finally over.

Critical Thinking

The relationship of facts and theories lies at the heart of the scientific method. Both Ptolemy's theory and Kepler's theory explain why the stars appear to move around Polaris at night. Kepler made a convincing argument by rebuttal to the Ptolemaic model because he could give a much simpler analysis. The history of astronomy is a history of arguments of rebuttal. Modern astronomy was made possible because Copernicus challenged the established relationship of theory and evidence in astronomy. This awareness of the relationship of factual and theoretical claims in science is one definition of **critical thinking** in the sciences. What is true for the history of astronomy is true for the sciences; critical thinking in the sciences relies on arguments of rebuttal.

Similar kinds of arguments of rebuttal are presented today in the debate over global warming. One of the main sources of data for arguments of rebuttal against global warming is the twenty-year record of temperature readings from NASA weather satellites orbiting the earth at the North and South poles. These satellites use microwave sensors to measure temperature variation in the atmosphere from the surface to about six miles above the earth. Computer models predict a gradual warming in the earth's lower atmosphere along with the surface because of the buildup of carbon dioxide and other greenhouse gases, the gases produced from burning fossil fuels. But while temperatures measured on the earth's surface have gradually increased, the corresponding rises in the atmosphere as recorded by satellites didn't appear to happen. In August 1998, however, two scientists discovered a flaw in the satellites that was making them lose altitude and therefore misreport temperature data. When adjusted, the satellite data confirm what thermometers on the ground tell us: The earth is getting warmer.

In some cases, particular disciplines have specialized training to assess the relationship of theory and evidence. But more often, people must engage in **general critical thinking** to assess the validity of claims based on evidence. Often, one has to weigh competing claims of people who have excellent qualifications. One group of nutritional experts says that people should take calcium supplements to strengthen their bones. Another group warns that people are in danger of suffering from kidney stones if they take too much calcium. Critical thinking is involved in all the kinds of arguments that are discussed in this book, but it is especially important in arguments of rebuttal.

Building a Rebuttal Argument

If you think back to the basic model of how arguments work, you can see that there are two primary strategies for rebuttal arguments:

CLAIM ◄─── LINK (because) ◄─── REASON ◄─── EVIDENCE
                 ▲
        CHALLENGES (So What?)

First, you can challenge the assumptions on which the claim is based. Copernicus did not question Ptolemy's data concerning how the stars and planets appear in the sky to an observer on the earth. Instead, he questioned Ptolemy's central assumption that the earth is the center of the solar system. Second, you can question the evidence. Sometimes, the evidence presented is simply wrong, as was the case for the satellites that lost altitude and reported faulty temperature data. Sometimes, the evidence is incomplete or unrepresentative, and sometimes, counterevidence can be found.

The great majority of issues that involve people cannot be decided with the certainty of the statement that the earth indeed orbits the sun. Even when the facts are generally agreed upon, there is often disagreement over the causes. Violent crime rates decreased from 1980 to 1992, and some politicians credited tougher sentencing that put more people in prison. But others pointed out that the drop could be attributed to the fact that older people, who commit fewer violent crimes, became a much larger segment of the overall population. The crime rates for the youngest age groups actually rose during this time. Those who disputed that putting more people in prison reduced violent crime argued that the drop was a reflection of the aging population of the United States.

Arguments over controversial issues lasting for many years often become primarily arguments of rebuttal. One such issue that has been debated throughout the twentieth century is drug policy in the United States. Today, almost everyone who writes about illegal drugs in the United States says that the current policy is bad. Even though U.S. jails and prisons are bursting with people who have been convicted and sentenced for drug offenses, millions of people still use illegal drugs. The social, political, and economic costs of illegal drugs are staggering, and the debate continues over what to do about these substances. On one side are those who want more police, more drug users in jail, and military forces sent to other countries to stop the drug traffic. On the other are those who compare current efforts to stop the flow of drugs to those of failed efforts under Prohibition (1919–1933) to halt the sale of alcohol. They want most illegal drugs to be legalized or decriminalized.

On September 7, 1989, Nobel prize–winning economist Milton Friedman published in the *Wall Street Journal* an open letter to William Bennett, then the drug czar (director of the Office of National Drug Policy) under President Bush. Friedman wrote:

Dear Bill:

In Oliver Cromwell's eloquent words, "I beseech you, in the bowels of Christ, think it possible you may be mistaken" about the course you and President Bush urge us to adopt to fight drugs. The path you propose of more police, more jails, use of the military in foreign countries, harsh penalties for drug users, and a whole panoply of repressive measures can only make a bad situation worse. The drug war cannot be won by those tactics without undermining the human liberty and individual freedom that you and I cherish.

You are not mistaken in believing that drugs are a scourge that is devastating our society. You are not mistaken in believing that drugs are tearing asunder our social fabric, ruining the lives of many young people, and imposing heavy costs on some of the most disadvantaged among us. You are not mistaken in believing that the majority of the public share your concerns. In short, you are not mistaken in the end you seek to achieve.

Your mistake is failing to recognize that the very measures you favor are a major source of the evils you deplore. Of course the problem is demand, but it is not only demand, it is demand that must operate through repressed and illegal channels. Illegality creates obscene profits that finance the murderous tactics of the drug lords; illegality leads to the corruption of law enforcement officials; illegality monopolizes the efforts of honest law forces so they are starved for resources to fight the simpler crimes of robbery, theft and assault.

Drugs are a tragedy for addicts. But criminalizing their use converts that tragedy into a disaster for society, for users and non-users alike. Our experience with the prohibition of drugs is a replay of our experience with the prohibition of alcoholic beverages. . . .

Had drugs been decriminalized 17 years ago [when Friedman first made an appeal that drugs be decriminalized], "crack" would never have been invented (it was invented because the high cost of illegal drugs made it profitable to provide a cheaper version) and there would today be far fewer addicts. The lives of thousands, perhaps hundreds of thousands of innocent victims would have been saved, and not only in the U.S. The ghettos of our major cities would not be drug-and-crime-infested no-man's lands. Fewer people would be in jails, and fewer jails would have been built.

Colombia, Bolivia, and Peru would not be suffering from narco-terror, and we would not be distorting our foreign policy because of narco-terror. Hell would not, in the words with which Billy Sunday welcomed Prohibition, "be forever for rent," but it would be a lot emptier.

In the first two paragraphs, Friedman carefully identifies the common ground he shares with Bennett. Both are political conservatives, as Friedman reminds Bennett when he mentions the "human liberty and individual freedom that you and I cherish." Friedman also agrees with Bennett about the severity of the drug problem, noting that it is "tearing asunder our social fabric, ruining the lives of many young people, and imposing heavy costs on some of the most disadvantaged among us."

Where Friedman differs from Bennett is in Bennett's central assumption: If drugs are now illegal and still being used, then the solution is to make them even more illegal, increasing penalties and extending law enforcement beyond U.S. borders. Friedman calls attention to the centrality of this assumption when he quotes Oliver Cromwell's famous words: "I beseech you, in the bowels of Christ, think it possible you may be mistaken." If, in fact, this central assumption is flawed, then the reason to spend millions of dollars, to violate civil liberties, and to antagonize other nations is suddenly taken away.

William Bennett responded to Friedman quickly. On September 19, 1989, the *Wall Street Journal* published an open letter of reply from Bennett to Friedman. Here is part of Bennett's response, which has a much more strident tone than Friedman's letter:

Dear Milton:

There was little, if anything, new in your open letter to me calling for the legalization of drugs. As your 1972 article made clear, the legalization argument is an old and familiar one, which has recently been revived by a small number of journalists and academics who insist that the only solution to the drug problem is no solution at all. What surprises me is that you would continue to advocate so unrealistic a proposal without pausing to consider seriously its consequences.

If the argument for drug legalization has one virtue it is its sheer simplicity. Eliminate laws against drugs, and street crime will disappear.

Take the profit out of the black market through decriminalization and regulation, and poor neighborhoods will no longer be victimized by drug dealers. Cut back on drug enforcement, and use the money to wage a public health campaign against drugs, as we do with tobacco and alcohol.

The basic premise of all these propositions is that using our nation's laws to fight drugs is too costly. To be sure, our attempts to reduce drug use do carry with them enormous costs. But the question that must be asked—and which is totally ignored by the legalization advocates—is, what are the costs of *not* enforcing laws against drugs?

In my judgment, and in the judgment of virtually every serious scholar in this field, the potential costs of legalizing drugs would be so large as to make it a public policy disaster.

Of course, no one, including you, can say with certainty what would happen in the U.S. if drugs were suddenly to become a readily purchased product. We do know, however, that wherever drugs have become cheaper and more easily obtained, drug use—and addiction—has skyrocketed. In opium and cocaine producing countries, addiction is rampant among the peasants involved in drug production.

Professor James Q. Wilson tells us that during the years in which heroin could be legally prescribed by doctors in Britain, the number of addicts increased forty-fold. And after the repeal of Prohibition—an analogy favored but misunderstood by legalization advocates—consumption of alcohol soared by 350%.

Could we afford such dramatic increases in drug use? I doubt it. Already the toll of drug use on American society—measured in lost productivity, in rising health insurance costs, in hospitals flooded with drug overdose emergencies, in drug caused accidents, and in premature death—is surely more than we would like to bear.

You seem to believe that by spending just a little more money on treatment and rehabilitation, the costs of increased addiction can be avoided. That hope betrays a basic misunderstanding of the problems facing drug treatment. Most addicts don't suddenly decide to get help. They remain addicts either because treatment isn't available or because they don't seek it out. . . .

As for the connection between drugs and crime, your unswerving commitment to a legalization solution prevents you from appreciating the complexity of the drug market. Contrary to your claim, most addicts do not turn to crime to support their habit. Research shows that many of them were involved in criminal activity before they turned to drugs. Many former addicts who have received treatment continue to commit crimes during their recovery. And even if drugs were legal, what evidence do you have that the habitual drug user wouldn't continue to rob and steal to get money for clothes, food or shelter? Drug addicts always want more drugs than they can afford, and no legalization scheme has yet come up with a way of satisfying that appetite.

Bennett goes on to maintain that "A true friend of freedom understands that government has a responsibility to craft and uphold laws that help educate citizens about right and wrong. That, at any rate, was the Founders' view of our system of government." He ends by describing Friedman's proposal as "irresponsible and reckless public policy."

Friedman was not content to let Bennett have the last word, so he in turn wrote a reply that appeared on September 29, 1989, in the *Wall Street Journal*. At this point, Friedman drops the open letter strategy and writes instead a more conventional response, referring to Bennett as *he* instead of *you*:

> William Bennett is entirely right (editorial page, Sept. 19) that "there was little, if anything, new in" my open letter to him—just as there is little, if anything, new in his proposed program to rid this nation of the scourge of drugs. That is why I am so disturbed by that program. It flies in the face of decades of experience. More police, more jails, more-stringent penalties, increased efforts at interception, increased publicity about the evils of drugs—all this has been accompanied by more, not fewer, drug addicts; more, not fewer, crimes and murders; more, not less, corruption; more, not fewer, innocent victims.
>
> Like Mr. Bennett, his predecessors were "committed to fighting the problem on several fronts through imaginative policies and hard work over a long period of time." What evidence convinces him that the same policies on a larger scale will end the drug scourge? He offers none in his response to me, only assertion and the conjecture that legalizing drugs would produce "a public policy disaster"—as if that is not exactly what we already have.

Friedman then claims that "legalizing drugs is not equivalent to surrender" but rather the precondition for an effective fight against drug use. He allows that the number of addicts might increase, but he argues that it is certain that the number of innocent victims would drop drastically. He adds that another category of victims are foreign nations when we base our foreign policy on drug control.

Friedman's sharpest criticism of Bennett comes over Bennett's claim to represent the tradition of the Founders of the United States. Friedman completely rejects Bennett's assertion that the Founders wanted government to educate citizens about what is right and what is wrong. Friedman says "that is a totalitarian view utterly unacceptable to the Founders. I do not believe, and neither did they, that it is the responsibility of government to tell free citizens what is right and wrong."

LANCE ARMSTRONG

A Defense of the Open Road

Lance Armstrong (1971–   ) grew up in Plano, Texas, as the child of a single mother. He won his first triathlon at age 13 and became a professional triathlete at 16. By the time he finished high school, swimming and running gave way to his passion for cycling. By age 25 he had become one of the top professional bicycle racers in the world. But in 1996, he found himself in a battle for his life with advanced testicular cancer, and his doctors gave him less than a 50 percent chance of survival. Armstrong's chemotherapy treatments were successful, and within a year he was training again. Few expected him to attain the level he achieved before his illness, but Armstrong returned a stronger and more determined rider. He won the most prestigious race in cycling—the three-week-long Tour de France—in 1999, in 2000, and in 2001.

"A Defense of the Open Road," published in the Austin American *Statesman in February 2001, was written in response to bills introduced into the Texas legislature banning bicycle teams from training in the state. Imagine being in Lance Armstrong's shoes, training hard to defend his Tour de France title, only to discover that instead of being supported, a few members of the Texas legislature were attempting to stop him from training. It is a good example of why people sometimes have to write rebuttal arguments to expose incredible stupidity. The public outrage in response to Armstrong's rebuttal led to an early death of the bike-banning bills.*

1   I learned to love Texas as a teenager cycling on a long, flat road past the plains of Plano to the ranch land and cotton fields, past the wildflowers and mesquite.

2   Sometimes I'd ride alone and sometimes with friends, racing or pulling each other as a team—working together against the dry, dusty wind. Drafting behind a friend, and then pulling ahead to pull your friends, is part of the camaraderie and teamwork of cycling.

3   That's why I'm so disappointed that two Hill Country legislators want to keep cyclists from riding the best roads in Texas. One legislator wants to ban riding with more than one friend on many rural roads, and another wants to ban all riding on certain rural roads.

4   Going further, Senate Bill 238, in a face-slap of an insult, would make all cyclists—children, adults, amateurs, and pros—ride single file on every road, with a "Slow Moving Vehicle" triangle hanging off our rear ends. This is the anti-sport, nanny-like equivalent of requiring golfers to use a putter off the tee to prevent a hook into the next fairway.

5   Although banning groups might be slightly more convenient for cars, it's vastly more dangerous for cyclists. Riding as a peloton, or group, is safer (not to mention more practical and efficient). Would you prefer your son or daughter to ride with a group or have to ride almost alone?

6   For example, when the U.S. Postal team holds training camp in Austin, we ride double pace lines through the Hill Country. The single-file rule and no-peloton rule would outlaw such team training rides. Plus, a single-file rule would make it illegal for riders to even pass each other.

7   The rules also would outlaw families riding together, Saturday-morning rides with friends, organized rides and races, charity rides and fund raisers and bicycle tours of Texas roads. From the forests of East Texas to the rugged mountains of West Texas, there is nothing like seeing Texas from a bike. These rules would make it an impossibility.

8   The current law—stay to the right, ride no more than two abreast and don't impede the reasonable flow of traffic—is based on common sense and thus easy to follow. The examples cited as reasons for the proposed laws seem to be based on a few cyclists disobeying the current law.

9   But a few bad acts shouldn't be the basis for passing a bad bill. Imposing new limits—potholed with exceptions for certain events, situations, speeds or roads—would be a nightmare to follow and to enforce. The more complex a rule, and the more distant it is from common sense, the less likely it can be followed.

10 Shoulders appear and disappear, and maps don't designate "roads with shoulders" and "roads without." Maps don't designate "high-traffic roads" and "low-traffic roads." Time of day, growth and other factors make this a moving target anyway. Often the road less traveled leads to the road more trafficked, which leads to another road less traveled. Restricting access to some roads is just not practical.

11 I am proud to be a Texan, and I want Texas to continue to attract riders with the beauty of our long, open roads. The rules of the road should be rules of reason and rules of respect, unencumbered by unworkable, excessive government regulation.

 ## Steps in Writing a Rebuttal Argument

If your instructor asks for a topic proposal, use steps 1–5 to guide you in writing the proposal.

1. **Identify an argument that you want to argue against.** Use this formula: It is wrong (or misguided or irresponsible) to claim X. You might consider using the open letter genre, addressing your rebuttal to a specific person but with the goal of having others read it too.

    Examples:
    - Requiring fine arts students to take math courses (or engineering students to take foreign language courses, or the like) is a bad idea.
    - Using tax dollars to pay for new stadiums for professional sports teams (or providing grants to artists and theater companies) is a misuse of public funds.
    - Requiring riders of bicycles and motorcycles to wear helmets is an unnecessary restriction of individual freedom.

2. **Identify the main claim(s) of the argument that you reject.** What exactly are you arguing against? If you are taking on affirmative action admissions policies for colleges and universities, then what do those policies involve and whom do they affect? Are there secondary claims attached to the main claim? A fair summary of your opponent's position should be in your finished argument.

3. **Examine the facts on which the claim is based.** Are the facts accurate? Are the facts a truly representative sample? Are the facts

current? Is there another body of facts that you can present as counterevidence? If the author uses statistics, is evidence for the validity of those statistics presented? Can the statistics be interpreted differently? If the author quotes from sources, how reliable are those sources? Are the sources treated fairly, or are quotations taken out of context? If the author cites outside authority, how much trust can you place in that authority?

4. **Examine the assumptions on which the claim is based.** What is the primary assumption of the claim you are rejecting? What other assumptions support that claim? How are those assumptions flawed? If you are arguing against a specific piece of writing, then how does the author fall short? Does the author resort to name calling? Use faulty reasoning? Ignore key facts?

5. **Analyze your potential readers.** To what extent do your potential readers support the claim that you are rejecting? If they strongly support that claim, then how might you appeal to them to change their minds? What common assumptions and beliefs do you share with them?

6. **Write a draft.**

   Identify the issue and the argument you are rejecting:
   - If the issue is not familiar to most of your readers, you might need to provide some background. Even if it is familiar, it might be helpful to give a quick summary of the competing positions. Remember that offering a fair and accurate summary is a good way to build credibility with your audience.

   Take on the argument that you are rejecting:
   - You might want to question the evidence that is used to support the argument. You can challenge the facts, present counterevidence and countertestimony, cast doubt on the representativeness of the sample, cast doubt on the currency and relevance of the examples, challenge the credibility of any authorities cited, question the way in which statistical evidence is presented and interpreted, and argue that quotations are taken out of context.
   - In most cases, you will want to question the assumptions and potential outcomes.

   Conclude with emphasis:
   - You should have a strong argument in your conclusion that underscores your objections. You might wish to close with a counterargument or counterproposal.

7. **Revise, revise, revise. See Chapter 11 for detailed instructions.**

   Stage 1. Read your argument aloud.

   Do no more in this stage than put checks in the margins that you can return to later. Think in particular about these things:

   ■ **Your claim.** When you finish reading, summarize in one sentence what you are arguing and why the primary assumption in the claim you are rejecting is faulty.

   ■ **Your good reasons.** What are the good reasons for your claim? Would a reader have any trouble identifying them?

   ■ **Your representation of yourself.** Forget for a moment that you wrote what you are reading. What impression do you have of you, the writer?

   ■ **Your consideration of your readers.** Do you give enough background if your readers are unfamiliar with the issue? Do you acknowledge opposing views that they might have? Do you appeal to common values that you share with them?

   Stage 2. Analyze your argument in detail.

   ■ **Examine your organization.** What are the topics of each of the paragraphs? Is the relationship of one paragraph to another clearly signaled? If any paragraphs appear out of order, think of another way to arrange them.

   ■ **Examine your evidence.** If you noted places where you could use more evidence when you read through the first time, now is the time to determine what kinds of additional evidence you need.

   ■ **Consider your title and introduction.** Be as specific as you can in your title and, if possible, suggest your stance. Does your introduction get off to a fast start and convince your reader to keep reading?

   ■ **Consider your conclusion.** Think about whether there is a summarizing point you can make, an implication you can draw, or another example you can include that sums up your position.

   ■ **Analyze the visual aspects of your text.** Do the font and layout you selected look attractive? Would headings and subheadings help to identify key sections of your argument? Would the addition of graphics augment key points?

   Stage 3. Focus on your style and proofread carefully.

   ■ **Check the connections between sentences.** Notice how your sentences are connected. If you need to signal the relationship from one sentence to the next, use a transitional word or phrase.

■ **Check your sentences for emphasis.** Elements at the beginning and the end of sentences tend to stand out more than things in the middle.

■ **Eliminate wordiness.** See how many words you can take out without losing the meaning.

■ **Use active verbs.** Anytime you can use a verb besides a form of *be* (*is, are, was, were*), take advantage of the opportunity to make your style more lively.

■ **Proofread your spelling carefully.** Your spelling checker will miss many mistakes.

■ **Use your handbook to check items of mechanics and usage.** Look up any item you are unsure of.

CHAPTER 10

Proposal Arguments

You no doubt have at least one friend who loves to argue. If you say you love a movie, your friend will trash it. If you mention that knowingly breaking the rules in a game is wrong, your friend will reply that it's fine as long as the referee doesn't catch you. These kinds of face-to-face arguments can become the basis for extended written arguments. But when someone finally gets motivated enough to write an extended argument, most often it is because she or he wants something to be changed or wants to stop something from being changed. These kinds of arguments are called **proposal arguments,** and they take the classic form: *We should (or should not) do X.*

> **Proposal arguments often include definition, causal, evaluation, narrative, and rebuttal arguments.**

At this moment, you might not think that you have anything you feel strongly enough about to write a proposal argument. But if you make a list of things that make you mad or at least a little annoyed, then you have a start toward writing a proposal argument. Some things on your list are not going to produce proposal arguments that many people would want to read. If your roommate or partner is a slob, you might be able to write a proposal for that person to start cleaning up more, but it is hard to imagine that anyone else would be interested. Similarly, it might be annoying to you that it stays too hot for too long in the summer where you live or too cold for too long in the winter, but unless you have a direct line to God, it is hard to imagine a serious proposal to change the climate where you live. (Cutting down on air pollution, of course, is something that people can change.) Short of those extremes, however, are a lot of things that you might think, "Why hasn't someone done something about this?" If you believe that others have something to gain if this problem is solved or at least made a little better, then you might be able to develop a good proposal argument.

For instance, suppose you are living off campus, and you buy a student parking sticker when you register for courses so that you can park in the student lot. However, you quickly find out that there are too many cars and trucks for the number of available spaces, and unless you get to campus by 8:00 A.M., you aren't going to find a place to park in your assigned lot. The situation makes you angry because you believe that if you pay for a sticker, you should have a reasonable chance of finding a space to park. You see that there are unfilled lots that are reserved for faculty and staff next to the student parking lot, and you wonder why more spaces aren't allotted to students. You decide to write to the president of your college. You want her to direct parking and traffic services to give more spaces to students or else build a parking garage that will accommodate more vehicles.

But when you start talking to other students on campus, you begin to realize that the problem may be more complex than your first view of it. Your college has taken the position that the fewer students who drive to campus, the less traffic there will be on and around your campus. The administration wants more students to ride shuttle buses, form car pools, or bicycle to campus instead of driving alone. You also find out that faculty and staff members pay ten times as much as students for their parking permits, so they pay a very high premium for a guaranteed space—much too high for most students. If the president of your college is your primary audience, you first have to argue that a problem really exists. You have to convince the president that many students have no choice but to drive if they are to attend classes. You, for example, are willing to ride the shuttle buses, but they don't run often enough for you to make your classes, get back to your car that you left at home, and then drive to your job.

Next, you have to argue that your solution will solve the problem. An eight-story parking garage might be adequate to park all the cars of students who want to drive, but parking garages are very expensive to build. Even if a parking garage is the best solution, the question remains: Who is going to pay for it? Many problems in life could be solved if you had access to unlimited resources, but very few people have such resources at their command. It's not enough to have a solution that can resolve the problem. You have to be able to argue for the feasibility of your solution. If you want to argue that a parking garage is the solution to the parking problem on your campus, then you must also propose how the garage will be financed.

Components of Proposals

Proposal arguments are often complex and involve the kinds of arguments that are discussed in Chapters 5 through 9. Successful proposals have four major components:

1. ***Identifying the problem.*** Sometimes, problems are evident to your intended readers. If your city is constantly tearing up the streets and then leaving them for months without doing anything to repair them, then you shouldn't have much trouble convincing the citizens of your city that streets should be repaired more quickly. But if you raise a problem that will be unfamiliar to most of your readers, you will first have to argue that the problem exists. As we saw in Chapter 1, Rachel Carson in *Silent Spring* had to use several kinds of arguments to make people aware of the dangers of pesticides, including narrative arguments, definition arguments, evaluation arguments, and arguments of comparison. Often, you will have to do similar work to establish exactly what problem you are attempting to solve. You will have to define the scope of the problem. Some of the bad roads in your city might be the responsibility of the state, not city government.

2. ***Stating your proposed solution.*** You need to have a clear, definite statement of exactly what you are proposing. You might want to place this statement near the beginning of your argument, or later, after you have considered and rejected other possible solutions.

3. ***Convincing your readers with good reasons that your proposed solution is fair and will work.*** When your readers agree that a problem exists and a solution should be found, your next task is to convince them that your solution is the best one to resolve the problem. If you're writing about the problem your city has in getting streets repaired promptly, then you need to analyze carefully the process that is involved in repairing streets. Sometimes there are mandatory delays so that competing bids can be solicited and unexpected delays when tax revenue falls short of expectations. You should be able to put your finger on the problem in a detailed causal

analysis. You should be able to make an evaluation argument that your solution is fair to all concerned. You should also be prepared to make arguments of rebuttal against other possible solutions.

4. ***Demonstrating that your solution is feasible.*** Your solution not only has to work; it must be feasible to implement. Malaysia effectively ended its drug problem by imposing mandatory death sentences for anyone caught selling even small amounts of drugs. Foreign nationals, teenagers, and grandmothers have all been hanged under this law. Malaysia came up with a good solution for its purposes, but this solution probably would not work in most countries because the punishment seems too extreme. If you want a parking garage built on your campus and you learn that no other funds can be used to construct it, then you have to be able to argue that the potential users of the garage will be willing to pay greatly increased fees for the convenience of parking on campus.

Building a Proposal Argument

Proposal arguments don't just fall out of the sky. For any problem of major significance—gun control, poverty, teenage pregnancy, abortion, capital punishment, drug legalization—you will find long histories of debate. An issue with a much shorter history can also quickly pile up mountains of arguments if it gains wide public attention. In 1972, for example, President Richard Nixon signed into law the Education Amendments Act, including Title IX, which prohibits sex discrimination at colleges that receive federal aid. Few people at the time might have guessed that Title IX would have such far-reaching consequences. When Title IX was first passed, 31,000 women participated in intercollegiate athletics. In the academic year 2000–2001, more than 163,000 women athletes participated in varsity college sports. Even more striking is the increase in girls' participation in high school sports. The number of boy athletes remains close to same as the figure for 1971 (approximately 3.6 million), while the number of girl athletes grew from 294,000 in 1971 to 2.7 million in 2001.

Proponents of Title IX are justifiably proud of the increased level of participation of women in varsity athletics. But for all the good that Title IX has done to increase athletic opportunities for women, critics blame Title IX for decreasing athletic opportunities for college men. According to the U.S. General Accounting Office (GAO), more than three hundred men's teams have been eliminated in college athletics since 1993. In 2000, the University of Miami dropped its men's swimming team, which had produced many

Girls' sports leagues were a rarity in many communities just thirty years ago.

Olympians, including Greg Louganis, who won gold medals in both platform and springboard diving in two consecutive Olympics. In 2001 the University of Nebraska also discontinued its men's swimming team, which had been in place since 1922, and the University of Kansas dropped men's swimming and tennis. Wrestling teams have been especially hard hit, dropping from 363 in 1981 to 192 in 1999. The effects were noticeable at the 2000 Olympics in Australia, where U.S. freestyle wrestlers failed to win any gold medals for the first time since 1968.

College and university administrators claim that they have no choice but to drop men's teams if more women's teams are added. Their belief comes not from the original Title IX legislation, which does not mention athletics, but from a 1979 clarification by the Office of Civil Rights (OCR), the agency that enforces Title IX. OCR set out three options for schools to comply with Title IX:

1. Bring the proportion of women in varsity athletics roughly equal to the percentage of women students.

2. Prove a "history and continuing practice" of creating new opportunities for women.

3. Prove that the school has done everything to "effectively accommodate" the athletic interests of women students.

University administrators have argued that the first option, known as *proportionality*, is the only one that can be argued successfully in a courtroom if the school is sued.

Proportionality is difficult to achieve at schools with football programs. Universities that play NCAA Division 1-A football offer eighty-five scholarships, the majority of athletic scholarships given to men. Since there is no equivalent sport for women, football throws the gender statistics way out of balance. Defenders of football ask that it be exempted from Title IX because it is the cash cow that pays most of the bills for both men's and women's sports. Only a handful of women's basketball programs make money. All other women's sports are money losers and, like men's "minor" sports, depend on men's football and basketball revenues and student fees to pay their bills. College officials maintain that if they cut the spending for football, football will bring in less revenue, and thus all sports will be harmed.

Those who criticize Title IX argue that it assumes that women's interest in athletics is identical to men's. They point out that male students participate at much higher rates in intramural sports, which have no limitations on who can play. In contrast, women participate at much higher rates in music, dance, theater, and other extracurricular activities, yet Title IX is not being applied to those activities.

Defenders of Title IX argue that women's interest in athletics cannot be determined until they have had equal opportunities to participate. They claim Title IX is being used as a scapegoat for college administrators who do not want to make tough decisions. They point out that in 2001, women made up 53 percent of all college students but only 42 percent of all college athletes. At major colleges and universities, men still received 73 percent of the funds devoted to athletics. Without Title IX, in their view, schools would have no incentive to increase opportunities for women.

The battle over Title IX is not likely to go away soon. In an increasing competition for the revenues produced by football bowl games, the NCAA basketball tournament, television revenue, and increased ticket prices, the schools that play big-time college football and basketball are now engaged in an "athletics arms race." Football coaches who win championships are paid over two million dollars a year, and some assistant coaches make more than their university's president. Men's athletics directors believe that they have to keep spending to stay competitive.

Defenders of Title IX reject this argument and maintain that a simple solution is available: If revenues do not increase, reduce the budgets of all sports by the same proportion rather than dropping some sports. They argue that football budgets are out of control, with luxuries such as staying in a hotel the night before home games and lavish spending on travel to away games now considered routine. One of the most powerful voices in this debate is Donna Lopiano's. In the essay that follows, Lopiano uses the analogy of a family to propose solutions for equality in college athletics.

DONNA LOPIANO

Don't Blame Title IX

Donna Lopiano (1947–) is the former director of women's athletics at the University of Texas at Austin and is the current executive director of the Women's Sports Foundation, founded in 1974 by the tennis star Billie Jean King. As an athlete, Lopiano participated in twenty-six national championships in four sports and was an All-American in softball in four different positions at Southern Connecticut State University. She has also coached men's and women's volleyball, and women's basketball, field hockey, and softball at the collegiate level. Lopiano is a member of the National Sports Hall of Fame and earned a Ph.D. from the University of Southern California.

Lopiano has been a tireless crusader for the rights of girls and women to have equal opportunities in athletics. She is proud to point out that in the early 1970s, one out of every twenty-seven high school girls played varsity sports. Today, that figure is one in three. But because one in two boys participates in sports, Lopiano believes one in three isn't good enough. She frequently attacks the argument that college football pays the bills for both women's and men's sports, using the NCAA's own statistics to point out that fewer than half of the major college football programs (Division 1-A) actually make a profit.

"Don't Blame Title IX" was published in 2001 on the Women's Sports Foundation Web site (www.womenssportsfoundation.org).

1

I'M often asked, "Is it fair to eliminate sports opportunities for men as a method of complying with Title IX of the Education Amendments of 1972, the federal law prohibiting sex discrimination in educational programs or activities at schools and colleges that receive federal funds?" Schools often cite insufficient finances to add more sports opportunities for women, cut a men's non-revenue sport and use these funds to start a new women's team.

When alumni and students complain about the decision, the institution blames the law (Title IX requires no such reduction in opportunities for men) and female athletes.

2   The real problem can be simply described. Your first two children are boys. You give them everything. Their rooms are palaces of athletics privilege—full of every sport gift imaginable—gloves, balls, bats, hockey sticks, football helmets, etc. They go to two or three sport camps every summer. They play Little League baseball, soccer, and Pop Warner football. One becomes an outstanding football player and the other excels in tennis. Then, you have another child, a girl, and your income doesn't change. She comes to you one day and says, "Mom, Dad—I want to play sports." What are your options?

3   Option A: Kill your last born son (i.e., drop the men's tennis team) so you still have only two children to provide for.

4   Option B: Tell your daughter she can't have the same privileges as her brothers. If she wants a glove she has to go to work and save up to buy it. Tell her she can't go to a summer sports camp unless she earns her own money and pays for it herself. Suggest that she sell cookies or get together with her girlfriends to have a bake sale (this is the way it was before Title IX) to scrape up enough money for equipment to play.

5   Option C: You gather the family around the kitchen table and explain to your children that your daughter is just as important as your sons and you don't have the dollars to provide the same privileges for your daughter as you did for your sons but that you are going to try your best to give all of your children every opportunity to participate in sports. You tell your sons that it is important to share their equipment and all you have provided for them. You probably come up with a system where each child gets to choose one summer sports camp instead of each attending several. The family gives up spring vacation in Disney World and tightens its belt. Everyone sacrifices and each child makes do with a smaller piece of the pie because now there are three (the Title IX situation).

6   The solution is Option C. Institutions that are dropping men's teams are choosing Option A not because of Title IX, but because they are being terrible parents (educational leaders). The answer to Title IX is very simple: If revenues don't increase, then everyone must make do with a smaller piece of the budget pie. The NCAA and its athletic conferences are simply refusing to legislate lower costs and a lower standard of living for men's sports in order to free up money for new women's teams.

7   Men's revenue sports are issuing threats regarding their own demise if their budgets are reduced in any way. First, tightening a sport's budget will

not cause this sport business to fail. Commercial entities initiate such cost cuts every day to eliminate fat, increase profit margins, and satisfy stockholders.

8   Second, and more important, there can never be an economic justification for discrimination. No one should ever be permitted to say that I can't comply with the law because I can't afford it. It is the same as saying, "I should be allowed to practice racism (or sexism) if I can't afford to initiate a change in the way I live or do business."

9   Using an employment discrimination example, the analogy would be that reducing the salaries of all employees is the preferred method of generating funds in an effort to increase salaries for the group that has historically experienced discrimination. This never happens. Rather, the salaries of the disadvantaged gender or individuals are always raised to the level of the advantaged group. As in the area of salary discrimination, the goal should be to bring the treatment of the group experiencing discrimination up to the level of the group that has received fair treatment, not to bring male athletes in minor sports down to the level of female athletes who simply were not provided with opportunities to play.

10   Even worse, when an institution eliminates a men's team in the name of Title IX, such action usually results in the development of destructive acrimony, pitting the men's non-revenue sports against women's sports. Alumni of the dropped men's sport get upset. An unnecessary domino effect results in the development of attitudes antithetical to solving discrimination in the long run. Gains for the underrepresented group come grudgingly and at a high cost to the previously advantaged group.

11   The last alternative should be cutting opportunities for students to participate in an educational activity. Other solutions, in order of preference, that should be considered are

12   1.   **Raising new revenues.** Gender equity can be used as an opportunity to raise new funds in much the same way as the need for a new building is used to initiate a capital campaign. However, it is essential that there be a positive spin on alumni solicitations for this purpose like adding one or two dollars to the current price of all sport tickets "so our daughters will have an equal chance to play" and other similarly creative revenue solutions. "Providing an equal opportunity for women to participate in varsity athletics" is also an excellent theme for an annual giving campaign targeted to female alumnae and supporters.

13   The demographic shift in higher education toward increasing percentages of women in undergraduate and graduate schools must also be noted. These are future generations of alumnae. Any position which antagonizes a group of future donors to the institution is short-sighted.

14   Presidential or school principal leadership is essential. The institution has the choice of "taking the high ground" and calling upon alumni and supporters of men's sports to "dig deeper" so our daughters are given the same chances to play as our sons, or pitting the have-nots against the have-nots by cutting men's sports teams. At many institutions, the resentment against Title IX has prevented athletic directors from "seeing the forest for the trees." The result has been the adoption of less than exemplary solutions to a very difficult problem.

15   2.   **Reducing excess expenditures on the most expensive men's sports and using the savings to expand opportunities and treatment for the underrepresented gender.** There are many expenditures in the budgets of well-funded sports which can be eliminated without having a negative impact on either competitiveness vis-a-vis other institutions or the quality of the athletics experience. Such reductions include: provision of hotel rooms the night before home contests, ordering new uniforms less frequently, reducing the distance traveled for non-conference competition by selecting others as competitive opponents in closer geographic proximity.

16   3.   **Athletic conference cost-saving.** The conference can adopt across-the-board mandated cost reductions that will assist all schools in saving funds while ensuring that the competitive playing field remains level (i.e., travel squad limits, adding the same sports for the underrepresented gender at the same time in order to ensure competition within a reasonable geographic area, etc.).

17   4.   **Internal across-the-board budget reductions.** All sports can be asked to cut their budgets by a fixed percentage, thereby allowing each sport to choose the way it might least be affected, to free up funds for expanded opportunities for women. This method is preferred in that it does not have a disproportionate impact on low-budget sports.

18   5.   **Moving to a lower competitive division.** At the college level, Division I programs can move to Division IAA or Division II competition, thereby reducing scholarship and other expenses.

19   6.   **Using tuition waiver savings to fund gender equity.** States can initiate legislation which provides for waiver of higher education tuition for athletic scholarships to members of the underrepresented gender, similar to the law adopted by the State of Washington. This legislation mandates the use of these scholarship savings to expand opportunities for the underrepresented gender. Such initiatives recognize that correcting gender inequities is an institutional obligation, not just an athletic department issue. There are other precedents for states to enact laws which confer

financial relief in an effort to remedy widespread discrimination. The states of Washington, Florida and Minnesota have all enacted state laws to provide funding to achieve gender equity in athletics.

20   Unfortunately, at most institutions, it is easier for a college president to cut wrestling or men's gymnastics than to deal with the politics of reducing the football or men's basketball budgets. Simply put, educational leaders need more guts to step up and do the right thing.

Steps in Writing a Proposal Argument

If your instructor asks for a topic proposal, use steps 1–6 to guide you in writing the proposal.

1. **Make a proposal claim advocating a specific change or course of action.** Use this formula: *We should (or should not) do* X. In an essay of five or fewer pages, it's difficult to propose solutions to big problems such as continuing poverty. Proposals that address local problems are not only more manageable; sometimes, they get actual results.

   Examples:
   - The process of registering for courses (getting appointments at the health center, getting email accounts) should be made more efficient.
   - Your community should create bicycle lanes to make bicycling safer and to reduce traffic (build a pedestrian overpass over a dangerous street; make it easier to recycle newspapers, bottles, and cans).

2. **Identify the problem.** What exactly is the problem? Who is most affected by the problem? What causes the problem? Has anyone tried to do anything about it? If so, why haven't they succeeded? What is likely to happen in the future if the problem isn't solved?

3. **Propose your solution.** State your solution as specifically as you can. What exactly do you want to achieve? How exactly will your solution work? Can it be accomplished quickly, or will it have to be phased in over a few years? Has anything like it been tried elsewhere? Who will be involved? Can you think of any reasons why your solution might not work? How will you address those arguments? Can you think of any ways of strengthening your proposed solution in light of those possible criticisms?

4. Consider other solutions. What other solutions have been or might be proposed for this problem, including doing nothing? What are the advantages and disadvantages of those solutions? Why is your solution better?

5. Examine the feasibility of your solution. How easy is your solution to implement? Will the people who will be most affected be willing to go along with it? (For example, lots of things can be accomplished if enough people volunteer, but groups often have difficulty getting enough volunteers to work without pay.) If it costs money, how do you propose paying for it? Who is most likely to reject your proposal because it is not practical enough? How can you convince your readers that your proposal can be achieved?

6. Analyze your potential readers. Who are you writing for? You might be writing a letter addressed to a specific person. You might be writing a guest editorial to appear in your campus newspaper or in your club's or organization's newsletter. You might be creating a Web site. How interested will your readers be in this problem? How much does this problem affect them? How would your solution benefit them directly and indirectly?

7. Write a draft.

Define the problem:
- Set out the issue or problem. You might begin by telling about your experience or the experience of someone you know. You might need to argue for the seriousness of the problem, and you might have to give some background on how it came about.

Present your solution:
- You might want to set out your solution first and explain how it will work, then consider other possible solutions and argue that yours is better; or you might want to set out other possible solutions first, argue that they don't solve the problem or are not feasible, and then present your solution.
- Make clear the goals of your solution. Many solutions cannot solve problems completely. If you are proposing a solution for juvenile crime in your neighborhood, for example, you cannot expect to eliminate all juvenile crime.
- Describe in detail the steps in implementing your solution and how they will solve the problem you have identified. You can impress your readers by the care with which you have thought through this problem.

■ Explain the positive consequences that will follow from your proposal. What good things will happen and what bad things will be avoided if your advice is taken?

Argue that your proposal is feasible:
■ Your proposal for solving the problem is a truly good idea only if it can be put into practice. If people have to change the ways they are doing things now, explain why they would want to change. If your proposal costs money, you need to identify exactly where the money would come from.

Conclude with a call for action:
■ Your conclusion should be a call for action. You should put your readers in a position such that if they agree with you, they will take action. You might restate and emphasize what exactly they need to do.

8. **Revise, revise, revise. See Chapter 11 for detailed instructions.**

Stage 1. Read your argument aloud.

Do no more in this stage than put checks in the margins that you can return to later. Think in particular about these things:
■ **Your good reasons.** What are the good reasons for your proposal? Would a reader have any trouble identifying them?
■ **Your representation of yourself.** Forget for a moment that you wrote what you are reading. What impression do you have of you, the writer?
■ **Your consideration of your readers.** Do you give enough background if your readers are unfamiliar with the issue? Do you acknowledge opposing views that they might have? Do you appeal to common values that you share with them?

Stage 2. Analyze your argument in detail.
■ **Review step 7.** Find where you define the problem and ask yourself whether you need to provide more evidence. Look at your solution, especially where you argue that good consequences can be achieved and negative consequences avoided and where you argue that the proposal is feasible.
■ **Examine your evidence.** If you noted places where you could use more evidence when you read through the first time, now is the time to determine what kinds of additional evidence you need.
■ **Consider your title and introduction.** Be as specific as you can in your title and, if possible, suggest your stance. In the introduction get off to a fast start and convince your reader to keep reading.

■ **Consider your conclusion.** Think about whether there is a summarizing point you can make, an implication you can draw, or another example you can include that sums up your position.

■ **Analyze the visual aspects of your text.** Do the font and layout you selected look attractive? Would headings and subheadings help to identify key sections of your argument? Would the addition of graphics augment key points?

Stage 3. Focus on your style and proofread carefully.

■ **Check the connections between sentences.** Notice how your sentences are connected. If you need to signal the relationship from one sentence to the next, use a transitional word or phrase.

■ **Check your sentences for emphasis.** Elements at the beginning and the end of sentences tend to stand out more than things in the middle.

■ **Eliminate wordiness.** See how many words you can take out without losing the meaning.

■ **Use active verbs.** Anytime you can use a verb besides a form of *be* (*is, are, was, were*), take advantage of the opportunity to make your style more lively.

■ **Proofread your spelling carefully.** Your spelling checker will miss many mistakes.

■ **Use your handbook to check items of mechanics and usage.** Look up any item you are unsure of.

CHAPTER 11

Revision: Putting It All Together

Skilled writers know that one secret to writing well is rethinking and rewriting. Even the best writers often have to reconsider their aims and methods in the course of writing and to revise several times to get the result they want. If you want to become a better writer, therefore, take three words of advice: revise, revise, revise.

The biggest trap you can fall into is seeking a fast resolution and skipping revision. The quality of an argument varies in

> **Revise, revise, revise.**

direct proportion to the amount of time devoted to it. You cannot revise a paper effectively if you finish it at the last minute. You have to allow your ideas to develop, and you have to allow what you write to sit for a while before you go back through it. So try your best to write your arguments over a period of several days. Be patient. Test your ideas against your reading and the informal advice of trusted friends and advisors. And once you are satisfied with what you have written, allow at least a day to let what you write cool off. With a little time you gain enough distance to "resee" it, which, after all, is what revision means. To be able to revise effectively, you have to plan your time.

Most of all, keep your eyes focused on the big picture, especially early in the process of making your argument. Don't sweat the small stuff at the beginning. If you see a word that's wrong or if you are unsure about a punctuation mark, you may be tempted to drop everything and fix the errors first. Don't do that: If you start searching for the errors early in the process, then it's hard to get back to the larger concerns that ultimately make your argument successful or unsuccessful.

Over time you have to develop effective strategies for revising if you're going to be successful. These strategies include the following:

1. Keep your goals in mind—but stay flexible about them.
2. Read as you write.
3. Switch your thinking from you and your argument to your reader.
4. Focus on your argument.
5. Attend to your style and proofread carefully.

In addition, plan to get responses to what you write in time for you to revise your work based on those responses.

Keep Your Goals in Mind— But Stay Flexible

People who argue effectively know what they want to achieve. They understand their readers' needs, know what they want to accomplish, and keep their goals in mind as they write and revise. But they also know that writing about a subject likely will change how they think about it, often in productive ways. Thus they remain flexible enough to modify their goals as they write. You may begin writing an argument because you have strong feeling about an issue; in fact, a rush of strong feelings can often motivate you to compose a strong statement at one sitting. That's good. But at some point before you commit what you write to a final version, give yourself a chance to rethink your goals. It may be that you can make a better argument in the end if you leave yourself open to adjustments in what you are arguing and to whom you are arguing it.

Consider, for example, the case of a student at a northeastern university, Nate Bouton (not his real name), who arrived on his campus in the midst of a controversy in 2000 over the raising of the Confederate Battle Flag over the South Carolina state capitol building. You probably recall the controversy: In 1999 the NAACP, in the conviction that the Confederate flag was a symbol of racism, called on citizens to boycott South Carolina tourist venues until the flag no longer was displayed over the state capitol building. After contentious debate and considerable thought, legislators decided to remove the flag. On July 1, 2000, it was taken down and displayed instead in a nearby memorial to Confederate soldiers. But public opinion within and outside South Carolina remained divided: Some citizens continued to ask that the flag be restored to the capitol, while others demanded that it be removed from the Confederate memorial as well.

As a native of South Carolina, Nate felt that students at his university were coming to uninformed, premature conclusions, which stemmed from faulty assumptions about the flag issue in particular and South Carolinians in general. When the players on the baseball team at Nate's university decided not to play previously scheduled games in South Carolina, he was ready to join the argument. He decided to write about the flag issue, in his words, "in order to straighten people out. People in the northeast just didn't know the facts and that ticked me off. I wanted to write an argument supporting what was being done in South Carolina."

Nate's interest and enthusiasm for his topic generated a series of notes and several draft paragraphs, and he was able to explain his goals forcefully in class. Here is what he wrote when his teacher asked for an account of what he planned to do in his essay: "I would like to evaluate the decision to remove the Confederate Battle Flag from the statehouse dome in Columbia, South Carolina. I do not believe it was handled properly and I do not think the valiant soldiers that fought in the war between the states and defended their way of life should be dishonored by a bunch of politicians who use people's feelings to their disadvantage. Now that politicians have won a battle, many more are springing up all over the South wanting to destroy a way of life and turn it into a politically correct zombie. I want to show that the flag is about pride, not prejudice."

But as Nate wrote a first draft, his goals gradually changed. In the course of discussing his ideas with his classmates and with his friends, he discovered that they had a number of what he considered to be misperceptions. They did not know much about the South and its traditions, and their conclusions on the flag issue, he was convinced, followed from their lack of knowledge. Nate also learned that several of his friends and classmates had different notions of what the Confederate flag stood for. African Americans in his dorm explained that when they stopped at a restaurant and saw the Confederate flag in the window, they understand from experience that it meant, "We don't want black people eating here."

Nate decided that one of his goals would be to educate people about the thinking of many South Carolinians and that the Confederate flag was not necessarily a symbol of racism. He would defend the decision of the South Carolina legislature, which had attempted to find some middle ground on the issue. Rather than calling for the return of the flag to the capitol, he would support the legislature's decision to raise the flag only at the monument to Confederate soldiers.

Read as You Write

Nate's conversations with his friends indicated to him that he had to become more knowledgeable before he could complete his argument. He continued reading in the library as he developed his points, using many of the search strategies we discuss in Chapter 15. Nate's decision reflects an important fact about effective arguments: They usually emerge from substantial knowledge. If you have not explored your topic fully, then you must read widely about the subject before going further. Not only will your reading alert you to arguments that you can cite in support of your own points, but it will also clarify for you the thinking of those who disagree with you so that you can take into account their points of view. Finally, reading will allow you to take seriously what we advise early in this book: that arguing is often more a contribution to a continuing conversation than a final resolution of all doubts, and that you can sometimes do far more good by persuading people to cooperate with you than by fervently opposing them.

Nate's reading gave him a number of insights into the flag issue. He learned about the original design of the flag, which was related to the crosses of St. Andrew and St. George. He also learned about the history of the flag's display at the capitol—including the fact that the flag was first raised there in 1962, in the midst of the civil rights movement. He also found that George Wallace began displaying the Battle Flag in Alabama shortly after his confrontations with Robert Kennedy over the issue of segregation. Nate read about the NAACP and the reasons for its opposition to the flag. He sampled Web sites that supported the flag's display over the capitol (including one that quoted the famous historian Shelby Foote), and he considered others that opposed that position. After several hours of note taking, Nate was ready to assemble a serious draft.

Switch from Writer to Reader

In most first drafts, it makes sense to get your ideas on paper without thinking about readers. Such a practice makes positive use of strong feelings and gets the skeleton of an argument out. (Nate's first draft expressed ideas that he had been formulating for some time.) The first draft, however, is only the beginning. You need to take time to think about how your argument will come across to your readers.

First, pretend you are someone who is either uninformed about your subject or informed but holding an opposing viewpoint. If possible think of an actual person and pretend to be that person. (Nate could easily imagine a person holding an opposing view because he knew people in his dorm who disagreed with him on this issue.) Then read your argument aloud all the way through. When you read aloud, you often hear clunky phrases and catch errors, but do no more in this stage than put checks in the margins that you can return to later. Once again, you don't want to get bogged down with the little stuff. Rather, what you are after in this stage is getting an overall sense of how well you accomplished what you set out to do. Think in particular about these things:

1. **Your claim.** When you finish reading, can you summarize in one sentence what you are arguing? If you cannot, then you need to focus your claim. Then ask yourself what's at stake in your claim. Who benefits by what you are arguing? Who doesn't? How will readers react to what you are arguing? If what you are arguing is obvious to everyone and if all or nearly all would agree with you, then you need to identify an aspect on which people would disagree and restate your claim.

2. **Your good reasons**. What are the good reasons for your claim? Would a reader have any trouble identifying them? Will those readers be likely to accept your reasons? What evidence is offered to support these good reasons and how is the evidence relevant to the claim (the "so what?" question in Chapter 2)? Note any places where you might add evidence and any places where you need to explain why the evidence is relevant.

3. **Your representation of yourself.** To the extent you can, forget for a moment that you wrote what you are reading. What impression do you have of you, the writer? Is the writer believable? Trustworthy? Has the writer done his or her homework on the issue? Does the writer take an appropriate tone? Note any places where you can strengthen your credibility as a writer.

4. **Your consideration of your readers.** Do you give enough background if your readers are unfamiliar with the issue? Do you acknowledge opposing views that they might have? Do you appeal to common values that you share with them? Note any places where you might do more to address the concerns of your readers.

Here is a sample paragraph from a first draft of Nate's essay on the Confederate flag:

The Confederate Battle Flag is not a racist sign; it is the most powerful and widely recognized symbol of Southern valor and independence. The flag honors the Confederate dead, who fought for their way of life and defended their homes from Northern aggression in the War Between the States. People today owe it to the men and women who fought for their belief in liberty and states' rights, a sacrifice rarely seen today. People ought to honor the memories of the Confederate fallen just as they remember people involved in every other war. While people are making monuments to war dead in Washington, including monuments to those who died in Vietnam and Korea, there are those who are trying to dishonor Confederate dead by taking the Battle Flag from the Confederate monument in Columbia.

When Nate put himself in the shoes of his readers, he quickly saw the need for substantial changes in that paragraph. He still felt strongly about his belief in the symbolism of the flag, but he also realized that people who disagreed with him—the people he was trying to persuade—would not appreciate his use of the term "War Between the States" because they would suspect him of thinking that the war was not fought over the issue of slavery and accuse him of resisting any racist notions associated with the flag. "States' rights" is a phrase that is honorable, but not when one of the rights is the right to own slaves. Here is how he revised his paragraph:

The Confederate Battle Flag is not a racist sign; it is the most powerful and widely recognized symbol of Southern valor and independence. It is true, unfortunately, that many racists today display the Confederate flag. But that unfortunate truth should not permit us to discontinue to honor the flag, any more than the use of the cross by the Ku Klux Klan should permit us to discontinue honoring the cross in our churches. It is also true that the Civil War was conducted in large part because of the issue of slavery, that many people therefore associate the Confederate flag with white supremacy, and that many whites during the Civil Rights era flew the flag as a sign of resistance to the end of segregation. But the Civil War was also fought for other reasons in the South by many people who neither owned slaves nor who had any use for slavery. The flag honors the Confederate dead who fought for their way of life and who believed they were defending their homes from Northern aggression. People today owe it to those who fought for their belief in liberty (our nation's most basic belief) to permit their monuments to include the flag they fought under. The Confederate flag needs to be restored to its original symbolism, and that can only take place if it continues to be displayed in honorable places. To change the Confederate monument in Columbia by taking away the Confederate flag would be to dishonor those who died under it. People ought to honor the memories of the Confederate fallen just as they remember people involved in every other war. Shelby Foote, the well known Southern historian and author of a three-volume history of the Civil War, said it best: "Many among the finest people this country ever produced died [under the Confederate flag]. To take it as a symbol of evil is a misrepresentation" (www.southerninitiative.com, April 30, 2001).

Do you think Nate's revisions were successful in answering his reader's objections and in creating a more effective ethos? How will his quotation from the Southern historian go over with his Northern readers?

Focus on Your Argument

Now it's time to go through your argument in detail.

1. Find your main claim.

What kind of claim is it? Are you writing a proposal, an evaluation, a rebuttal, a narrative, or what? What things follow from that? (All arguments, as we have emphasized in Chapters 5 through 10, tend to develop in certain ways, depending on their kind.) Nate's argument that the Confederate flag ought to be permitted to remain on the Confederate monument (but not over the state capitol building) is a proposal argument. Identifying the type of claim helps you to think about how it might be developed further. We offer guidelines for proposal arguments in Chapter 10.

2. How will you support your claim?

What good reasons will you use? Will you use definitions, an evaluation, a causal argument, a list of consequences, a comparison or contrast, or a combination of these? Nate's paragraph, one segment of his overall proposal, offers a definition: "The Confederate Battle Flag is not a racist sign; it is the most powerful and widely recognized symbol of Southern valor and independence." If Nate can get his readers to accept that definition, that "good reason" for agreeing to his overall thesis, he will have gone a long way toward achieving his goals. It may take him several paragraphs to argue for the definition, but eventually it will be worth the effort. Nate might also use other good reasons to support his overall position on the flag issue: the good consequences that will follow if his advice is heeded (e.g., goodwill; an end to polarization in the community), the bad consequences that might be avoided (e.g., continued controversy and divisiveness in South Carolina), the useful comparisons or contrasts that can be cited as support (e.g., the comparison between the Klan's use of the cross and racists' use of the Confederate flag), and so forth. Altogether, those good reasons will make up a complete and satisfactory argument.

3. Analyze your organization.

Turn to one of the Steps in Writing guides at the end of Chapters 5 though 10 that best fits your argument (or Chapter 4 if you are doing an analysis). The guides will help you determine what kind of overall organization you need. For example, if you have a definition argument, go to the Steps in Writing guide at the end of Chapter 5. You should be able to identify the criteria for your definition. How many criteria do you offer? Where are they located? Are they clearly connected to your claim? In what order should they be offered?

In addition, think about other effective ordering principles. Since readers often remember things that come first or last, do you want to put your strongest good reasons early and repeat them toward the end? Or do you want to build toward a climactic effect by ordering your reasons from least important to most important? Can you group similar ideas? Should you move from least controversial to most controversial? Or from most familiar to least familiar?

4. Examine your evidence.

If you noted places where you could use more evidence when you first read through your draft, now is the time to determine what kinds of additional evidence you need. Evidence can come in the shape of examples, personal experiences, comparisons, statistics, calculations, quotations, and other kinds of data that a reader will find relevant and compelling. Decide what you need and put it in.

5. Consider your title and introduction.

Many students don't think much about titles, but titles are important: A good title makes the reader want to discover what you have to say. Be as specific as you can in your title and, if possible, suggest your stance. In the introduction get off to a fast start and convince your reader to keep reading. You may need to establish right away that a problem exists. You may have to give some background. You many need to discuss an argument by someone else that you are addressing. But above all, you want to convince your reader to keep reading.

6. Consider your conclusion.

Restating your claim usually isn't the best way to finish. The worst endings say something like "in my paper I've said this." Think about whether there is a summarizing point you can make, an implication you can draw, or another example you can include that sums up your position. If you are writing a proposal, your ending might be a call for action or a challenge. If you have a telling quotation from an authority, sometimes that can make an effective clincher.

7. Analyze the visual aspects of your text.

Do the font and layout you selected look attractive? Do you use the same font throughout? If you use more than one font, have you done so consistently? Would headings and subheadings help to identify key sections of your argument? If you include statistical data, would charts be effective? Would illustrations help to establish key points? For example, a map could be very useful if you are arguing about the location of a proposed new highway.

Focus on Your Style and Proofread Carefully

In our advice about revision, we have ignored so far issues of style and correctness. We did that not because we think style and correctness are unimportant but because some people forget that revision can involve much more than those things. In your final pass through your text, you should definitely concentrate on the style of your argument and eliminate as many errors as you can. Here are some suggestions that may help.

1. Check the connections between sentences.

Notice how your sentences are connected. If you need to signal the relationship from one sentence to the next, use a transitional word or phrase. For example, compare the following:

Silent Spring was widely translated and inspired legislation on the environment in nearly all industrialized nations. *Silent Spring* changed the way we think about the environment. $\rightarrow$

Silent Spring was widely translated and inspired legislation on the environment in nearly all industrialized nations. **Moreover**, the book changed the way we think about the environment.

2. Check your sentences for emphasis.

When most people talk, they emphasize points by speaking louder, using gestures, and repeating themselves. You should know that it is possible to emphasize ideas in writing too.

- **Things in main clauses tend to stand out more than things in subordinate clauses.** Compare these two sentences: "Kroger, who studied printing in Germany, later organized a counterfeiting ring"; and "Before he organized a counterfeiting ring, Kroger studied printing in Germany." These two sentences contain exactly the same information, but they emphasize different things. The second sentence suggests Kroger studied printing in order to organize a counterfeit ring. Signal what you want to emphasize by putting it into main clauses, and put less important information in subordinate clauses or in modifying phrases. (If two things are equally important, signal that by using coordination: "Kroger studied printing in Germany; he later organized a counterfeiting ring.")

- **Things at the beginning and at the end of sentences tend to stand out more than things in the middle.** Compare these three sentences: "After he studied printing in Germany, Kroger organized a counterfeiting ring"; "Kroger, after he studied printing in Germany, organized a counterfeiting ring"; and "Kroger organized a counterfeiting ring after he studied printing in Germany." All three sentences contain the exact same words and use the same main clause and subordinate clause, but they emphasize different things, depending on which items are placed in the beginning, middle, and end.

- **Use punctuation for emphasis.** Dashes add emphasis; parentheses de-emphasize. Compare these two sentences: "Kroger (who studied printing in Germany) organized a counterfeiting ring"; and "Kroger—who studied printing in Germany—organized a counterfeiting ring."

3. Eliminate wordiness.

Drafts often contain unnecessary words. When you revise, often you can find long expressions that can easily be shortened ("at this point in time" → "now"). Sometimes you become repetitive, saying about the same thing you said a sentence or two before. See how many words you can take out without losing the meaning.

4. Use active verbs.

Anytime you can use a verb besides a form of *be* (*is, are, was, were*), take advantage of the opportunity to make your style more lively. Sentences that begin with "There is (are)" and "It is" often have better alternatives:

> "It is true that exercising a high degree of quality control in the manufacture of our products will be an incentive for increasing our market share."
> → "If we pay attention to quality when we make our products, more people will buy them".

Notice too that active verbs often cut down on wordiness.

5. Know what your spelling checker can and can't do.

Spelling checkers are the greatest invention since peanut butter. They turn up many typos and misspellings that are hard to catch. But spelling checkers do not catch wrong words (e.g. "to much" should be "too much"), incorrect word endings ("three dog"), and other, similar errors. You still have to proofread carefully to eliminate misspellings and word choice errors.

6. Use your handbook to check items of mechanics and usage.

Nothing hurts your credibility more than leaving mechanics and usage errors in what you write. A handbook will help you identify the most common errors and answer questions of usage. Readers probably shouldn't make such harsh judgments when they find errors, but in real life they do. We've seen job application letters tossed in the rejected pile because an applicant made a single, glaring error. The conventions of punctuation, mechanics, and usage aren't that difficult to master, and you'll become a lot more confident when you know the rules or at least know how to look up the rules. You should also trust your ear: If you noticed that a sentence was hard to read aloud or that it doesn't sound right, think about how you might rephrase it. If a sentence seems too long, then you might break it into two or more sentences. If you notice a string of short sentences that sound choppy, then you might combine them. If you notice any run-on sentences or sentence fragments, fix them.

Get Help on Your Draft

Don't trust your own ears (and eyes) exclusively. Most good writers let someone else—a trusted advisor or several of them—read what they write before they share it with their audience. You too need to develop a way of getting advice that you can use to shape your revisions. Be sure to leave enough time for someone else to review your work and for you to make revisions.

A good reviewer is one who is willing to give you their time and honest opinion, and who knows enough about the subject of your paper to make useful suggestions. A roommate or close friend can serve, but often such a friend will be reluctant to give negative evaluations. Perhaps you can develop a relationship with people with whom you can share drafts—you read theirs; they read yours. Whomever you choose, give that person time to read your work carefully and sympathetically. You need not take every piece of advice you get, but you do need to consider suggestions with an open mind.

PART 3

Making Effective Arguments

Designing, Presenting, and Documenting

Advances in digital technology have made it possible for almost anyone to publish color images along with text, both on paper and on the World Wide Web. Programs such as PowerPoint make it easy to prepare visuals for oral presentations. Furthermore, many students now routinely publish animations, audio, and video clips along with images on Web sites. What is now possible using relatively common and inexpensive computers and software is staggering in comparison to what could be done just a decade ago.

But if new technologies for writing have given us a great deal of potential power, they have also presented us with a variety of challenges. Designing a piece of writing wasn't much of an issue with a typewriter. You could either single or double space, and increase or decrease the margins. But today with a word processing program you can change the typeface, typestyle, and type size, insert illustrations, create and insert tables and other graphics, and print in color. If you are publishing on the Web, you can introduce sound, animation, and video. Sometimes it seems like there are too many choices.

Likewise when you do research on the Web, you often find too much rather than too little. Much of what you find is of little value for a serious argument. And if the physical act of making changes to what you write is easier with a computer, the mental part is still hard work. Even experienced writers struggle with getting what they write into the shape they want it. In the chapters in Part 3, we offer you strategies for creating effective arguments using both new and old technologies.

CHAPTER 12

Effective Visual Design

Understanding Visual Arguments

The average American is exposed to over 3,000 arguments each day, the great majority of which come in the form of advertisements. Many rely on images in addition to text. A typical example is a magazine ad for a leading department store that includes only a picture of a handsome professional woman dressed in a black suit looking at herself in a mirror, the name of the store, and the caption "Somehow you just know." Because the effects of such ads are difficult to explain, some people have called them irrational and even deceptive. But they are anything but irrational. We don't need to be told that being well dressed is important for a professional image.

Products such as clothing, detergent, deodorant, cigarettes, and soft drinks rely heavily on images to sell their products. Nonetheless, as was discussed in the previous chapters, writers also offer images of themselves in order to be convincing. The key difference, of course, is that we are presented with visual images when we encounter advertising, while we have to construct our image of a writer from the voice in the text. Yet it isn't quite that

Figure 12.1 Advertisement for Harrison K-9 Security Services

simple. Some ads include a fair amount of text, and increasingly, writers incorporate graphics in what they write.

Let's take a look at an ad that has both text and images. The text of the ad for Harrison K-9 Security Services in Figure 12.1 is framed by a header across the top: the word "VIGILANCE" imposed over an image of a woman, a child, and a dog and a proportionally much larger image of a German shepherd positioned in the left third of the frame. We can describe three main elements of this ad: the text, the images, and the graphic design.

TEXT

The text fills the center right of the frame. The first paragraph gives the argument of the ad:

> When you're away from home, you need to know that your family is safe. There is no substitute for the vigilant eyes and ears of Harrison K-9 Security Services European German Shepherd protectors.

The second paragraph describes the training the dogs receive and who has bought them: "families, business executives, entertainers, and professional athletes." The third paragraph describes training for the purchasers of the dogs, and finally, the logo of the company is followed by its address and phone number.

IMAGES

The image of the German shepherd on the left of the frame is shot from a low angle, making the dog appear quite large. Its coat is thick, and its ears point up toward the word "VIGILANCE" at the top. The smaller second image shows a woman seated on a carpet, a young child kneeling beside her, and a dog resting nearby. The woman and child are looking at something in the child's hand. They are dressed casually in jeans, and the viewer assumes that they are a mother and daughter at home. The dog looks both relaxed and alert, its gaze fixed on the viewer.

This small image is consistent with the text in several ways. First, since there is no man in the frame, the father is presumably absent. The text says that people who have bought dogs include "families, business executives, entertainers, and professional athletes." The image thus suggests that the buyer of the dog will likely be a man who travels, leaving his wife and children at home, rather than a woman who is employed as a business executive, entertainer, or professional athlete. But the image can also be viewed from the perspective of the "intruder" mentioned in the text. The dog is between the intruder and the woman and child. To get to them requires getting past the dog.

GRAPHIC DESIGN

Graphic designers consider the relationship of the elements when they design an ad. The images and text support each other in this ad, but through good graphic design, these relationships can be enhanced. When you page through the magazine where the ad appeared, your eyes are first drawn to the image of the dog. The background color of the ad is maroon, which enhances the rich, light brown tones of the dog's coat. The dog's ears direct attention to the word "VIGILANCE," printed in a color very similar to that of the dog's coat. "VIGILANCE" is superimposed over the image of the woman, child, and dog; thus, even a quick glance at the ad takes in the two images and the word. If you continue looking at the ad, you next move clockwise to the text, which is set in a sans serif typeface (we'll explain typefaces shortly) in white letters against the dark maroon background. The typeface and background color set the text of the ad apart from the text of the magazine, which uses black serif type against a white background.

This ad demonstrates how a graphic designer coordinates images with the message of an ad. A designer organizes words and images to achieve a desired effect for a particular audience and purpose. These principles of graphic design are not so very different from the rhetorical principles that were discussed in the previous chapters. It all has to do with understanding how particular effects can be achieved for particular readers in particular situations. Best of all, you too can use graphic design to your own advantage.

Print Is a Visual Medium

Perhaps the most important thing to know about design is that there are very few hard-and-fast rules. As for all arguments, everything depends on the rhetorical situation. All your decisions hinge on your purpose, your subject, and the type of document you are writing, your intended audience(s), and how you want your reader(s) to perceive you. Sometimes, you succeed by breaking the rules.

Let's start with how your readers perceive you. You see an ad for a part-time position designing Web sites, brochures, and newsletters for a copy shop that pays good money, and since you have the necessary skills, you decide to apply. You write your letter of application:

Jennifer Barnes

308 Bruffee Street
Minneapolis, MN 55423

January 5, 2002

Andrew J. Johnson, Vice President
Copy Mart
742 Church Street S.E.
Minneapolis, MN 55454

Dear Mr. Johnson:

I wish to apply for the design position that you advertised in the *Minneapolis Tribune* on January 3, 2002.

I am a communications major at the University of Minnesota, and I have three years experience designing brochures, newsletters, and Web pages for businesses and nonprofit organizations in the Twin Cities. I am skilled in using JavaScript, Adobe PageMaker, Photoshop, and Illustrator, and Macromedia Director, Dreamweaver, and Flash. My résumé is enclosed, complete with a list of Web sites that I have designed and the names, addresses, and phone numbers of people who have employed me.

You may reach me by email or at my home phone, (612) 634-5789, on most afternoons. I look forward to hearing from you.

Sincerely,

Jennifer Barnes

The letter is fine, but it looks a little bland. You are, after all, applying for a design position. So you decide to change your letterhead using the WordArt feature of your word processing program and use a different font for the body to make it more snappy. After a little while, you come up with this:

Jennifer Barnes

308 Bruffee Street
Minneapolis, MN 55423

January 5, 2002

Andrew J. Johnson, Vice President
Copy Mart
742 Church Street S.E.
Minneapolis, MN 55454

Dear Mr. Johnson:

I wish to apply for the design position that you advertised in the *Minneapolis Tribune* on January 3, 2002.

I am a communications major at the University of Minnesota, and I have three years experience designing brochures, newsletters, and Web pages for businesses and nonprofit organizations in the Twin Cities. I am skilled in using JavaScript, Adobe PageMaker, Photoshop, and Illustrator, and Macromedia Director, Dreamweaver, and Flash. My résumé is enclosed, complete with a list of Web sites that I have designed and the names, addresses, and phone numbers of people who have employed me.

You may reach me by email or at my home phone, (612) 634-5789, on most afternoons. I look forward to hearing from you.

Sincerely,

Jennifer Barnes

This is better, you think, but maybe still not professional enough. You try one more time, simply using shading and a different font for the letterhead:

308 Bruffee Street
Minneapolis, MN 55423

January 5, 2002

Andrew J. Johnson, Vice President
Copy Mart
742 Church Street S.E.
Minneapolis, MN 55454

Dear Mr. Johnson:

I wish to apply for the design position that you advertised in the *Minneapolis Tribune* on January 3, 2002.

I am a communications major at the University of Minnesota, and I have three years experience designing brochures, newsletters, and Web pages for businesses and nonprofit organizations in the Twin Cities. I am skilled in using JavaScript, Adobe PageMaker, Photoshop, and Illustrator, and Macromedia Director, Dreamweaver, and Flash. My résumé is enclosed, complete with a list of Web sites that I have designed and the names, addresses, and phone numbers of people who have employed me.

You may reach me by email or at my home phone, (612) 634-5789, on most afternoons. I look forward to hearing from you.

Sincerely,

Jennifer Barnes

That's the professional look you want. You send the letter, and you get the job.

Your first newsletter assignment comes from a local group, Stop Stadium Welfare (SSW), which is opposed to using taxpayer dollars to pay for a new stadium. Like most people, the members of SSW want their newsletter in a hurry, and what they bring you is a visual mess. They hand you several short articles and no model to follow, since this is the group's first newsletter.

You start reading what they hand you. The first article has the title "Do Stadiums Really Bring in Jobs and New Businesses?" It begins:

Stadium boosters like to claim fabulous economic impacts from building new stadiums with taxpayers' dollars. But the record suggests just the opposite. Most sports stadiums lose money. Stadiums built in the 1970s and 1980s, including the Superdome in New Orleans, the Silverdome in suburban Detroit, and the Meadowlands in New Jersey, are now considered obsolete, and each loses over a million government dollars a year. They are drains on the local economy, not economic multipliers.

There are four other, shorter articles, so there's plenty of material for a four-page newsletter. But how will you put it together?

You start out by making a header and then type in the stories one after the other (see Figure 12.2). You quickly realize that putting the stories in 1, 2, 3 order is not the solution. Your newsletter looks like a term paper with long stretches of unbroken text. It has little visual interest, and it's not easy to read. You remember that a professor once said that lines with more than twelve to fourteen words become hard to read. So the first thing you do is to divide the page into two columns. That's simple to do using the columns command in your word processing program. But you still haven't solved the problem of the long article that you started out with. You then decide to make the columns into text boxes so that you can carry over some text to later pages. That allows you to get three stories on the first page.

Next you change the typeface from Times Roman to Arial, which allows you to use smaller type to get more on the page and gives your newsletter a clean, simple look. You decide that a photo would be nice, and you quickly find a shot of the Metrodome in your office's photo file. Since the

Stop Stadium Welfare

Volume 1, Issue 1   2002

Do Stadiums Really Bring in Jobs and New Businesses?
By Reginald Alexander

Stadium boosters like to claim fabulous economic impacts from building new stadiums with taxpayers' dollars. But the record suggests just the opposite. Most sports stadiums lose money. Stadiums built in the 1970s and 1980s, including the Superdome in New Orleans, the Silverdome in suburban Detroit, and the Meadowlands in New Jersey, are now obsolete, and each lose over a million government dollars a year. They are drains on the local economy, not multipliers.

Before the Metrodome, we had Metropolitan Stadium, south of Minneapolis in the suburb of Bloomington. It was built with local business support in an open field. The old Met virtually made the Hwy 494 "strip," a belt of restaurants, clubs, hotels and stores. It was an outdoor stadium, like the ones the owners want built now. The controversial government-built successor, the Metrodome, has not had the same impact on downtown Minneapolis. Downtown Minneapolis has continued to decline.

What is most amazing is that the same arguments used to justify the Metrodome are being made for a new stadium. If the Metrodome failed to revive downtown, why would another stadium be different? The Metrodome's primary economic spinoffs appear to be a few $5 parking lots.

A study by the Brookings Institution published in 1997 examined sports facilities from a variety of economic perspectives. The authors conclude that the economic impact of a new sports facility is very small at best and often negative. In no case do the effects justify the enormous investment in a new stadium. Probably the most successful new stadium has been Oriole Park in Baltimore, which brings in many people from outside the area. Nevertheless, the net gain for Baltimore's economy in terms of tax revenues and jobs created is only $3 million a year—a minimal return on a $200 million investment.

Meanwhile, local politicians talk about giving the Twins an even bigger subsidy to help reduce their losses. These losses are not documented, or at least the figures not shown to the public. And the owner of the Twins, Carl Pohlad, is a billionaire. Even if the Twins are losing money, why would Mr. Pohlad expect taxpayers to cover his baseball losses any more than they would bail out another venture?

North Carolina Voters Just Say No to Stadium Tax
By Arlene Smith

North Carolina voters rejected the use of taxes to help build a new stadium so theTwins could move to North Carolina. Referendum results show Forsythe County 41-59% against, Guilford County 33-67% against. Commisioner of Baseball Bud Selig made the following statement: "There's no other way to say it: The people in the Twin Cities have to deal with it. They still have to deal with the stadium issue."

Figure 12.2   Version 1 of Stop Stadium Welfare Newsletter

Metrodome has become a symbol of Minneapolis, it works well to point out that people want to tear it down only twenty years after it was built. You add some headings and subheadings to break up the text and give emphasis. Finally, you put in a table of contents so that people will know what else is in the newsletter besides what is on the front page. You're pleased with the result (see Figure 12.3), and it took nothing more than using the commands on your word processing program. Good design doesn't necessarily require fancy tools.

Stop Stadium Welfare

Volume 1, Issue 1   2002

North Carolina Voters Just Say No to Stadium Tax

Arlene Smith

North Carolina voters rejected the use of taxes to help build a new stadium so the Twins could move to North Carolina. Referendum results show Forsythe County 41-59% against, Guilford County 33-67% against. Commissioner of Baseball Bud Selig made the following statement: "There's no other way to say it: The people in the Twin Cities have to deal with it. They still have to deal with the stadium issue."

Deal with what, Bud? Do you think we are too stupid to know what is in our best interest? We're tired of paying for sweetheart deals that benefit only the rich owners and overpaid players. We're tired of giving welfare payments to rich owners who then complain they need even more money out of our pockets.

Entertainment for the Elite

Sports stadiums used to bring people together. The rich people had the best seats, but they were only a few rows in front of where ordinary people sat. Now the wealthy want to sit in luxury boxes, separated from the crowd. What's wrong with most older stadiums is not that they are obsolete but that they lack dozens of luxury boxes.

continued on page 2

INSIDE THIS ISSUE

Do Stadiums Really Bring in Jobs and New Businesses?

Reginald Alexander

Stadium boosters like to claim fabulous economic impacts from building new stadiums with taxpayers' dollars. But the record suggests just the opposite. Most sports stadiums lose money. Stadiums built in the 1970s and 1980s, including the Superdome in New Orleans, the Silverdome in suburban Detroit, and the Meadowlands in New Jersey, are now obsolete, and each lose over a million government dollars a year. They are drains on the local economy, not multipliers.

The Metrodome Hasn't Delivered on the Promise to Revive Downtown

Before the Metrodome, we had Metropolitan Stadium, south of Minneapolis in the suburb of Bloomington. It was built with local business support in an open field. The old Met virtually made the Hwy 494 "strip," a belt of restaurants, clubs, hotels and stores. It was an outdoor stadium, like the ones the owners want built now. The controversial government-built successor, the Metrodome, has not had the same impact on downtown Minneapolis. Downtown Minneapolis has continued to decline.

The Metrodome was opened in 1982 and remains one of the newer baseball stadiums.

What is most amazing is that the same arguments used to justify the Metrodome are being made for a new stadium. If the Metrodome failed to revive downtown, why would another stadium be different? The Metrodome's primary economic spinoffs appear to be a few $5 parking lots.

continued on page 3

Figure 12.3   Version 2 of Stop Stadium Welfare Newsletter

 Design Basics

Before a discussion of principles of graphic design, it is important to know, in the most basic terms, how language and visual design work. Language is extremely well adapted for describing things that fall into a linear order. Because humans perceive time as linear, language allows them from a very young age to tell stories. It's also possible to tell stories with images; indeed, images have become the preferred medium with the invention of movies and later television in the twentieth century. But it's not so easy to put together a video story, say of your last vacation, no matter how easy the editing features are on your camcorder. Telling someone the story of your vacation, however, is easy. You just have to remember where you went and what you did.

Even if you are describing a place, you still have to decide what to tell about first. Suppose someone asks you how your house is laid out. You might begin by saying that inside the front door, there is an entryway that goes to the living room. The dining room is on the right, and the kitchen is adjacent. On the left is a hallway, which connects to two bedrooms on the right, one on the left, and a bathroom at the end. But if you draw a floor plan, you can show at once how the house is arranged. That's the basic difference between describing with spoken language and describing with visual images. Spoken language forces you to put things in a *sequence*; visual design forces you to arrange things in *space*. Written language—especially writing on a computer—permits you to do both: to use sequence and space simultaneously. Some of the same principles apply for both language and design when you write. Three of the most important groups of design principles are arrangement, consistency, and contrast.

ARRANGEMENT

Place every item on a page in a visual relationship with the other items.

Many people get through high school by mastering the five-paragraph theme. When they get the assignment, they first have to figure out exactly three points about the topic. Then they write an introduction announcing that they have three points, write a paragraph on each of the three points, and conclude with a paragraph that repeats the three points. It is amazing how far that formula can carry one. The basic structure of announcing the subject, developing it sequentially, and concluding with a summary works well enough in a great many circumstances—from business letters to short reports. Even many PhD dissertations are five-paragraph themes on a larger scale.

But if you translate the five-paragraph formula to space, it's not so simple. Think about putting it on a business card. How would you do it?

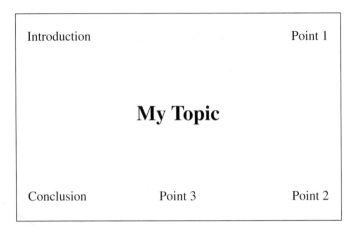

Your eyes naturally go to the center, where the topic is boldfaced. But where do they go after that? It's not a given that a reader will start in the upper left-hand corner and go clockwise around the card.

Let's switch to an example business card.

(919) 684-2741	23 Maple Street
	Durham, NC 27703
Todd Smith	
Westin Associates	Management
	Consulting

Again, the name in the middle is where you go first, but where do your eyes go after that? The problem is that nothing on the card has any obvious visual relationship with anything else.

The way beginning designers often solve this problem is to put everything in the center. This strategy forces you to think about what is most important, and you usually put that at the top. On the following card, the information is grouped so that the relationship of the elements is clear. One of the most important design tools—white space—separates the main elements.

Todd Smith

Westin Associates

Management Consulting

23 Maple Street
Durham, NC 27703
(919) 684-2741

But centering everything isn't the only solution for showing the relationship of elements. Another way is by **alignment.** In the next example, the elements are aligned on the right margin and connected by an invisible line. This alignment is often called **flush right.**

Todd Smith

Westin Associates

Management Consulting

23 Maple Street
Durham, NC 27703
(919) 684-2741

If you are in the habit of centering title pages and other elements, try using the flush left and flush right commands along with grouping similar elements. You'll be surprised what a difference it makes and how much more professional and persuasive your work will appear. Turn back to the revised Stop Stadium Welfare newsletter on page 234 to see how the strong flush left alignment of text, headings, and the picture produces a professional look.

Consistency

> Make what is similar look similar.

You learned the principle of consistency in elementary school when your teacher told you to write on the lines, make the margins even, and indent your paragraphs. When you write using a computer, these things are done for you by your word processing program. However, too many people stop there when they use a computer to write. You can do a whole lot more.

Sometime during your college years, you likely will write a report or paper that uses headings. Readers increasingly expect you to divide what you write into chunks and label those chunks with headings. It's easy enough to simply center every heading so that your report looks like this:

Title

Xxxxxxxx xxxxxxxx xxxxxxx xxxxxxx xxxxxxxx xxxxxxxx
xxxxxxx xxxxxxx xxxxxxxx xxxxxxx xxxxxxx xxxxxxxx
xxxxxxx xxxxxxx xxxxxxx xxxxxxx xxxxxxx xxxxxxx xxxxx
xxxxxxx xxxxxxx xxxxxxx xxxxxxx xxxxxxx xxxxxxx
xxxxxxx xxxxxxx

Heading 1

Xxxxxxxx xxxxxxxx xxxxxxx xxxxxxx xxxxxxxx xxxxxxxx
xxxxxxx xxxxxxx xxxxxxxx xxxxxxx xxxxxxx xxxxxxxx
xxxxxxx xxxxxxx xxxxxxx xxxxxxx xxxxxxx xxxxxxx xxxxx
xxxxxxx xxxxxxx xxxxxxx xxxxxxx xxxxxxx xxxxxxx
xxxxxxx xxxxxxx xxxxxxx xxxxxxxx xxxxxxxxx xxxxxxx
xxxxxxxx xxxxxxx

Heading 2

Xxxxxxxx xxxxxxxx xxxxxxx xxxxxxx xxxxxxxx xxxxxxxx
xxxxxxx xxxxxxx xxxxxxxx xxxxxxx xxxxxxx xxxxxxxx
xxxxxxx xxxxxxx xxxxxxx xxxxxxx xxxxxxx xxxxxxx xxxxx
xxxxxxx xxxxxxx xxxxxxx xxxxxxx xxxxxxx xxxxxxx
xxxxxxx xxxxxxx

If you write a report that looks like this one, you can make it much more visually appealing by devising a system of consistent headings that indicate the overall organization. You first have to determine the level of importance of each heading by making an outline to see what fits under what. Then you make the headings conform to the different levels so that what is equal in importance will have the same level of heading.

Title

Xxxxxxxx xxxxxxxx xxxxxxx xxxxxxx xxxxxxxx xxxxxxxx
xxxxxxx xxxxxxx xxxxxxxx xxxxxx xxxxxxx xxxxxxxx
xxxxxxx xxxxxxx xxxxxxx xxxxxxx xxxxxx xxxxxxx
xxxxxxx xxxxxxx xxxxxxx xxxxxx xxxxxx xxxxxxx
xxxxxx xxxxxxx

Major Heading

Xxxxxxxx xxxxxxxx xxxxxxx xxxxxxx xxxxxxxx xxxxxxxx
xxxxxxx xxxxxxx xxxxxxxx xxxxxx xxxxxxx xxxxxxxx
xxxxxxx xxxxxxx xxxxxxx xxxxxx xxxxxx xxxxxxx
xxxxxxx xxxxxxx xxxxxxx xxxxxxxx xxxxxxxxx xxxxxxx
xxxxxxxx xxxxxxx

Level 2 Heading   Xxxxxxxx xxxxxxxx xxxxxxx xxxxxxx
xxxxxxxxx xxxxxxxx xxxxxx xxxxxxx xxxxxxxx xxxxxxx
xxxxxxx xxxxxxxx xxxxxxx xxxxxx xxxxxx xxxxxxx
xxxxxx xxxxxxx xxxxxx xxxxxx

Other useful tools that word processing programs offer are ways of making lists. Bulleted lists are used frequently to present good reasons for claims and proposals. For example:

The proposed new major in Technology, Literacy, and Culture will:

- Prepare our students for the changing demands of the professions and public citizenship.
- Help students to move beyond technical skills and strategies to understand the historical, economic, political, and scientific impacts of new technologies.
- Allow students to practice new literacies that mix text, graphics, sound, video, animation, hypermedia, and real-time communication.
- Help to ensure that wise decisions are made about the collection, organization, storage, and distribution of and access to information via new technologies.
- Provide students with a deeper, richer, and more profound understanding of the dynamic relationships among technology, culture, and the individual.

A bulleted list is an effective way of presenting a series of items or giving an overview of what is to come. However, bulleted lists can be ineffective if the items in the list are not similar.

CONTRAST

Make what is different look different.

We tend to follow the principle of consistency because that's what we've been taught and that's what writing technologies—from typewriters to computers—do for us. But the principle of contrast takes some conscious effort on our part to implement. Take a simple résumé as an example:

Roberto Salazar

Address: 3819 East Jefferson Avenue, Escondido, CA 92027

Send email to: salazar@capaccess.org

Job Title: Financial Consultant, Credit Reviewer, Financial Analyst

Relocation: Yes—particular interest in Latin America.

Experience

1997-present. Credit Services Group, Carpenter & Tokaz LLP, 3000 Wilshire Boulevard, Los Angeles, California 90017

CONSULTING: Presented Directorate with report findings, conclusions, and recommendations for operation improvements. Coordinated a process improvement engagement for a large finance company, which resulted in the consolidation of credit operations.

SUPERVISION: Supervised, trained, and assessed the work of staff (1–4) involved in audit assists. Reviewed real estate investments, other real estate owned, and loan portfolios for documentation, structure, credit analysis, risk identification, and credit scoring.

Education

1997 San Diego State University, San Diego, California, Bachelor of Business Administration

Languages

Fluent in English and Spanish. Experience in tutoring students with Spanish lessons at San Diego State University, San Diego, California

Computers

Proficient with Microsoft Word and Excel, Lotus Notes, AmiPro, Lotus 1-2-3, WordPerfect, and Sendero SV simulation modeling software. Familiarity with several online information retrieval methods.

References Available On Request.

The résumé has consistency but there is no contrast between what is more important and what is less important. The overall impression is that the person is dull, dull, dull.

Your résumé, along with your letter of application, might be the most important piece of persuasive writing you'll do in your life. It's worth taking some extra time to distinguish yourself. Your ability to write a convincing letter and produce a handsome résumé is a good reason for an employer to hire you. Remember why you are paying attention to graphic design. You want your readers to focus on certain elements, and you want to create the right ethos. Use of contrast can emphasize the key features of the résumé and contribute to a much more forceful and dynamic image.

Roberto Salazar

3819 East Jefferson Avenue
Escondido, CA 92027
salazar@capaccess.org

Position Titles Sought

Financial Consulting
Credit Reviewer
Financial Analyst
(Willing to relocate, especially to Latin America)

Education

1997   **Bachelor of Business Administration.** San Diego State University.

Experience

1997-present   **Credit Services Group, Carpenter & Tokaz, LLP.**
3000 Wilshire Boulevard
Los Angeles, California 90017

Consulting: Presented Directorate with report findings, conclusions, and recommendations for operation improvements. Coordinated a process improvement engagement for a large finance company, which resulted in the consolidation of credit operations.

Supervision: Supervised, trained, and assessed the work of four staff involved in audit assists. Reviewed real estate investments, other real estate owned, and loan portfolios for documentation, structure, credit analysis, risk identification, and credit scoring.

Languages

Fluent in English and Spanish. Experience as a Spanish Tutor at SDSU.

Computer Skills

Proficient with Microsoft Word & Excel, Lotus Notes, AmiPro, Lotus 1-2-3, WordPerfect, and Sendero SV simulation modeling software. Familiarity with several online information retrieval methods.

References

Available on request.

Notice that arrangement and consistency are also important to the revised résumé. Good design requires that all elements be brought into play to produce the desired results.

The Rhetoric of Type

Until computers and word processing software came along, most writers had little or no control over the type style they used. If they typed, they likely used Courier, a fact that many typists didn't even know. Furthermore, the typewriter gave no choice about type size. Writers worked with either 10-point type or 12-point type. (A point is a printer's measure. One inch equals 72 points.) You had no way to include italics. The convention was to underline the word so that the printer would later set the word in italics. Boldfacing could be accomplished only by typing the word over again, making it darker.

Even if the general public knew little about type styles and other aspects of printing before computers came along, printers had five hundred years' experience learning about which type styles were easiest to read and what effects different styles produced. Type styles are grouped into families of **typefaces.** When you open the pull-down font menu of your word processing program, you see a small part of that five-hundred-year tradition of developing typefaces. At first, many of the typefaces will look about the same to you, but after you get some practice with using various typefaces, you will begin to notice how they differ.

The two most important categories of typefaces are **serif** and **sans serif.** Serif (rhymes with "sheriff") type was developed first, imitating the strokes of an ink pen. Serifs are the little wedge-shaped ends on letter forms, which scribes produced with wedge-tipped pens. Serif type also has thick and thin transitions on the curved strokes. Five of the most common serif typefaces are the following:

Times

Palatino

Bookman

· Garamond

New Century Schoolbook

If these typefaces look almost alike to you, it's not an accident. Serif typefaces were designed to be easy to read. They don't call attention to themselves. Therefore, they are well suited for long stretches of text and are used frequently.

Sans serif type (*sans* is French for "without") doesn't have the little wedge-shaped ends on letters, and the thickness of the letters is the same. Popular sans serif typefaces include the following:

- Helvetica

  Avant Garde

  Arial

Sans serif typefaces work well for headings and short stretches of text. They give the text a crisp, modern look. And some sans serif typefaces are easy to read on a computer screen.

Finally, there are many script and decorative typefaces. These typefaces tend to draw attention to themselves. They are harder to read, but sometimes they can be used for good effects. Some script and decorative typefaces include the following:

Zapf Chancery

STENCIL

Mistral

Tekton

Changing typefaces will draw attention. It is usually better to be consistent in using typefaces within a text unless you want to signal something.

It's easy to change the size of type when you compose on a computer. A specific size of a typeface is called a **font.** The font size displays on the menu bar. For long stretches of text, you probably should use at least 10-point or 12-point type. For headings, you can use larger type.

type	8 point
type	10 point
type	12 point
type	14 point
type	18 point
type	24 point
type	36 point

type

48 point

type

72 point

Fonts also have different weights. **Weight** refers to the thickness of the strokes. Take a look at the fonts on your font menu. You probably have some fonts that offer options ranging from light to bold, such as Arial Condensed Light, Arial, Arial Rounded MT Bold, and Arial Black. Here's what each of these looks like as a heading:

1. *Arial Condensed Light*

Position Titles Sought

Financial Consultant
Credit Reviewer
Financial Analyst
(Willing to relocate, especially to Latin America)

2. *Arial*

Position Titles Sought

Financial Consultant
Credit Reviewer
Financial Analyst
(Willing to relocate, especially to Latin America)

3. *Arial Rounded MT Bold*

Position Titles Sought

Financial Consultant
Credit Reviewer
Financial Analyst
(Willing to relocate, especially to Latin America)

4. *Arial Black*

Position Titles Sought

Financial Consultant
Credit Reviewer
Financial Analyst
(Willing to relocate, especially to Latin America)

You can get strong contrasts by using heavier weights of black type for headings and using white space to accent what is different.

Finally, most word processing programs have some special effects that you can employ. The three most common are **boldface,** *italics*, and <u>underlining</u>. All three are used for emphasis, but underlining should be avoided because it makes text harder to read.

Graphic Presentation of Information

Tables and Charts

Word processing software gives you the capability of creating tables, graphs, and charts in one software program and then importing those graphics into a text file. For example, tables and charts created with Microsoft Excel can easily be imported into Microsoft Word files. Many arguments can be made more effective with the visual presentation of important information. If you have statistical information to support your argument, you should consider whether to present that information in words, as a table, or as a graphic—or in some combination of these.

Let's take as an example the ongoing debate between gun rights advocates and gun control advocates. Gun rights advocates typically rely on definitional arguments. Their foremost argument is based on their interpretation of the Second Amendment to the U.S. Constitution, which reads "A well regulated Militia, being necessary to the security of a free State, the right of the people to keep and bear Arms, shall not be infringed." What exactly the Second Amendment means today is much disputed. Gun control advocates interpret the Second Amendment in its historical context, in which the newly formed states of the United States required local armies to battle against Native Americans. The Supreme Court reached the same conclusion in a 1939 case (*U.S. v. Miller,* 307 U.S. 174), finding that possession of a firearm is not protected by the Second Amendment unless it has some reasonable relationship to the preservation or efficiency of a well-regulated militia. No gun control law ever brought before the Supreme Court or other federal courts has ever been overturned on Second Amendment grounds. Nevertheless, the National Rifle Association and other gun rights advocates continue to argue that ownership of guns is protected by the Bill of Rights.

Those who wish to regulate firearms, however, often bypass the constitutional argument in favor of arguments of consequence. Gun control advocates point to comparisons between the United States and other advanced nations of the world, all of which have much stricter gun laws than the United States and much lower rates of deaths by firearms. The rate of firearm deaths in the United States is three times higher than Canada's, four times higher than Australia's, nine times higher than Germany's, twenty-four times higher than the United Kingdom's (even including Northern Ireland), and almost two hundred times higher than Japan's.

The problem when you start giving a lot of statistics in words is that your readers shortly lose track of your numbers. If you want to argue effectively using statistics, you have to put the numbers in formats that permit your readers to take them in. Tables are quite useful for presenting much numerical data at one glance. If you have the numbers, you can make the table quickly and easily with a program like Microsoft Excel.

Table 12.1 shows a tabular comparison of the death rates due to firearms in the United States and other advanced nations.

	Total Firearm Deaths		Firearm Homicides		Firearm Suicides		Fatal Firearm Accidents	
	Rate	Number	Rate	Number	Rate	Number	Rate	Number
United States (1995)	13.7	35,957	6	15,835	7	18,503	0.5	1,225
Australia (1994)	3.05	536	0.56	96	2.38	420	0.11	20
Canada (1994)	4.08	1,189	0.6	176	3.35	975	0.13	38
Germany (1995)	1.47	1,197	0.21	168	1.23	1,004	0.03	20
Japan (1995)	0.07	93	0.03	34	0.04	49	0.01	10
Sweden (1992)	2.31	200	0.31	27	1.95	169	0.05	4
Spain (1994)	1.01	396	0.19	76	0.55	219	0.26	101
United Kingdom (1994)	0.57	277	0.13	72	0.33	193	0.02	12

(rates are per 100,000 people)
Source: United Nations, *United Nations International Study on Firearms Regulation* (Vienna, Austria: United Nations Crime Prevention and Criminal Justice Division, 1997) 109.

Table 12.1 Firearm Deaths by Country

Although tables can present an array of numbers at once, they lack the dramatic impact of charts. Charts visually represent the magnitude and proportion of data. The differences in death rates due to firearms is striking when presented as a chart. One of the easiest charts to make is a simple bar chart (Figure 12.4).

The tools available in a software program such as Microsoft Excel allow you a number of options. For example, you can represent the bars in three dimensions (Figure 12.5). Be aware, though, that three-dimensional bars can distort the data and make it more difficult to compare the heights of the columns.

Alternatively, you can make a horizontal bar chart instead of a vertical bar chart (Figure 12.6).

The options available to you involve rhetorical decisions. You can manipulate the length of the axes on a bar chart, either exaggerating or minimizing differences. Or in the case of firearm deaths, you can use the total numbers instead of the rate. Notice how much more exaggerated the number of firearm deaths in the United States appears when the total number is used instead of the rate per 100,000 people (compare Figures 12.7 and 12.8). As always it's important to keep your rhetorical goals in mind when you make a chart.

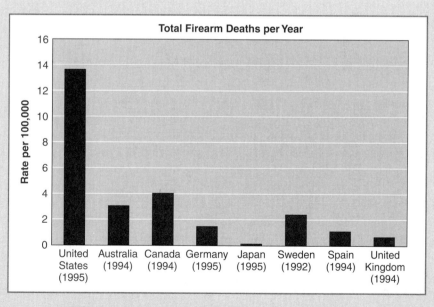

Figure 12.4 Bar Chart of Firearm Deaths by Country

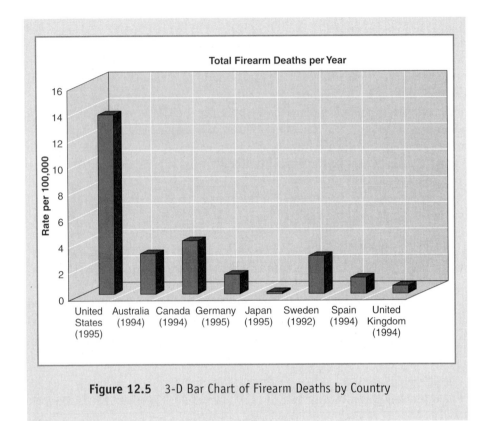

Figure 12.5 3-D Bar Chart of Firearm Deaths by Country

Another family of charts that are very easy to create are pie charts. As the name suggests, **pie charts** illustrate how the pie is divided. They are especially useful for representing percentages, but they work only if the percentages of the parts add up to 100 percent. Gun control advocates frequently cite a study done in Seattle that identified all gunshot deaths over a six-year period (A. L. Kellermann and D. L. Reay, "Protection or Peril: An Analysis of Firearm-Related Deaths in the Home," *New England Journal of Medicine* 314 (1986): 1557–1560). Of the 733 deaths by firearms, a majority (398) occurred in the home in which the firearm involved was kept. Of those 398 deaths, 333 (83.6 percent) were suicides, 41 (10.3 percent) were criminal homicides, 12 (3.0 percent) were accidental, 7 (1.7 percent) were justifiable self-defense, and only 2 (0.5 percent) involved an intruder shot during an attempted entry (see Figure 12.9). Gun control advocates use this study to question the advisability of keeping firearms in the home for protection. Gun rights advocates, however, fault the study because there is no evidence on how many attempts to enter the home were prevented because intruders feared that the owner was armed.

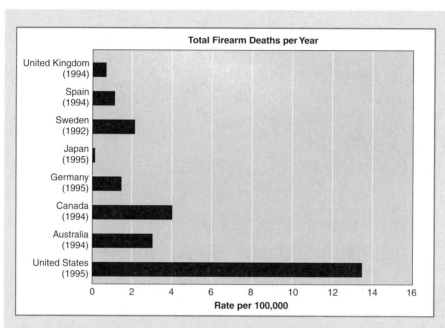

Figure 12.6   Horizontal Bar Chart of Firearm Deaths by Country

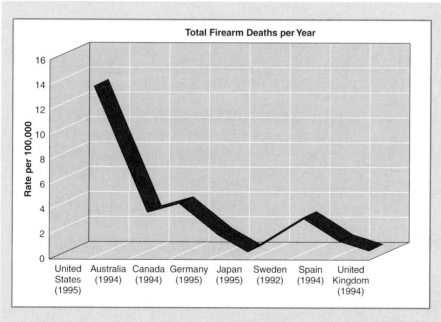

Figure 12.7   3-D Line Chart of Firearm Deaths by Rate per 100,000

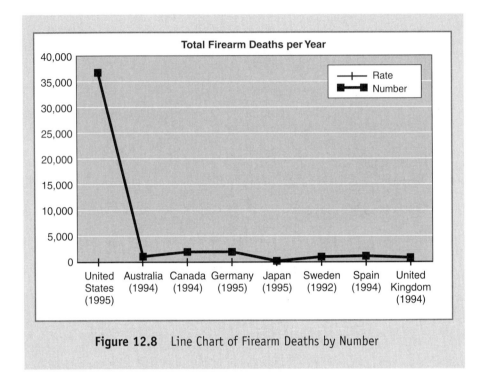

Figure 12.8 Line Chart of Firearm Deaths by Number

MISLEADING CHARTS

Charts can be misleading as well as informative. Line graphs are useful for representing changes over time, and from Table 12.2, you can make a line chart of energy consumption from 1970 to 1995. The line chart would appear to rise significantly from 1970 to 1995, from 66.4 to 90.6 quadrillion British thermal units, indicating a 36 percent increase. If plotted on a line chart, the increase would appear steep. But if the growth in population in the United States is taken into consideration, the increase is not nearly as great, from 327 to 345, only a 5.5 percent increase. A line chart would appear relatively flat.

OTHER GRAPHICS

Other graphics, such as maps and pictures, can also be useful in arguments. If you want to argue for the preservation of old-growth forests, for example, including maps of the surviving old-growth forests are a good tactic because so little of this type of forest survives. The problem is that good maps and images take a long time to create. You can find maps and images on the Web that may

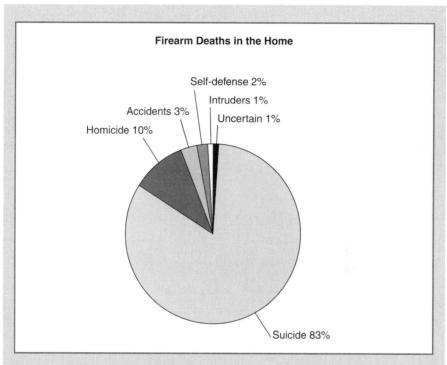

Figure 12.9 Pie Chart of Firearm Deaths in the Home

Year	Energy Consumption in Quadrillion British Thermal Units	Energy Consumption per Capita in BTUs
1970	66.4	327
1975	70.6	327
1980	76	334
1985	74	311
1990	84.2	337
1995	90.6	345

Source: Bureau of the Census. *Statistical Abstract of the United States, 1997* (Washington, D.C.: U.S. Department of Commerce, 1997) 592.

Table 12.2 Table of Energy Consumption in the United States, 1970–1995

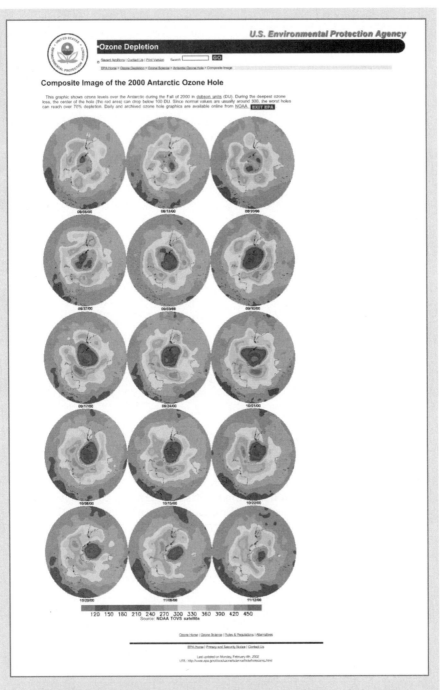

Figure 12.10 Composite Image of the Antarctic Ozone Hole in 2000
(http://www.epa.gov/docs/ozone/science/hole/holecomp.html)

be useful. For example, if you are writing about the depletion of the ozone layer over the earth, you can find this composite image of the Antarctic ozone hole on the Environmental Protection Agency's Web site (Figure 12.10).

If you download maps and images from the Web, you might have to change their format. Images on the Web are usually in JPEG or GIF format, and if your word processing program does not do the conversion for you, you might have to convert the file yourself with a program such as Graphic Converter or Adobe Photoshop.

The main thing you want to avoid is using images strictly for decoration. Readers quickly get tired of pictures and other graphics that don't contribute to the content. Think of pictures, charts, and graphics as alternative means of presenting information. Good use of graphics contributes to your overall argument.

CHAPTER 13

Effective Web Design

Arguments on the Web

Because the Web is a grassroots medium with millions of people putting up Web sites, it's no surprise that the Web has turned out to be a vast forum for arguments. Many organizations and individuals have taken advantage of the low cost of using the Web to publicize their stands on issues. To get a sense of the range of interest groups that use the Web to publicize their views, go to Yahoo! (www.yahoo.com), where you'll find under the "Society and Culture" heading, the subheading "Issues and Causes." As you can see from the list (see Figure 13.1), the issues extend from abortion, affirmative action, and animal rights to weight and nutrition, welfare reform, and xenotransplantation.

It seems that if anyone has an opinion about anything, there's a Web site representing that position. If you have strong feelings about any broad issue, you can find on the Web people who think like you do.

The problem with many argument sites on the Web is that they don't provide much depth. Their links, if any, take you to similar sites, with no context for making the link. It's up to you to figure out the relevance of the link. This strategy works for people who are already convinced of the position

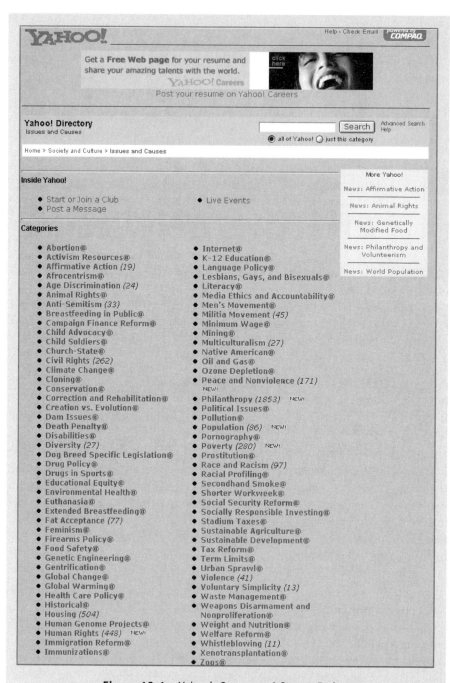

Figure 13.1 Yahoo's Issues and Causes Index
http://www.yahoo.com/Society_and_Culture/Issues_and_Causes/

being advocated, but it's not a strategy that works well with people who haven't made up their mind. When you create a Web site that advocates a position, the ease of linking on the Web doesn't make your work any easier. Good arguments still require much thinking on your part and careful planning. You cannot expect your readers to do your work for you. You still have to supply good reasons.

Creating a Web Site

Creating a Web site used to be a chore because the files for the site had to be hand-coded in Hypertext Markup Language (HTML). HTML works in the same way early word processing programs worked. If you wanted boldface type, you had to insert a switch to turn on the boldfacing and another to turn off the boldfacing. HTML uses switches called tags. If you want to boldface a word, you have to insert <b> before the word and </b> after the word so it looks like this:

<p style="text-align:center"><b>**boldface**</b></p>

As word processing programs improved and computer memory expanded, you no longer had to insert tags in the text. Word processing programs displayed on the screen what gets printed on the page—known as WYSIWYG ("what you see is what you get").

Until recently, you had to know how to write HTML code to make Web pages. Now, you don't have to know any HTML to make Web pages. Web authoring software makes it very easy to compose Web pages. Most of them work much like word processing programs. When you want to make a heading or a link, you simply highlight that text with your mouse and then click to get what you want—bigger or smaller text, boldface, italics, centering, links, and so on. The most popular Web authoring programs are

- Netscape Composer (free as part of Netscape Communicator)
- Adobe PageMill
- Claris Home Page
- Microsoft FrontPage

One of the most popular Web authoring software programs for professional Web designers is Macromedia Dreamweaver. You may want to learn to use a professional software package if you intend to create extensive Web sites.

Tutorials and other guides show you how to put text on the Web, but they don't tell you how reading is different on the Web. In most printed books, magazines, and newspapers, the text is continuous. Printed text isn't necessarily linear—witness the boxes and sidebars in this book. While it's possible to go back and forth in print, the basic movement in print is linear and the basic unit is the paragraph. By contrast the basic movement on the Web is nonlinear and the basic unit is the screen. Perhaps the most important fact to remember is that fewer than 10 percent of people who click on a Web site ever scroll down the page. Their eyes stop at the bottom of the screen. And those who do scroll down usually don't scroll down very far.

THE FIRST SCREEN IS THE MOST IMPORTANT

People who browse Web sites don't stay long if they aren't interested or if it takes too long to find out what's on the Web site. That's why the first screen is critical. If you have something to tell your visitors, tell them right away. They probably aren't going to click through a bunch of screens or scroll though long stretches to find out where you stand on an issue. You have to let your readers know on the first screen what your site is about.

The first screen is also the front door to your site, and when visitors enter your front door, they need to know where to go next. Supplying navigation tools on the first page is critical. These can take the form of menu bars, buttons, or clickable images. Whatever form you choose, the labels should indicate what the visitor will find on the next screen.

The Web page in Figure 13.2 was created by Grace Bernhardt for a class project on the conflict surrounding the Balcones Canyonlands Preserve (BCP), a nature reserve located within the city limits of Austin, Texas, and the habitat for six endangered species. The text on the first page describes the place and the various stakeholders in the Balcones Canyonlands Preserve. It also provides a menu to the main areas of the site.

DIVIDE YOUR TEXT INTO CHUNKS

Long stretches of text on the Web tend not to get read. Part of the problem is that most people do not have large-screen monitors. For those people, reading text on the Web is like trying to read a newspaper through a three-inch-square hole. It's possible to do but not much fun. Newspapers grew to their present size because our eyes can take in a large expanse of information when we scan the page. Perhaps in the next few years, large-screen monitors will

Figure 13.2 Balcones Canyonlands Preserve: A Look at the Controversy from Several Sides
http://www.tlc.utexas.edu/courses/2001s_321/bcp/p4d.htm

give us a similar experience, but for now, most of us are still using small-screen monitors.

Given the limitations of the monitors that most people now use, many Web designers try to divide text into chunks whenever possible. For example, when they present a list of facts, they often put space between items or use a bulleted list rather than a long paragraph. The page in Figure 13.3 is from a student Web site designed by Chungpei Hu on safety issues for Sixth Street, the entertainment district in Austin, Texas. It uses a bulleted list to enumerate frequent fire code violations in bars and clubs along Sixth Street.

You can put a great deal of background information on a Web site connected by links to the main argument. Thus you can offer a short summary on the main page with links to other pages that give background and evidence. One advantage of this strategy is that you design a single site both for those who know a great deal about the subject and want to skip the background information, and for those who know little and need to know the background. You can include additional evidence that would be hard to work into a paper otherwise. Furthermore, the act of clicking on particular words can make readers aware of the links in an argument.

But because text on the Web is usually truncated and readers skim quickly and jump from one page to another, it's more difficult to place a detailed, sustained argument on a Web site. Some people don't even try. They simply place a long text on the Web and assume those who are really inter-

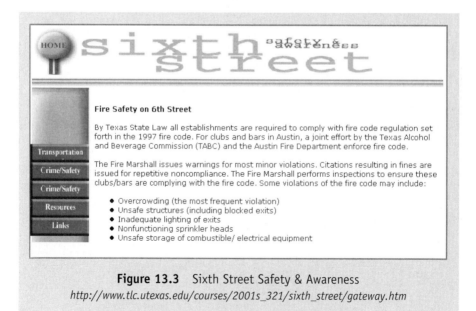

Figure 13.3 Sixth Street Safety & Awareness
http://www.tlc.utexas.edu/courses/2001s_321/sixth_street/gateway.htm

ested will download that text, print it, and read it. Making that assumption, however, means risking losing all but the most interested readers on a particular subject. Readers increasingly expect arguments on the Web to be designed for the Web.

MAKE THE TEXT READABLE

Above all, make your text readable. Remember that other people's monitors may be smaller than yours; thus what appears as small type on your monitor may require a magnifying glass for others. Also, dark backgrounds make for tough reading. If you use a dark background and want people to read what you write, be sure to increase the font size, make sure the contrast between text and background is adequate, and avoid using all caps and italics.

TEXT IN ALL CAPS IS HARD TO READ ON A BLACK BACKGROUND, *ESPECIALLY IF THE TEXT IS IN ITALICS.*

Stay Organized

When you decide to put up a Web site, it's critical that you do some planning in advance.

1. **Make an outline of your site.** You should draw on paper how you want your site organized.

2. **Collect all the source materials for your site.** These materials may include text and images. Keep the materials together in a manila folder. When you have this material in digital form, put it in a folder, labeled "Sources" or the name of your project, on your hard drive and on a backup disk.

3. **Use a system for naming files.** Use only lowercase letters because later you may forget which letters you capitalized. Don't use punctuation marks like semicolons, which have specific meanings

(continued)

Stay Organized (continued)

you may not intend, because they may cause you problems down the road. All Web pages have to end in .htm (on PCs) or .html (on Macs). Label image files by their type, such as .gif (for GIF files) or .jpg (for JPEG files).

4. **Put your files in a folder.** You're going to put the files on your Web site server in a folder just like you do on your computer. The simplest way is to put the whole folder on the server when you are ready. You probably will need only one folder, but if you are creating a site that may become bigger down the road, you might think about using more than one folder.

5. **Save, save, save.** It always is a good idea to make backup copies. You should make copies on a diskette or even better, on a Zip disk, which can store large files.

Principles of Web Design

When you design your Web site, you have many tools available that you don't have with ordinary text. You can add graphics and create links to your own pages and pages made by others. When you become more advanced, you can even add animations and audio and video clips. Pictures and other multimedia elements can make your Web site appealing and give your content visual impact. But pictures that do not contribute to your content can also be confusing, distracting readers from the substance of your argument. Furthermore, pictures and graphics also have a great deal to do with the performance of your site—how long it takes for pages to load on the screen.

Determine the Visual Theme of Your Site

Most Web sites contain more than one page, and because it is so easy to move from one page to another on the Web, it's important to make your site as unified as possible. Using common design elements, such as color, icons, typeface, and layout, contributes to the unity of the site. The Balcones Canyonlands Preserves site shown in Figure 13.2 repeats the image of its most famous resident—the endangered golden-cheeked warbler—on each page, along with images of foliage. Even without the text, the images on the site make it evident that the site deals with environmental issues.

DIRECT THE VIEWER'S EYES

The design principles we discuss in Chapter 12 also apply to Web design, with one important addition. The top of a Web page is even more critical than the top of a printed page because, as discussed earlier, many people have monitors that do not display an entire Web page. And because many people never scroll down, you have to pay special attention to the top of the page.

Many Web pages use jarring colors for striking effects—hot pinks and fluorescent greens on black backgrounds. Many others have visually intense backgrounds that distract from the text or make the text hard to read. If you want people to read your text, you have to use lighter tones for backgrounds and supporting images. Reserve the bright colors for points you most wish to emphasize or avoid bright colors altogether, as they may overwhelm the rest of the text on your site.

KEEP THE VISUALS SIMPLE

The students who produced the Web sites in this chapter could have included many large pictures if they had chosen to. But they deliberately kept the visual design simple. A less complicated site is not only more friendly because it loads faster, but if it is well designed, it can be elegant. Simple elements are also easier to repeat. Too many icons, bullets, horizontal rules, and other embellishments give a page a cluttered appearance. A simple, consistent design is always effective for pages that contain text.

Finally, keep in mind that although good graphic design provides visual impact and can help the visitor navigate a Web site, it has little value if it is not supported by substance. People still expect to come away from a Web site with substantial information. Good visual design makes your Web site more appealing, but it does not do the work of argument for you.

NAVIGATIONAL DESIGN

People don't read Web sites the same way they read a book. They scan quickly and move around a lot. They don't necessarily read from top to bottom. If you are trying to make an argument on the Web, you have to think differently about how the reader is going to encounter your argument. If you

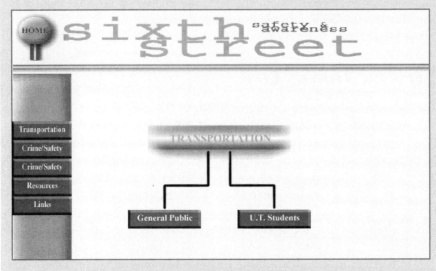

Figure 13.4   Sixth Street Safety & Awareness
*http://www.tlc.utexas.edu/courses/2001s_321/sixth_street/html/transportation/
transportation.htm*

put the argument on more than one page, you have to plan the site so that readers can navigate easily.

Designing navigational tools for your Web site is a three-step process. First, you should decide on the overall structure of your Web site, assuming you plan to include more than one page. Web sites that have a main page should have clear navigation tools. For example, the transportation section of Sixth Street Safety & Awareness (Figure 13.4) offers sections for both the general public and University of Texas students. The navigation icons make the possibilities obvious.

Audience Considerations on the Web

A Web site can potentially reach millions of people, which is its greatest benefit but at the same time can present a major difficulty in planning your site. The concept of audience becomes more complicated on the Web. Not only do you not know who will click on your Web site, but you also don't know exactly how each visitor will see or hear what you put up. Some people will have the latest Web browsers, powerful computers, big-screen monitors, and very fast ethernet, DSL, or cable modem connections. Others may be connecting to your Web site by slow dial-up modem connections and may have older, less-powerful computers that cannot run the latest versions of Web browsers. You can include sound, image, and even movie files, but not everyone can download these files. If you want all your visitors to see everything on your Web site without waiting minutes for your pages to load, you have to think about them when you are designing your site. The Sixth Street Safety & Awareness site (Figures 13.3 and 13.4) is posted in two versions, allowing those with fast and slow connections to experience the site.

A famous architect, Ludwig Mies van der Rohe, once said "less is more." He was talking about a general principle for the design of buildings: Simple is better. This principle is a good one to keep in mind when you are designing your Web site. "Less is more" means using fewer, simpler typefaces, fewer colors, and fewer potentially distracting elements. On the Web, less size also means more speed. So we might change van der Rohe's aphorism to "less is faster." Pay attention to size when you put images on the Web. Smaller images not only load faster but they also look better.

Evaluating a Web Site

You can use the following criteria to evaluate Web sites you have designed or those designed by others.

1. **Audience:** How does the site identify its intended audience? How does it indicate what else is on the site?

2. **Content:** How informative is the content? Where might more content be added? What do you want to know more about? Are there any mechanical, grammar, or style problems?

3. **Readability:** Is there sufficient contrast between the text and the background to make it legible? Are the margins wide enough? Are there any paragraphs that go on too long and need to be divided? Are headings inserted in the right places, and if headings are used for more than one level, are these levels indicated consistently? Is text in boldface and all caps kept short?

4. **Visual Design:** Does the site have a consistent visual theme? Where is the focal point on each page? Do the images contribute to the visual appeal or do they detract from it?

5. **Navigation:** How easy or difficult is it to move from one page to another on the site? Are there any broken links?

CHAPTER 14

Effective Oral Presentations

Becoming effective in oral communication is just as important as in written communication. You may be asked to give oral presentations in your later life and perhaps in your college career. Oral presentations can be developed from written assignments and supported by visual elements such as slides, overheads, film clips, and other media.

Planning an Oral Presentation

GETTING STARTED

Successful oral presentations, like written arguments, require careful planning. You first step is to find out what kind of oral presentation you are being asked to give. Kinds of oral presentations include the following:

- **Persuasive speeches** attempt to change the audience's attitudes and beliefs or convince them that a particular course of action is best.

■ **Informative speeches** explain a subject or demonstrate a process.

■ **Entertaining speeches** keep the audience's attention with stories and jokes.

■ **Debates** directly confront an opposing viewpoint.

■ **Group presentations** involve team members who present aspects of a subject individually.

Look closely at your assignment. If the kind of presentation is not stated explicitly, words such as *argue for*, *report*, and *propose* are important clues about what is expected.

Another important consideration is length. How much time you have to give a speech determines the depth you can go into. Speakers who ignore this simple principle often announce near the end of their time that they will have to omit major points and rush to finish. Their presentations end abruptly and leave the audience confused about what the speaker had to say.

You also should consider early on where you will be giving the speech. If you want to use visual elements to support your presentation, you need to make sure the room has the equipment you need. If you know the room is large or has poor acoustics, you will need to bring audio equipment. If you know the visual equipment available is inadequate or the lighting is difficult to control you may choose not to use presentation software or overheads. You often can adjust for room conditions if you plan in advance.

SELECTING YOUR TOPIC

Choosing and researching a topic for an oral presentation is similar to choosing and researching a topic for a written assignment. If you have a broad choice of topics, make a list of subjects that interest you. Then go through your list and ask yourself these questions:

■ Will you enjoy speaking on this topic?

■ Will your audience be interested in this topic?

■ Does the topic fit the situation for your presentation?

■ Do you know enough to speak on this topic?

■ If you do not know enough, are you willing to do research to learn more about the topic?

Remember that enthusiasm is contagious, so if you are excited about a topic, chances are your audience will become interested too.

Research for an oral presentation is similar to the research you must do for a written argument. You will find guidelines in Chapter 15 for planning your research. Remember that you will need to develop a bibliography for an oral presentation that requires research just as you would for a written argument. You will need to document the sources of your information and provide those sources in your talk.

THINKING ABOUT YOUR AUDIENCE

Unlike writing, when you give a speech, you have your audience directly before you. They will give you concrete feedback during your presentation by smiling or frowning, by paying attention or losing interest, by asking questions or sitting passively.

When planning your presentation, you should think about the general characteristics of your audience.

- What is the age range of your audience?
- What occupations are represented?
- What is the likely mix of men and women?
- What is the educational background?
- What is the ethnic and cultural background?

You should also think about your audience in relation to your topic.

- Will your audience be interested in your topic?
- Are there ways you can get them more interested?
- What is your audience likely to know or believe about your topic?
- What does your audience probably not know about your topic?
- What key terms will you have to define or explain?
- What assumptions do you hold in common with your audience (such as political or religious beliefs, or business philosophy)?
- Where is your audience most likely to disagree with you?
- What questions are they likely to ask?

SUPPORTING YOUR PRESENTATION

The steps for writing listed in Part 2 can be used to organize an oral presentation. When you have organized your main points, you need to decide how to support those points. Look at your research notes and think about how best to incorporate the information you found. Consider using one or more of these strategies:

- **Facts.** Speakers who know their facts build credibility.
- **Statistics.** Good use of statistics gives the impression that the speaker has done his or her homework. Statistics also can indicate that a particular example is representative. One tragic car accident doesn't mean a road is dangerous, but an especially high accident rate relative to other nearby roads does make the case.
- **Statements by authorities.** Quotations from credible experts are another common way of supporting key points.
- **Narratives.** Narratives are small stories that can illustrate key points. Narratives are a good way of keeping the attention of the audience. Keep them short so they don't distract from your major points.
- **Humor.** In most situations audiences appreciate humor. Humor is a good way to convince an audience that you have common beliefs and experiences, and that your argument may be one they can agree with.

PLANNING YOUR INTRODUCTION

No part of your speech is more critical than the introduction. You have to get the audience's attention, introduce your topic, convince the audience that it is important to them, present your thesis, and give your audience either an overview of your presentation or a sense of your direction. Accomplishing all this in a short time is a tall order, but if you lose your audience in the first two minutes, you won't recover their attention. You might begin with a compelling example or anecdote that both introduces your topic and indicates your stance.

PLANNING YOUR CONCLUSION

The next most important part of your speech is your conclusion. You want to end on a strong note. First, you need to signal that you are entering the conclusion. You can announce that you are concluding, but you also can give signals in other ways. Touching on your main points again will help your audience to remember them. But simply summarizing is a dull way to close. Think of an example or an idea that captures the gist of your speech, something that your audience can take away with them.

Delivering an Oral Presentation

THE IMPORTANCE OF PRACTICE

There is no substitute for rehearsing your speech several times in advance. You will become more confident and have more control over the content. The best way to overcome nervousness about speaking in front of others is to be well prepared. When you know what you are going to say, you can pay more attention to your audience, making eye contact and watching body language for signals about how well you are making your points. When you rehearse you can also become comfortable with any visual elements you will be using. Finally, rehearsing your speech is the only reliable way to find out how long it will take to deliver.

Practice your speech in front of others. If possible, go to the room where you will be speaking and ask a friend to sit in the back so you can learn how well you can be heard. You can also learn a great deal by videotaping your rehearsal and watching yourself as an audience member.

SPEAKING EFFECTIVELY

Talking is so much a part of our daily lives that we rarely think about our voices as instruments of communication unless we have some training in acting or public speaking. You can become better at speaking by becoming more aware of your delivery. Pay attention to your breathing as you practice your speech. When you breathe at your normal rate, you will not rush your speech. Plan where you will pause during your speech. Pauses allow you to take a sip of water and give your audience a chance to sum up mentally what you have said. And don't be afraid to repeat key points. Repetition is one of the easiest strategies for achieving emphasis.

Most of the time nervousness is invisible. You can feel nervous and still impress your audience as being calm and confident. If you make mistakes while speaking, know that the audience understands and will be forgiving.

Stage fright is normal; sometimes it can be helpful in raising the energy level of a presentation.

NONVERBAL COMMUNICATION

While you are speaking, you are also communicating with your presence. Stand up unless you are required to sit. Move around instead of standing behind the podium. Use gestures to emphasize main points, and only main points; if you gesture continually, you may appear nervous.

Maintaining eye contact is crucial. Begin your speech by looking at the people directly in front of you and then move your eyes around the room, looking to both sides. Attempting to look at each person during a speech may seem unnatural, but it is the best way to convince all the members of your audience that you are speaking directly to them.

TIPS For Effective Speeches

Usually more effective	Usually less effective
Practice in advance	Don't practice
Talk	Read
Stand	Sit
Make eye contact	Look down
Move around	Stand still
Speak loudly	Mumble
Use visual elements	Lack visual elements
Focus on main points	Get lost in details
Give an overview of what you are going to say in the introduction	Start your talk without indicating where you are headed
Give a conclusion that summarizes your main points and ends with a key idea or example	Stop abruptly
Finish on time	Run overtime

HANDLING QUESTIONS

Your presentation doesn't end when you finish. Speakers are usually expected to answer questions afterward. How you handle questions is also critical to your success. Speakers who are evasive or fail to acknowledge questions sometimes lose all the credibility they have built in their speech. But speakers who listen carefully to questions and answer them honestly build their credibility further.

Keep in mind a few principles about handling questions:

- Repeat the question so that the entire audience can hear it and to confirm you understood it.
- Take a minute to reflect on the question. If you do not understand the question, ask the questioner to restate it.
- Some people will make a small speech instead of asking a question. Acknowledge their point of view but avoid getting into a debate.
- If you cannot answer a question, don't bluff and don't apologize. You can offer to research the question or you can ask the audience if they know the answer.
- If you are asked a question during your speech, answer it if it is a short, factual question or one of clarification. Postpone questions that require long answers until the end to avoid losing the momentum of your speech.

Multimedia Presentations

VISUAL ELEMENTS

Visual elements can both support and reinforce your major points. They give you another means of reaching your audience and keeping them stimulated. Visual elements range from simple transparencies and handouts to elaborate multimedia presentations. Some of the easier visual elements to create are

- Outlines
- Text
- Statistical charts
- Flow charts

- Photographs
- Models
- Maps

At the very minimum, you should consider putting an outline of your talk on an overhead transparency. Some speakers think that they will kill interest in their talk if they show the audience what they are going to say in advance. Just the opposite is the case. An outline allows an audience to keep track of where you are in your talk. Outlines also help you to make transitions to your next point.

Most printers can make transparencies from blank transparency sheets fed through the paper feeder. Charts, maps, photographs, and other graphics in digital format can thus be printed onto transparencies. Many photocopiers can also make transparencies.

Keep the amount of text short. You don't want your audience straining to read long passages on the screen and neglecting what you have to say. Except for quotations, use single words and short phrases—not sentences—on transparencies and slides.

Readable Transparencies and Slides

If you put text on transparencies or slides, make sure that the audience can read the text from more than 10 feet away. You may depend on your transparencies and slides to convey important information, but if your audience cannot read the slides, not only will the information be lost but the audience will become frustrated.

Use these type sizes for transparencies and slides.

	Transparencies	Slides
Title:	36 pt	24 pt
Subtitles:	24 pt	18 pt
Other text:	18 pt	14 pt

Preview your transparencies and slides from a distance equal to the rear of the room where you will be speaking. If you cannot read them, increase the type size.

One major difficulty with visual elements is that they tempt you to look at the screen instead of at your audience. You have to face your audience while your audience is looking at the screen. Needless to say, you have to practice to feel comfortable.

PRESENTATION SOFTWARE

You likely have seen many presentations that use Microsoft PowerPoint because it has become a favorite of faculty who lecture. If you have Microsoft Word on your computer, you likely have PowerPoint since they are often bundled together. PowerPoint is straightforward to use, which is one of the reasons it has become so popular. You can quickly get an outline of your presentation onto slides, and if projection equipment is available in the room where you are speaking, the slides are easily displayed.

PowerPoint offers a choice of many backgrounds, which is a potential pitfall. Light text on a dark background is hard to read. It forces you to close every window and turn off all the lights in order for your audience to see the text. Darkened rooms create problems. You may have difficulty reading your notes in a dark room, and your audience may fall asleep. Instead, always use dark text on a white or light-colored background. Usually your audience can read your slides with a light background in a room with the shades up or lights on.

Usually you can leave a slide on the screen for about one to two minutes, which allows your audience time to read and connect the slide to what you are saying. You will need to practice to know when to display a new slide. Without adequate practice, you can easily get too far ahead or behind in your slide show and then be forced to interrupt yourself to get your slides back in synch with your speech. You also need to know how to darken the screen if you want the audience to focus on you during parts of your presentation.

Another pitfall of PowerPoint is getting carried away with all the special effects possible such as fade-ins, fade-outs, and sound effects. Presentations heavy on the special effects often come off as heavy on style and light on substance. They also can be time-consuming to produce.

CHAPTER 15

Effective Research

Research: Knowing What Information You Need

The writing that you do in school sometimes seems isolated from the real world. After all, when you write for a class, your real audience is usually the teacher. For the same reason, the research associated with writing for school tends to get isolated from real-world problems. Instead of asking questions such as how compounds that mimic estrogen might be causing reproductive abnormalities in certain animal species, students ask questions such as "What do I need to know to write this paper?" This approach tends to separate research from writing. If you've ever said to yourself, "I'll go to the library to do the research tonight, and then tomorrow afternoon I'll start writing the paper," you might be making some assumptions about the nature of research and writing that will actually make your task harder instead of easier. So for now, set aside what you already know about how to do research and think instead in terms of gathering information to solve problems and answer questions.

Effective research depends on two things: knowing what kind of information you are looking for and knowing where to get it. What you already know about writing arguments will help you to make some decisions about what kind of information you should be looking for. For instance, if you have decided to write a proposal for solving the problem of HMOs limiting subscribers' health care options, you already know that you will need to find statistics (to help your readers understand the urgency and scope of the problem) and several different analyses of the situation by writers from different camps (to help you make sure your own understanding of the situation is accurate, complete, and fair to all participants). But if you keep thinking about the demands of the proposal as a type of argument, you might also decide that you need to look at how this problem has been solved in the British or Canadian health system or how programs like Medicare and Medicaid are dealing with it.

Even if you don't yet know enough about your subject to know what type of argument you will want to write, there are still some basic questions you can use to plan your research. To make a thoughtful and mature contribution to any debate in the realm of public discourse, you will need to know the background of the issue. As you begin your research, then, you can use the following questions as a guide.

1. Who are the speakers on this issue and what are they saying?

Subdividing the group of everyone who has something to say on this issue and everything that is being said into narrower categories will help you to gain a better understanding of what the debate looks like. For example, you might make the following divisions:

- Who are the experts on this issue? What do the experts say?
- Who else is talking about it? What do they say?
- Are the people whose interests are most at stake participating in the debate? What are they saying?

In addition to the categories of experts, nonexpert speakers, and those whose interests are at stake, there are other general categories you can begin from, such as supporters and opponents of a position, liberals and conservatives, and so on.

Also remember that any given debate will have its own specific set of opponents. In a debate about constructing a storage facility for nuclear waste in Nevada, for instance, conservationists and proponents of growth in the state of Nevada are lining up against the federal government. On another significant issue—water usage—proponents of growth stand in opposition to conservationists, who object to the demands Las Vegas makes on the waters of the Colorado River. On yet other issues, conservationists depend on the federal government to use its power to protect land, water, and other resources that are vulnerable to the activities of businesses and individuals.

2. What is at stake?

Political debates often boil down to arguments about control of, or access to, resources or power. Therefore, resources and power are good places to start looking for what is at stake in any given debate. Depending on the nature of the debate, you might also look at what is at stake in terms of ethical and moral issues. For example, as a country and as a human community, what does this nation stand to lose if a whole generation of African-American urban young people grows up alienated from other people in the United States? To help narrow down your search, you might rephrase this question in several different ways:

- How or why does this issue matter: to the world, to the citizens of this country, to the people whose interests are at stake, to me?
- What stands to be gained or lost for any of these stakeholders?
- Who is likely to be helped and hurt the most?

3. What kinds of arguments are being made about this issue?

Just as it is helpful to subdivide the whole field of speakers on your issue into narrower groups that line up according to sides, it is also helpful to subdivide the whole field of what is being said according to types or categories of arguments. It might help to set up a chart of speakers and their primary arguments to see how they line up.

- What are the main claims being offered?
- What reasons are offered in support of these claims?
- What are the primary sources of evidence?
- Is some significant aspect of this issue being ignored or displaced in favor of others?
- If so, why?

4. Who are the audiences for this debate?

Sometimes, the audience for a debate is every responsible member of society, everyone living in a certain region, or everyone who cares about the fate of the human species on this planet. More often, however, arguments are made to specific types of audiences, and knowing something about those audiences can help you to understand the choices that the writers make. Even more important, knowing who is already part of the audience for a debate can help you to plan your own strategies.

- Do you want to write to one of the existing audiences to try to change its mind or make it take action?
- Or do you want to try to persuade a new, as-yet-uninvolved audience to get involved in the debate?
- How much do they know about the issues involved?
- Where do they likely stand on these issues?
- Will they define the issues the same way you do?

5. What is your role?

At some point, as you continue to research the issue and plan your writing strategies, you will need to decide what your role should be in this debate. Ask yourself:

- What do I think about it?
- What do I think should be done about it?
- What kind of argument should I write, and to whom?

What Makes a Good Subject for Research

- **Find a subject that you are interested in.** Research can be enjoyable if you are finding out new things rather than just confirming what you already know. The most exciting part of doing research is making small discoveries.

(continued)

What Makes a Good Subject for Research *(continued)*

- **Make sure that you can do a thorough job of research.** If you select a topic that is too broad, such as proposing how to end poverty, you will not be able to do an adequate job.

- **Develop a strategy for your research early on.** If you are researching a campus issue such as a parking problem, then you probably will rely most on interviews, observations, and possibly a survey. But if you find out that one of the earliest baseball stadiums, Lakefront Park in Chicago (built in 1883), had the equivalent of today's luxury boxes and you want to make an argument that the trend toward building stadiums with luxury boxes is not a new development, then you will have to do library research.

- **Give yourself enough time to do a thorough job.** You should expect to find a few dead ends, and you should expect to better focus your subject as you proceed. If you are going to do research in the field, by survey, or in the library, remember the first principle of doing research: *Things take longer than you think they will.*

Use these questions to take inventory of how much you already know about the issue and what you need to find out more about. When you have worked through these questions, you are ready to make a claim that will guide your research efforts. See the Steps in Writing exercises at the end of Chapters 5 through 10 to get started.

Planning Your Research

Once you have a general idea about the kind of information you need to make your argument, the next step is to decide where to look for it. People who write on the job—lawyers preparing briefs, journalists covering news stories, policy analysts preparing reports, engineers describing a manufacturing process, members of Congress reporting to committees, and a host of others—have general research strategies available to them. The first is to gather the information themselves, which is called **primary** or **firsthand evidence.** We can distinguish two basic kinds of primary research.

Experiential research involves all the information you gather just through observing and taking note of events as they occur in the real world. You meet with clients, interview a candidate, go to a committee meeting, talk to coworkers, read a report from a colleague, observe a manufacturing process, witness an event, or examine a patient. In all these ways, you are adding to your store of knowledge about a problem or issue. In many cases, however, the knowledge that is gained through experience is not enough to answer all the questions or solve all the problems. In that case, writers supplement experiential research with empirical research and research in the library.

Empirical research is a way of gathering specific and narrowly defined data by developing a test situation and then observing and recording events as they occur in the test situation. Analysis of tissue samples and cell cultures in a laboratory, for instance, can add important information to what a doctor can learn by examining a patient. Crash tests of cars help automakers and materials engineers understand why crumpling is an important part of a car's ability to protect its passengers in a crash. Surveys of adult children of divorced parents make it possible for psychologists to identify the long-term effects of divorce on family members. Many people believe that this kind of research is what adds new information to the store of human knowledge; so for many audiences, reporting the results of empirical research is an important part of making a strong argument. (Therefore, writers often use statistics and reports of research done by experts in the field to support their claims.)

For the most part, however, debates about public issues occur outside the fairly narrow intellectual spaces occupied by the true experts in any given field. Experts do, of course, participate in public debates, but so do all other interested citizens and policymakers. The majority of speakers on an issue rely on the work of others as sources of information—what is known as **secondary** or **secondhand evidence.** Many people think of library research as secondary research—the process of gathering information by reading what other people have written on a subject. In the past, library research was based almost exclusively on collections of printed materials housed in libraries; in addition to public and university libraries, organizations of all kinds had their own collections of reference materials specific to their work. Today, the Internet has brought significant changes in the way people record, store, view, distribute, and gain access to documents. For most issues, searching the Internet will be an important part of your library research.

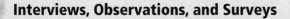

Interviews, Observations, and Surveys

Interviews

- Decide first why one or more interviews could be important for your argument. Knowing the goals of your interview will help you to determine whom you need to interview and to structure the questions in the interview. You might, for example, learn more about the history of a campus issue than you were able to find out in the campus newspaper archives.

- Schedule each interview in advance, preferably by email or letter. Let the person know why you are conducting the interview. Then follow up with a phone call to find out whether the person is willing and what he or she might be able to tell you.

- Plan your questions. You should have a few questions in mind as well as written down. Listen carefully so that you can follow up on key points.

- Come prepared with at least a notebook and pencil. If you use a tape recorder, be sure to get the person's permission in advance and be sure that the equipment is working.

Observations

- Make detailed observations that you can link to your claim. For example, if you believe that the long lines in your student services building are caused by inefficient use of staff, you could observe how many staff members are on duty at peak and slack times.

- Choose a place where you can observe without intrusion. Public places work best because you can sit for a long time without people wondering what you are doing.

- Carry a notebook and write extensive notes whenever you can. Write down as much as you can. Be sure to record where you were, the date, exactly when you arrived and left, and important details such as the number of people present.

(continued)

Interviews, Observations, and Surveys *(continued)*

Surveys

- Like interview questions, questions on surveys should relate directly to the issue of your argument. Take some time to decide what exactly you want to know first.

- Write a few specific, unambiguous questions. The people you contact should be able to fill out your survey quickly, and they should not have to guess what a question means. It's always a good idea to test the questions on a few people to find out whether they are clear before you conduct the survey.

- You might include one or two open-ended questions, such as "What do you like about X?" or "What don't you like about X?" Answers to these questions can be difficult to interpret, but sometimes they provide insights.

- Decide whom you want to participate in your survey and how you will contact them. If you are going to use your survey results to claim that the people surveyed represent the views of undergraduates at your school, then you should match the gender, ethnic, and racial balance to the proportions at your school.

- If you are going to mail or email your survey, include a statement about what the survey is for and how the results will be used.

- Interpreting your results should be straightforward if your questions require definite responses. Multiple-choice formats make data easy to tabulate, but they often miss key information. If you included one or more open-ended questions, you need to figure out a way to analyze responses.

Finding What You Are Looking for in Print Sources

Large libraries can be intimidating, even to experienced researchers when they begin working on a new subject. You can save time and frustration if you have some idea of how you want to proceed when you enter the library.

Libraries have two major kinds of sources: books and periodicals. Periodicals include a range of items from daily newspapers to scholarly journals that are bound and put on the shelves like books.

Most books are shelved according to the Library of Congress Classification System, which uses a combination of letters and numbers to give you the book's unique location in the library. The Library of Congress call number begins with a letter or letters that represent the broad subject area into which the book is classified. The Library of Congress system has the advantage of shelving books on the same subject together, so you can sometimes find additional books by browsing in the stacks. You can use the *Library of Congress Subject Headings*, available in print in your library's reference area or on the Web (http://lcweb.loc.gov), to help you find out how your subject might be indexed.

If you want to do research on cloning, you might type "cloning" in the subject index of your online card catalog, which would yield something like the following results:

1 Cloning—23 item(s)
2 Cloning—Bibliography.—1 item(s)
3 Cloning—Congresses.—2 item(s)
4 Cloning—Fiction.—6 item(s)
5 Cloning—Government policy—United States.—2 item(s)
6 Cloning—History.—1 item(s)
7 Cloning, Molecular—36 item(s) Indexed as: MOLECULAR CLONING
8 Cloning—Moral and ethical aspects.—13 item(s)
9 Cloning—Moral and ethical aspects—Government policy—United States.—1 item(s)
10 Cloning—Moral and ethical aspects—United States.—2 item(s)
11 Cloning—Religious aspects—Christianity.—2 item(s)
12 Cloning—Research—History.—1 item(s)
13 Cloning—Research—Law and legislation—United States.—1 item(s)
14 Cloning—Research—United States—Finance.—1 item(s)
15 Cloning—Social aspects.—1 item(s)
16 Cloning—United States—Religious aspects.—1 item(s)

This initial search helps you to identify more precisely what you are looking for. If you are most interested in the ethical aspects of cloning, then the books listed under number 8 would be most useful to you.

Finding articles in periodicals works much the same way. To find relevant newspaper and magazine articles, use a periodical index. These indexes are located in the reference area of your library. They may be in print form, on CD-ROM, or sometimes available on your library's Web site. General indexes that list citations to articles on popular and current topics include

> *ArticleFirst* (electronic)
>
> *CARL Uncover* (electronic)
>
> *Expanded Academic ASAP* (electronic)
>
> *InfoTrac* (electronic)
>
> *Lexis/Nexis* (electronic)
>
> *Readers' Guide to Periodical Literature* (print)
>
> *Periodical Abstracts* (electronic)
>
> *ProQuest* (electronic)

Some of these indexes contain the full text of articles, which you can print out. Others will give you a reference, which you then have to find in your library. In addition to these general periodical indexes, there are many specialized indexes that list citations to journal articles in various fields. Deciding which kind of articles you want to look for—scholarly, trade, or popular—will help you to select the right index.

Follow these steps to find articles:

1. Select an index that is appropriate to your subject.
2. Search the index using the relevant subject heading(s).
3. Print or copy the complete citation to the article(s).
4. Check the periodicals holdings to see whether your library has the journal.

Scholarly, Trade, and Popular Journals

Some indexes give citations for only one kind of journal. Others include more than one type. Although the difference between types of journals is not always obvious, you should be able to judge whether a journal is scholarly, trade, or popular by its characteristics.

Characteristics of Scholarly Journals

- Articles are long with few illustrations.
- Articles are written by scholars in the field, usually affiliated with a university or research center.
- Articles have footnotes or a works-cited list at the end.
- Articles usually report original research.
- Authors write in the language of their discipline, and readers are assumed to know a great deal about the field.
- Scholarly journals contain relatively few advertisements.

Examples: *American Journal of Mathematics, College English, JAMA: Journal of the American Medical Association, Plasma Physics*

Characteristics of Trade Journals

- Articles are frequently related to practical job concerns.
- Articles usually do not report original research.
- Articles usually do not have footnotes or have relatively few footnotes.

(continued)

Scholarly, Trade, and Popular Journals (continued)

- Items of interest to people in particular professions and job listings are typical features.

- Advertisements are aimed at people in the specific field.

Examples: *Advertising Age, Industry Week, Macworld, Teacher Magazine*

Characteristics of Popular Journals

- Articles are short and often illustrated with color photographs.

- Articles seldom have footnotes or acknowledge where their information came from.

- Authors are usually staff writers for the magazine or freelance writers.

- Advertisements are aimed at the general public.

- Copies can be bought at newsstands.

Examples: *Cosmopolitan, Newsweek, Sports Illustrated, GQ, People*

Finding What You Are Looking for in Electronic Sources

If you are familiar with searchable electronic databases like your library's cata-log, you might want to think of the Internet as just another database. How-ever, there are two significant differences between the Internet and your li-brary's catalog and other indexes you might have used in the library. The first difference, obviously, is that while catalogs and indexes of print material give you information *about* books, articles, and other resources, they don't usually contain the documents themselves. An Internet search, on the other hand, can give you direct access to sources that are available all over the world. In the early days of public access to the Internet, when Internet resources were very limited and not as useful as readily available print resources, the Internet was not very helpful in most areas of research. But as the Internet grows up, it is becoming accepted as a legitimate—and even essential—part of our ability to record and share knowledge.

The other significant difference between the Internet and other research databases is that while only "authorized personnel" can add entries to or delete them from a traditional database, anyone who has access to a server can create a Web site (add an entry), and anyone who has a Web site can shut it down (delete an entry) or move it to a different location. There are literally millions of Web sites (entries) in the Internet's giant database, and sites are being added, moved, and deleted every day. To navigate this global library, we have search engines, programs that are so fast and sophisticated that they can sort through the wealth of available material and return a list of sites that match your search request (called *hits*) within seconds if you have a fast connection.

KINDS OF SEARCH ENGINES

A search engine is a set of programs that sort through millions of items with incredible speed. There are four basic kinds of search engines.

1. **Keyword search engines** (e.g., AltaVista, Google, Hotbot, Lycos). Keyword search engines use both a **robot**, which moves through the Web capturing information about Web sites, and an **indexer**, which organizes the information found by the robot. Each keyword search engine gives different results because each assigns different weights to the information it finds. These search engines often use words in the title of a Web site or words in a meta tag to order the results they report.

2. **Web directories** (e.g., Britannica, Galaxy, LookSmart, WebCrawler, Yahoo!). Web directories classify Web sites into categories and are the closest equivalent to the cataloging system used by libraries. On most directories professional editors decide how to index a particular Web site. Web directories also allow keyword searches.

3. **Metasearch agents** (e.g., Dogpile, Mamma, Metacrawler, ProFusion, SavvySearch). Metasearch agents allow you to use several search engines simultaneously. While the concept is sound, metasearch agents are limited by the number of hits they can return and their inability to handle advanced searches.

4. **Natural language search engines** (e.g., Ask Jeeves). Natural or real language search engines allow you to search by asking questions such as "Where can I find a recipe for pound cake?" Natural language search engines are still in their infancy, and no doubt they will become much more powerful in the future.

Search Engines

If you don't have much experience with search engines, try out a few different ones until you find one or two favorites, then learn how to use them well. Keyword search engines can be frustrating because they turn up so much, but you become better at using them with practice.

- To start your search, open your browser and select "Search." You may be offered a selection of Web navigators and search engines.

- To use a keyword search, enter a word, name, or phrase. Some search engines require quotation marks to indicate a phrase or full name. If you type Gwyneth Paltrow without quotation marks, you will get hits for all instances of Gwyneth and all instances of Paltrow.

(continued)

Search Engines *(continued)*

- When you want the search to retrieve any form of a word, for example both child and children, you can use "child*" to get both terms. The asterisk is sometimes referred to as a wild card.

- Most search engines will retrieve only exact matches to the terms you use in your search request. Try all the variations you can think of if you want to do a thorough search.

- Some search engines use a plus sign (+) to indicate that a term is required (as in "+ADHD +children") and a minus sign (–) to indicate that sites containing that term should not be included. For example, "+ADHD –children" will exclude sites on ADHD that mention children. Other search engines use AND, OR, and NOT in capital letters. The pluses, minuses, ANDs, ORs, and NOTs, are called Boolean operators.

- Use the search tips or help button on a search engine for particular advice.

Evaluating Sources

Not only is the volume of information on the Web overwhelming, but the quality varies a great deal too. No one polices the Web; therefore a great deal of misinformation is posted.

The reliability and relevance of sources are not new problems with the Web. Print sources also contain their share of biased, inaccurate, and misleading information. Other print sources may be accurate but not suited to the purpose of your project. A critical review can help you to sort through the sources you have gathered. Even though print and Internet sources differ in many ways, some basic principles of evaluation can be applied to both.

TRADITIONAL CRITERIA FOR EVALUATING PRINT SOURCES

Over the years librarians have developed criteria for evaluating print sources.

1. *Source.* Who printed the book or article? Scholarly books that are published by university presses and articles in scholarly journals are assessed by

experts in the field before they are published. Because of this strict review process, they contain generally reliable information. But since the review process takes time, scholarly books and articles are not the most current sources. For people outside the field, they also have the disadvantage of being written for other experts. Serious trade books and journals are also generally reliable, though magazines devoted to politics often have an obvious bias. Popular magazines and books vary in quality. Often, they are purchased for their entertainment value, and they tend to emphasize what is sensational or entertaining at the expense of accuracy and comprehensiveness. Many magazines and books are published to represent the viewpoint of a particular group or company, so that bias should be taken into account. Newspapers also vary in quality. National newspapers, such as the *New York Times, Washington Post,* and *Los Angeles Times,* employ fact checkers and do a thorough editorial review and thus tend to be more reliable than newspapers that lack such resources.

2. **Author.** Who wrote the book or article? Is the author's name mentioned? Are the author's qualifications listed?

3. **Timeliness.** How current is the source? Obviously, if you are researching a fast-developing subject such as cloning, then currency is very important. But if you are interested in an issue that happened years ago, then currency might not be as important.

4. **Evidence.** How adequate is the evidence to support the author's claims? Where does the evidence come from—interviews, observations, surveys, experiments, expert testimony, or counterarguments? Does the author acknowledge any other ways in which the evidence might be interpreted?

5. **Biases.** Can you detect particular biases of the author? Is the author forthright about his or her biases? How do the author's biases affect the interpretation that is offered?

6. **Advertising.** Is the advertising prominent in the journal or newspaper? Is there any way that ads might affect what gets printed? For example, some magazines that ran many tobacco ads refused to run stories about the dangers of smoking.

Traditional print criteria can be helpful in evaluating some Internet sources. For example, if you evaluate messages sent to a Usenet newsgroup, most do not list the qualifications of the author or offer any support for the validity of evidence. Sources on the Web, however, present other difficulties. Some of these are inherent in the structure of the Web, with its capability for linking to other pages. When you are at a site that contains many links, you often find that some links go to pages on the same site but others take you off the site. You have to pay attention to the URLs to know where you are in relation to where you started. Furthermore, when you find a Web page using a search engine, often you go deep into a complex site without having any sense of the context of that page. You might have to spend thirty minutes or more just to get some idea of what is on the overall site. Another difficulty of doing research on the Web is that you are limited by the equipment you are using and the speed of your connection.

ADDITIONAL CRITERIA FOR EVALUATING WEB SOURCES

Traditional criteria for evaluating print sources remain useful for evaluating sources on the Web, but you should keep in mind how the Web can be different.

1. *Source.* If a Web site indicates what organization or individual is responsible for the information found on it, then you can apply the traditional criteria for evaluating print sources. For example, most major newspapers maintain Web sites where you can read some of the articles that appear in print. If a Web site doesn't indicate ownership, then you have to make judgments about who put it up and why. Documents are easy to copy and put up on the Web, but they are also very easily quoted out of context or altered. For example, you might find something that is represented as an "official" government document that is in fact a fabrication.

2. *Author.* Often, it is difficult to know who put up a particular Web site. Even when an author's name is present, in most cases the author's qualifications are not listed.

3. *Timeliness.* Many Web pages do not list when they were last updated; therefore, you do not know how current they are. Furthermore, there are thousands of ghost sites on the Web—sites that the owners have abandoned but have not bothered to remove. You can stumble onto these old sites and not realize that the organization might have a more current site elsewhere. Also, many Web site maintainers do not update their links, and when you start clicking, you get many error messages.

4. *Evidence.* The accuracy of any evidence found on the Web is often hard to verify. There are no editors or fact checkers guarding against mistakes or misinformation. The most reliable information on the Web stands up to the tests of print evaluation, with clear indication of an edited source, credentials of the author, references for works cited, and dates of publication.

5. ***Biases.*** Many Web sites are little more than virtual soapboxes. Someone who has an ax to grind can potentially tell millions of people why he or she is angry. Other sites are equally biased but conceal their attitude with a reasonable tone and seemingly factual evidence such as statistics.

6. ***Advertising.*** Many Web sites are "infomercials" of one sort or another. While they can provide useful information about specific products or services, the reason the information was placed on the Web is to get you to buy the product or service. Advertising on the Web costs a fraction of broadcast ads, so it's no wonder that advertisers have flocked to the Web.

Taking Notes

Before personal computers became widely available, most library research projects involved taking notes on notecards. This method was cumbersome, but it had some big advantages. You could spread out the notecards on a table or pin them to a bulletin board and get an overview of how the information that you gathered might be connected. Today, many people make notes in computer files. If you make notes in a computer file, then you don't have to retype when you write your paper. For example, if you copy a direct quote and decide to use it, you can cut and paste it. It is, of course, possible to print all your notes from your computer and then spread them out, or you can even paste your notes on cards, which will let you enjoy the best of both systems. Whatever way works best for you, there are a few things to keep in mind.

Make sure you get the full bibliographic information when you make notes. For books, you should get the author's name, title of the book, place of publication, publisher, and date of publication. This information is on the front and back of the title page. For journals, you need the author's name, title of the article, title of the journal, issue of the journal, date of the issue, and page numbers. For Web sites, you need the name of the page, the author if listed, the sponsoring organization if listed, the date the site was posted, the date you visited, and the complete URL.

Make photocopies of sources you plan to use in your paper. Photocopies save you the time of copying and lessen the chances you'll make mistakes. If you do take notes, be sure to indicate which words are the author's and which words are yours. It's easy to forget later. If you're using electronic sources, then print the sources you plan to use. Attach the bibliographic information to photocopies and printouts so that you won't get mixed up about where the source came from.

Finally, know when to say you have enough information. Many topics can be researched for a lifetime. It's not just the quantity of sources that counts. You should have enough diversity that you are confident you know the major points of view on a particular issue. When you reach a possible stopping point, group your notes and see whether a tentative organization for your paper becomes evident. People who like to work with notecards sometimes write comment cards to attach to each card, indicating how that piece of information fits. People who work with computer files sometimes type in caps how they see their notes fitting together. The method doesn't matter as much as the result. You should have a sketch outline by the time you finish the information-gathering stage.

CHAPTER 16

MLA Documentation

Intellectual Property and Scholastic Honesty

Hasbro had the hit toy of the holidays in 1998 with Furby, but if Furby reminded you of Gizmo, the cuddly creature in the Warner Bros. movies *Gremlins* and *Gremlins 2: The New Batch*, you weren't alone. The executives at Warner Bros. also noticed the similarities, and reportedly, Hasbro paid Warner Bros. a large out-of-court settlement for recasting the image of Gizmo. The flap over Furby is but one of many instances of the complex issues surrounding the concept of intellectual property. Copyright laws were established in the 1700s to protect the financial interests of publishers and authors, but over the last century, the domain of intellectual property has spread to music scores and lyrics, recordings, photographs, films, radio and television broadcasts, computer software, and, as the Furby example illustrates, all sorts of other likenesses. During the past decade, the legal battles over intellectual property rights have involved the Internet, which eventually will have major consequences for how much information will be freely available on the World Wide Web.

However, intellectual property rights are not the main reason that college writing requires strict standards of documentation. Writing at the college level follows a long tradition of scholarly writing that insists on accuracy in referencing other work so that a reader can consult a writer's sources. Often, scholarly arguments build on the work of others, and experiments almost always identify an area that other researchers have addressed. Sometimes, other pieces of writing are the primary data, as when a historian uses letters and public documents to construct what happened in the past. It is important for other historians to be able to review the same documents to confirm or reject a particular interpretation.

There is also a basic issue of fairness in recognizing the work of others. If you find an idea in someone else's work that you want to use, it seems only fair to give that person proper credit. In Chapter 6, we discuss Robert H. Frank and Phillip J. Cook's controversial argument that changes in attitudes help to account for the increasing divide between rich and poor people since 1973, a shift that they summarize as the winner-take-all society. The phrase "winner-take-all society" has become common enough that you might hear it in news features describing the contemporary United States, but certainly any extended treatment of the concept should acknowledge Frank and Cook for coming up with the idea. Many students now acknowledge the work of other students if they feel that their classmates have made an important contribution to their work. And why not? It's only fair.

In our culture in general and in the professions in particular, work that people claim is their own is expected to be their own. Imagine that you are the director of marketing at a company that paid a consulting firm to conduct a survey, only to find out that the work the firm presented to you had been copied from another survey. Wouldn't you be on the phone right away to your company's attorneys? Even though the unethical copying of the survey might have been the failure of only one employee, surely the reputation of the consulting firm would be damaged, if not ruined. Many noteworthy people in political and public life have been greatly embarrassed by instances of plagiarism; in some cases, people have lost their positions as a result. Short of committing a felony, plagiarism is one of the few things that can get you expelled from your college or university if the case is serious enough. So it's worth it to you to know what plagiarism is and isn't.

AVOIDING PLAGIARISM

Stated most simply, you plagiarize when you use the words or ideas of someone else without acknowledging the source. That definition seems easy enough, but when you think about it, how many new ideas are there? And how could you possibly acknowledge where all your ideas came from? In practical terms, you are not expected to acknowledge everything. You do not have to acknowledge what is considered general knowledge, such as facts that you could find in a variety of reference books. For example, if you wanted to assert that Lyndon Johnson's victory over Barry Goldwater in the 1964 presidential election remains the largest popular vote percentage (61 percent) in presidential election history, you would not have to acknowledge the source. This information should be available in encyclopedias, almanacs, and other general sources.

But if you cite a more obscure fact that wouldn't be as readily verifiable, you should let your readers know where you found it. Likewise, you should acknowledge the sources of any arguable statements, claims, or judgments. The sources of statistics, research findings, examples, graphs, charts, and illustrations also should be acknowledged. People are especially skeptical about statistics and research findings if the source is not mentioned. For example, if you argue that the Internet has led to even greater marginalization of the rural poor in the United States, you might include statistics that in 1995, the households of rural poor (incomes less than $10,000) had the lowest levels of computer penetration—only 4.5 percent—of any population group. By contrast, 7.6 percent of households of the poor in central cities had computers. Failing to give the source of these statistics could undercut your argument, but since these statistics are from the U.S. Department of Commerce ("Falling through the Net: A Survey of the 'Have Nots' in Rural and Urban America," Washington, DC: U.S. Department of Commerce, July 1995), the source adds credibility.

Where most people get into plagiarism trouble is when they take words directly and use them without quotation marks or else change a few words and pass them off as their own words. It is easiest to illustrate where the line is drawn with an example. Suppose you are writing an argument about attempts to censor the Internet, and you want to examine how successful other nations have been. You find the following paragraph about China:

> China is encouraging Net use for business, but not what it considers seditious or pornographic traffic and "spiritual pollution." So the state is building its communications infrastructure like a mammoth corporate system—robust within the country, but with three gateways to the world, in Beijing, Shanghai, and Shenzhen. International exchanges can then be monitored and foreign content "filtered" at each information chokepoint, courtesy of the Public Security Bureau.
>
> —Jim Erickson. "WWW.POLITICS.COM." *Asiaweek* 2 Oct. 1998: 42.

You want to mention the point about the gateways in your paper. You have two basic options: to paraphrase the source and to quote it directly.

If you quote directly, you must include all words you take from the original inside quotation marks:

> According to one observer, "China is encouraging Net use for business,
> but not what it considers seditious or pornographic traffic and 'spiritual
> pollution'" (Erickson 42).

This example is typical of MLA style. The citation goes outside the quotation marks but before the period. The reference is to the author's last name, which refers you to the full citation in the works-cited list at the end. Following the author's name is the page number where the quotation can be located. Notice also that if you quote material that contains quotation marks, then the double quotation marks change to the single quotation mark. If you include the author's name, then you need to cite only the page number:

> According to Jim Erickson, "China is encouraging Net use for business,
> but not what it considers seditious or pornographic traffic and 'spiritual
> pollution'" (42).

If an article appears on one page only, you do not need to include the page number:

> According to Jim Erickson, "China is encouraging Net use for business, but
> not what it considers seditious or pornographic traffic and 'spiritual
> pollution.'"

If the newspaper article did not include the author's name, you would include the first word or two of the title. The logic of this system is to enable you to find the reference in the works-cited list.

The alternative to quoting directly is to paraphrase. When you paraphrase, you change the words without changing the meaning. Here are two examples:

Plagiarized

China wants its citizens to use the Internet for business, but not for circulating views it doesn't like, pornography, and "spiritual pollution." So China is building its communications infrastructure like a mammoth corporate system—well linked internally but with only three ports to the outside world. The Public Security Bureau will monitor the foreign traffic at each information choke-point (Erickson).

This version is unacceptable. Too many of the words in the original are used directly here, including much of one sentence: "is building its communications infrastructure like a mammoth corporate system." If an entire string of words is lifted from a source and inserted without using quotation marks, then the passage is plagiarized. The first sentence is also too close in structure and wording to the original. Changing a few words in a sentence is not a paraphrase. Compare the following example:

Acceptable paraphrase

The Chinese government wants its citizens to take advantage of the Internet for commerce while not allowing foreign political ideas and foreign values to challenge its authority. Consequently, the Chinese Internet will have only three ports to the outside world. Traffic through these ports will be monitored and censored by the Public Security Bureau (Erickson).

There are a few words from the original in this paraphrase, such as *foreign* and *monitored*, but these sentences are original in structure and wording while accurately conveying the meaning of the original.

USING SOURCES EFFECTIVELY

The purpose of using sources is to *support* your argument, not to make your argument for you. Next to plagiarism, the worst mistake you can make with sources is stringing them together without building an argument of your own. Your sources help to show that you've done your homework and that you've thought in depth about the issue.

One choice you have to make when using sources is when to quote and when to paraphrase. Consider the following example about expressways:

Urban planners of the 1960s saw superhighways as the means to prevent inner cities from continuing to decay. Inner-city blight was recognized as early as the 1930s, and the problem was understood for four decades as one of circulation (hence expressways were called "arterials"). The planners argued that those who had moved to the suburbs would return to the city on expressways. By the end of the 1960s, the engineers were tearing down thousands of units of urban housing and small businesses to build expressways with a logic that was similar to the logic of mass bombing in Vietnam—to destroy the city was to save it (Patton 102). Shortly the effects were all too evident. Old neighborhoods were ripped apart, the flight to the suburbs continued, and the decline of inner cities accelerated rather than abated.

Not everyone in the 1950s and 1960s saw expressways as the answer to urban dilapidation. Lewis Mumford in 1958 challenged the circulation metaphor. He wrote: "Highway planners have yet to realize that these arteries must not be thrust into the delicate tissue of our cities; the blood they circulate must rather enter through an elaborate network of minor blood vessels and capillaries" (236). Mumford saw that new expressways produced more congestion and aggravated the problem they were designed to overcome, thus creating demand for still more expressways. If road building through cities were allowed to continue, he predicted the result would be "a tomb of concrete roads and ramps covering the dead corpse of a city" (238).

Notice that two sources are cited: Phil Patton, *Open Road: A Celebration of the American Highway*. New York: Simon & Schuster, 1986; and Lewis Mumford, "The Highway and the City," *The Highway and the City*. New York: Harcourt, Brace, 1963. 234-46.

The writer decided that the point from Patton about tearing down thousands of units of urban housing and small businesses to build expressways in the 1960s should be paraphrased but Mumford's remarks should be quoted directly. In both direct quotations from Mumford, the original wording is important. Mumford rejects the metaphor of arteries for expressways and foresees the future of cities as paved-over tombs in vivid language. As a general rule, you should use direct quotations only when the original language is important. Otherwise, you should paraphrase.

If a direct quotation runs more than four lines, then it should be indented one inch and double-spaced. But you still should integrate long quotations into the text of your paper. Long quotations should be attributed; that is, you should say where the quotation comes from in your text as well as in the reference. And it is a good idea to include at least a sentence or two after the quotation to describe its significance for your argument. The original wording in the long quotation in the following paragraph is important because it gives a sense of the language of the Port Huron Statement. The sentences following the quotation explain why many faculty members in the

1960s looked on the Port Huron Statement as a positive sign (of course, college administrators were horrified). You might think of this strategy as putting an extended quotation in an envelope with your words before and after:

> Critiques of the staleness and conformity of American education made the first expressions of student radicalism in the 1960s such as the "Port Huron Statement" from the Students for a Democratic Society (SDS) in 1962 appear as a breath of fresh air. The SDS wrote:
>
>> Almost no students value activity as a citizen. Passive in public, they are hardly more idealistic in arranging their private lives; Gallup concludes they will settle for "low success, and won't risk high failure." There is not much willingness to take risks (not even in business), no setting of dangerous goals, no real conception of personal identity except one manufactured in the image of others, no real urge for personal fulfillment except to be almost as successful as the very successful people. Attention is being paid to social status (the quality of shirt collars, meeting people, getting wives or husbands, making solid contacts for later on); much, too, is paid to academic status (grades, honors, the med-school rat race). But neglected generally is real intellectual status, the personal cultivation of mind. (238)
>
> Many professors shared the SDS disdain for the political quietism on college campuses. When large-scale ferment erupted among students during the years of the Vietnam War, some faculty welcomed it as a sign of finally emerging from the intellectual stagnation of the Eisenhower years. For some it was a sign that the promise of John F. Kennedy's administration could be fulfilled, that young people could create a new national identity.

Note three points about form in the long quotation. First, there are no quotation marks around the extended quotation. Readers know that the material is quoted because it is blocked off. Second, words quoted in the original retain the double quotation marks. Third, the page number appears after the period at the end of the quotation.

Whether long or short, make all quotations part of the fabric of your paper while being careful to indicate which words belong to the original. A reader should be able to move through the body of your paper without having to stop and ask: Why did the writer include this quotation? or Which words are the writer's and which are being quoted?

MLA Works-Cited List

Different disciplines use different styles for documentation. The two styles that are used most frequently are the APA style and the MLA style. APA stands for American Psychological Association, which publishes a style manual used widely in the social sciences (see Chapter 17). MLA stands for the Modern Language Association, and its style is the norm for humanities disciplines, including English and rhetoric and composition.

Both MLA and APA styles use a works-cited list placed at the end of a paper. Here is an example of an MLA works-cited list:

Center "Works Cited."

Double-space all entries. Indent all but the first line five spaces.

Alphabetize entries by last name of authors or by title if no author is listed.

Underline the titles of books and periodicals.

Works Cited

Bingham, Janet. "Kids Become Masters of Electronic
    Universe: School Internet Activity Abounds." Denver
    Post 3 Sept. 1996, sec. A: 13.

Dyrli, Odvard Egil, and Daniel E. Kinnaman.
    "Telecommunications: Gaining Access to the World."
    Technology and Learning 16.3 (Nov. 1995): 79-84.

Ellsworth, Jill H. Education on the Internet: A Hands-On
    Book of Ideas, Resources, Projects, and Advice.
    Indianapolis: Sams, 1994.

Engardio, Pete. "Microsoft's Long March." Business Week 24
    June 1996: 52-54.

National Center for Education Statistics. "Internet Access
    in Public Education." Feb. 1998. NCES. 4 Jan. 1999
    <http://nces.ed.gov/pubs98/98021.html>.

"UK: A Battle for Young Hearts and Minds." Computer
    Weekly 4 Apr. 1996: 20.

The works-cited list eliminates the need for footnotes. If you have your sources listed on notecards, then all you have to do when you finish your paper is to find the cards for all the sources that you cite, alphabetize the cards, and type your works-cited list. For works with no author listed, alphabetize by the first content word in the title (ignore *a*, *an*, and *the*).

Some of the more common citation formats in MLA style are listed in the following section. If you have questions that these examples do not address, you should consult the *MLA Handbook for Writers of Research Papers* (5th edition, 1999) and the *MLA Style Manual and Guide to Scholarly Publishing* (2nd edition, 1998).

CITING BOOKS

The basic format for listing books in the works-cited list is the author's name (last name first), the title (underlined), the place of publication, the short name of publisher, and the date of publication. You will find the exact title on the title page (not on the cover), the publisher, and the city (use the first city if several are listed). The date of publication is included in the copyright notice on the back of the title page.

Book by One Author

Ellsworth, Jill H. Education on the Internet: A Hands-On Book of

    Ideas, Resources, Projects, and Advice. Indianapolis: Sams,

    1994.

Book by Two or More Authors

Sturken, Marita, and Lisa Cartwright. Practices of Looking: An Introduction

    to Visual Culture. New York: Oxford UP, 2001.

Two or More Books by the Same Author

Berger, John. About Looking. New York: Pantheon, 1980.

- - - . Ways of Seeing. New York: Viking, 1973.

Translation

Martin, Henri-Jean. The History and Power of Writing. Trans. Lydia G.

    Cochrane. Chicago: U of Chicago P, 1994.

Edited Book

Bizzell, Patricia, and Bruce Herzberg, eds. The Rhetorical Tradition:
Readings from Classical Times to the Present. Boston: Bedford,
1990.

One Volume of a Multivolume Work

Habermas, Jürgen. Lifeworld and System: A Critique of Functionalist
Reason. Trans. Thomas McCarthy. Boston: Beacon, 1987. Vol. 2 of
The Theory of Communicative Action. 2 vols. 1984-87.

Selection in an Anthology or Chapter in an Edited Collection

Merritt, Russell. "Nickelodeon Theaters, 1905-1914: Building an Audience
for the Movies." The American Film Industry. Rev. ed. Ed. Tino Balio.
Madison: U of Wisconsin P, 1985. 83-102.

Government Document

Malveaux, Julianne. "Changes in the Labor Market Status of Black Women."
A Report of the Study Group on Affirmative Action to the Committee
on Education and Labor. U.S. 100th Cong., 1st sess. H. Rept. 100-L.
Washington: GPO, 1987. 213-55.

Bible

Holy Bible. Revised Standard Version Containing the Old and New
Testaments. New York: Collins, 1973. [Note that "Bible" is not
underlined.]

CITING PERIODICALS

When citing periodicals, the necessary items to include are author's name
(last name first), the title of the article inside quotation marks, the title of the
journal or magazine (underlined), the volume number (for scholarly journals), the date, and page numbers. Many scholarly journals are printed to be
bound as one volume, usually by year, and the pagination is continuous for
that year. If, say, a scholarly journal is printed in four issues and the first issue
ends on page 278, then the second issue will begin with page 279. For jour-

nals that are continuously paginated, you do not need to include the issue number. Some scholarly journals, however, are paginated like magazines with each issue beginning on page 1. For journals paginated by issue, you should list the issue number along with the volume (e.g., for the first issue of volume 11, you would put "11.1" in the entry after the title of the journal).

Article in a Scholarly Journal—Continuous Pagination

Berlin, James A. "Rhetoric and Ideology in the Writing Class." College English
50 (1988): 477-94.

Article in a Scholarly Journal—Pagination by Issue

Kolby, Jerry. "The Top-Heavy Economy: Managerial Greed and Unproductive
Labor." Critical Sociology 15.3 (1988): 53-69.

Review

Chomsky, Noam. Rev. of Verbal Behavior, by B. F. Skinner. Language 35
(1959): 26-58.

Magazine Article

Engardio, Pete. "Microsoft's Long March." Business Week 24 June 1996:
52-54.

Newspaper Article

Bingham, Janet. "Kids Become Masters of Electronic Universe: School
Internet Activity Abounds." Denver Post 3 Sept. 1996, sec. A: 13.

Letter to the Editor

Luker, Ralph E. Letter. Chronicle of Higher Education 18 Dec. 1998, sec. B: 9.

Editorial

"An Open Process." Editorial. Wall Street Journal 30 Dec. 1998, sec. A: 10.

CITING ONLINE SOURCES

Online sources pose special difficulties for systems of citing sources. Many on-line sources change frequently. Sometimes you discover to your frustration that what you had found on a Web site the previous day has been altered or in some cases no longer exists. Furthermore, basic information such as who put up a Web site and when it was last changed are often absent. Many print sources have also been put on the Web, which raises another set of difficulties. The basic format for citing a generic Web site is author's name (last name first), the title of the document (in quotation marks), the title of the complete work or name of the journal (underlined), the date of Web publication or last update, the sponsoring organization, the date you visited, and the URL (enclosed in angle brackets).

Web Site

"Composite Image of the 1995 Antarctic Ozone Hole." United States
Environmental Protection Agency's Home Page 10 June 1998.
4 Jan. 1999 <http://www.epa.gov/docs/ozone/science/hole/
holecomp.html>.

Book on the Web

Rheingold, Howard. Tools for Thought: The People and Ideas of the
Next Computer Revolution. New York, 1985. 1996. Brainstorms.
4 Jan. 1999 <http://www.well.com/user/hlr/texts/
tftindex.html>.

Article in a Scholarly Journal on the Web

Browning, Tonya. "Embedded Visuals: Student Design in Web Spaces."
Kairos. 2.1 (1997). 4 Jan. 1999 <http://www.as.ttu.edu/kairos/2.1/
features/browning/index.html>.

Article in a Magazine on the Web

"Happy New Euro." Time Daily 30 Dec. 1998. 4 Jan. 1999
<http://cgi.pathfinder.com/time/daily/
0,2960,17455-101990101,00.html>.

Personal Web Site

Vitanza, Victor. Victor's Uncanny Web Site. 4 Jan. 1999
<http://www.uta.edu/english/V/Victor_.html>.

CD-ROM

Boyer, Paul, et al. The Enduring Vision, Interactive Edition. 1993 ed. CD-
  ROM. Lexington, MA: Heath, 1993.

CITING OTHER SOURCES

Interview

Williams, Errick Lynn. Telephone interview. 4 Jan. 1999.

Unpublished Dissertation

Rouzie, Albert. "At Play in the Fields of Writing: Play and Digital Literacy in
  a College-Level Computers and Writing Course." Diss. U of Texas at
  Austin, 1997.

Film

Saving Private Ryan. Dir. Stephen Spielberg. Perf. Tom Hanks, Matt Damon,
  Tom Sizemore. Paramount, 1998.

Television Program

"The Attitude." Dir. Allan Arkush, Daniel Attias, et al. Writ. David E. Kelley.
  Perf. Calista Flockhart, Courtney Thorne-Smith. Ally McBeal. Fox.
  WFXT, Boston. 3 Nov. 1997.

Recording

Glass, Phillip. "Low" Symphony. Point Music, 1973.

Speech

Khrushchev, Sergei. "Russia, Putin, and the War on Terrorism." National
  Press Club, Wasington. 6 Dec. 2001.

Sample Argument Paper Using Sources

The paper that follows, by Chris Thomas, is an example of a student argument that uses sources well and that documents those sources appropriately.

Chris Thomas

Professor Selzer

Eng. 15 Sect. 20

24 October 1998

Should Race Be a Qualification to Attend College?

An Examination of Affirmative Action

Imagine that you are an African American student like me and that it is your first day of classes at a prestigious university. As you make your rounds on campus, you become increasingly aware of the swift glances that you are receiving from some of your predominately white classmates. You assume that the looks are generated because you are among the few African American students around, but you soon learn that your assumptions were too shallow. A student that you begin to have a conversation with asks what you received on your SATs. You initially believe that this inquiry is just a piece of general freshman curiosity, but your classmate's line of questioning ends with the question, "Do you think that you got into school because of your race and affirmative action?" That leads you to feel resented by the classmate because of your presence in this university.

Believe it or not, thousands of African American students experience similar scenarios every year. These predicaments force African Americans to question their merit and sense of belonging and draw attention to the controversial issue of affirmative action and its relevance to college admissions. Let me explore both sides of the issue by clearly defining the policy, looking at its causes, assessing the facts, evaluating the policy, and examining conflicting ideas on what should be done in the future about affirmative action.

This page follows MLA recommendations for a student research paper that does not use a title page. If you have a title page, you need only your name and title on the first page.

With reference to college admission, the definition of affirmative action is relatively simple. In his book Preferential Policies: An International Perspective, Thomas Sowell states, "What is called 'affirmative action' in the United States is [. . .] [a] government-mandated preferential policy toward government-designated groups" (13). There is general understanding that affirmative action is a program that aims to overcome the effects of past discrimination by giving preferential treatment to ethnic minorities and women. Barbara R. Bergmann's In Defense of Affirmative Action confirms that "Affirmative Action planning and acting [are designed] to end the absence of certain kinds of people—those who belong to groups that have been subordinated or left out from certain jobs and schools. The term is usually applied to those plans that set forth goals, required since the early 1970s, for government contractors and universities receiving public funds" (7). The Equal Opportunities Act of 1972 set up a right to act on such plans. Bergmann goes on to state, "[affirmative action] is an insurance company taking steps to break its tradition of promoting only white men to executive positions." The program is also seen as a means to producing a diverse learning and working environment.

In the case of African Americans, affirmative action was created to compensate for a history of slavery and systemic racial discrimination. The program was initiated because American society had produced an atmosphere that was strictly conducive to white men's success and dominance. Affirmative action programs arose out of governmental and judicial decisions requiring efforts to remedy continuing discrimination based on sex and race (Ponterotto et al. 6). This program is an effort to "level the playing field" and to try to make it possible for African Americans to have an equal, fair, and just opportunity to succeed. One aim of the program is to help curb the negative stereotypes and stigmas that American society has bestowed upon African Americans. The ultimate goal of such programs is to enable these individuals, through educational and vocational achievement, to have greater access to socioeconomic opportunity and stability (Ponterotto et al. 6). (For a full account of the history and intent of affirmative action, I recommend Affirmative Action on Campus by Joseph G. Ponterotto et al.)

How does affirmative action work with reference to college admission? It is understood that preferential treatment in some respects is given to African American applicants. On college campuses, affirmative action's ideals are translated into combating sexism and racism and social acceptance of minority-group members (Ponterotto et al. 6). In Ending Affirmative Action, Terry Eastland notes, "[Supreme Court] Justice Powell said in his Bakke opinion [referring to the University of California v. Bakke affirmative action case], that a university has the First Amendment freedom to make judgments about its educational mission. This freedom includes the latitude to select a student body [which] can help promote the educational environment most conducive to 'speculation, experiment, and creation' in which all students, minorities and non-minorities alike, benefit" (77).

If it is understood that affirmative action is implemented to compensate for past discriminations of African Americans, then what's the problem? The debate lies not in the definition, causes, or goals of affirmative action in the college admission process, but in the contradictory evaluation policies that develop out of the process. Is affirmative action a good, bad, or fair program that should be used to assist African Americans in the college admission process? There are opposing arguments on this issue; there are those who believe that it is a just and necessary program and those who strongly oppose the issue. The components of the issue that have caused the greatest controversy are the qualifications of the African American applicants, the aims of the program, and the progression of the program.

Thomas   4

Shouldn't the most qualified applicants to a university receive top priority in admissions? "The answers to such a question require a critical examination of just what is meant by 'best qualified,'" states Norman Matloff in "Toward Sensible Affirmative Action Policies." Consider the question of admissions policy for any famous university, with many more applicants than open slots. Let us ask whether, say, applicants with higher SAT scores should get automatic priority in admissions over those with lower scores (Matloff 1). It goes without saying that "test scores alone [are] not the way to determine admission," according to John Furedy, professor of psychology at the University of Toronto (qtd. in Saha 1); standardized test scores are not perfect measurement tools, and thus they should not be overapplied in admissions decisions. Yet for most students, test scores will at least reliably predict whether the student's academic skills are "in the league with" those of typical students at the given school. In "Why Not a Lottery to Get into UC?" Norman Matloff affirms that "first one must keep in mind that neither SAT scores nor any other numeric measure will be a very accurate predictor of future grades. It thus makes no sense to admit one applicant over another simply because the first applicant had higher test scores." Even the staunchest supporters of standardized tests seem to agree "that the scores reflect only a small part of the factors that predict freshman grades, and far less of what it takes to graduate from college" (Lederman A36).

Supporters of affirmative action believe that an overemphasis shouldn't be placed solely on SAT scores. They believe that "you need to understand the degree to which race, gender, and religion affect that person. You need to look at that person as a whole," notes Earl Lewis, interim dean of the graduate school at the University of Michigan (qtd. in Saha 2), and family and collegiate background of the applicant should be taken into consideration. Supporters agree that academic strength should be the most important component of college admissions, but they also believe that an applicant's family background also influences the probability that a person will succeed in college. It is widely understood that students with parents or family members that attended college have a better chance at college success than those without such a history. Supporters of affirmative action also argue that past societal limitations have restricted African American students from colleges, thus producing a situation in which relatively few African Americans have a history of attending college to pass on to their children. Moreover, past discrimination has created a college environment for African Americans that isn't as conducive to college pursuits as white applicants. Supporters argue that affirmative action will help to gradually increase the number of African American family members that attend college. Supporters also believe that admissions should look at the well-roundedness of the applicant. They should look at situations such as the applicant's involvement in school, his or her living environment, and possible required work experiences which would account for not so stellar grades.

On the other hand, opponents of affirmative action say that the preferential aspects of the program overlook academically qualified white students. Opponents believe that preferential treatment should be given to those of strong academic caliber, not to those of a particular race, and they see admissions decisions as central to maintaining high institutional standards. "The students who are denied at Berkeley will move down one notch," says David Murray; "we must not throw out the thermometer [of test scores] because we don't like the temperature it's taking" (qtd. in Lederman A37). As this quotation indicates, critics of affirmative action have a high regard for test scores: "Much of the discussion presumes that the tests are a very profound measure of academic preparation, and can really predict how well people do in college," notes Claude Steele, a psychology professor at Stanford University (qtd. in Lederman A37).

Another element of debate is the actual goals of affirmative action in college admissions. Supporters contend that the main goal of the program is to "level the playing field" in all aspects of society by giving qualified African American applicants the opportunity to attend college. The supporters argue that giving this preferential treatment to African Americans will provide minorities the opportunity "to defy the pernicious stereotypes and stigmas cast upon them by others"—for example, that African Americans are lazy, unsuccessful, and are strictly drug and sex driven (Lewis 2). Upholders of affirmative action argue that "the whole point of employing racial preferences in admissions is to change the composition of the student body—to bring more members of 'favored' groups into the institution," thus diversifying the college atmosphere (Thernstrom 36).

While opponents of affirmative action in college admission often concede that the program has been needed as an aid to stop past discrimination, they strongly believe that now "a dual system of criteria, based solely on race, strikes most Americans of all races as offensive" (Maguire 52). They vehemently argue that affirmative action is "reverse discrimination." They believe that affirmative action is "the 'ignorant' way of fighting discrimination. There is one simple rule to fight discrimination: do not discriminate," notes Furedy (qtd. in Saha 2). They affirm that one cannot fight discrimination with reverse discrimination targeted toward white Americans.

Opponents also claim that the supposed beneficiaries of the program, African Americans, in fact get hurt the most by negative effects of affirmative action. Clint Bolick, for instance, in The Affirmative Action Fraud, states that "preference policies may do their beneficiaries more harm than good. Race-based diminution of admissions standards inevitably causes a mismatch between students' abilities and the demands of the school" (79). Eastland too concedes that "being treated differently in order to be treated equally—a 'benign' act, according to advocates of affirmative action—has had its costs" (72), which can be described as a general idea that African Americans' degrees will have a low value. Furedy observes that this degree-devaluing of African Americans is possible because "people who are accepted [to college with the help of affirmative action] have a smear attached to them; it will be assumed that they were accepted not for their merit, but for their race" (qtd. in Saha 1), that they were able to obtain it because of their race, not because of their academic abilities. It will also lead African American students to question their sense of belonging. Opponents state that if standards for admission are lowered when considering the admission of African American students, then these programs will "distort what is now a level playing field and bestow preferential treatment on undeserving minorities because of their skin" (Lewis 1).

There is, then, much debate over the evaluation of affirmative action and its link to college admission of African Americans. Both supporters and opponents have strong arguments on the issue. Both sides state why the program is good or bad and have an arguable and justifiable argument for their beliefs. Where, then, should we go from here?

Supporters believe that affirmative action in college admission of African Americans should continue to be practiced. Syndicated columnist William Raspberry states that he has thoroughly interviewed "two eminent American educators [who] have taken a good hard look at affirmative action in college admissions, and their conclusion is that by virtually any reasonable measure, affirmative action works." Advocates believe that affirmative action is still needed because "without the deconstruction of white power and privilege, how can we legitimately claim that the playing field is level" (Lewis 22), even if African Americans

Thomas   8

are no longer discriminated against and suppressed to quite the extent
that they once were. In the words of Kerry Colligan, "you need to talk
about the debt this country has to pay. You cannot negate 300 years of
slavery and 100 years of oppression" (2).

On the other hand, opponents believe that the affirmative action
policies college admissions follow should be curbed because it is an
unfair act of "reverse discrimination" that causes racial tension from
resentful white Americans. Opponents believe that "[g]roups seen as
newly favored because of their race or ethnicity may become targets of
the majority's animosity, or they may be seen as needing special
treatment because of their supposed inferiority" (Ponterotto et al. 6).
They suggest that the program be made unconstitutional because it
violates both the 14th Amendment, which guarantees equal protection
under the law, and Title VI of the 1964 Civil Rights Act, which forbids
discrimination in programs receiving federal financial aid (Colligan 1).
Realizing that discrimination is still a problem, some opponents suggest
that "the focus should be on education in the K-12 sector in order to
prepare everyone equally well [. . .] for entrance exams" (Doyle 1).

Exactly where does this leave us? The critics that attack affirmative
action are correct when they say that affirmative action corrupts the
purity of the process. Extreme care must be taken in determining if
affirmative action in the admission of African Americans to college
should be practiced, for how long, and to what degree. While the policies
of affirmative action are not perfect and they do raise some legitimate
concerns, they take us away from a system that is inherently unfair to
some groups. "The active deconstruction of the white privilege that grew
out of virulent American racism affords African Americans a greater
chance at equal opportunity and will have the side effect of forcing us to
re-evaluate a society that unfairly disadvantages minorities" (Lewis 4).

The issue is more confusing if you consider that "affirmative action prefers individuals on the basis of their group membership, [not considering that] those minorities with academic credentials competitive with regularly admitted students may nonetheless be regarded with skepticism as affirmative action admittees" (Eastland 90). Therefore, further research on and evaluation of the issue is definitely needed to see if the progression or regression of the program's aims will uphold the aims of the respective arguing sides of the issue.

Thomas   10

Works Cited

Barr, Margaret J., et al. Affirmative Action on Campus. San Francisco:
Jossey-Bass, 1990.

Bergmann, Barbara R. In Defense of Affirmative Action. New York: Basic,
1996.

Bolick, Clint. The Affirmative Action Fraud. Washington: Cato Institute,
1996.

Colligan, Kerry. "Panelists Discuss History of Affirmative Action, Lawsuit."
The University Record 26 Nov. 1997. 14 Dec. 1998 <http://www.
umich.edu/~newinfo/U_Record/Issues97/Nov/afhist.htm>.

Doyle, Rebecca A. "Students Express Views on Racism, Discrimination."
The University Record 26 Nov. 1997. 14 Dec. 1998
<http://www.umich.edu/~newinfo/U_Record/Issues97/Nov/
afhist.htm>.

Eastland, Terry. Ending Affirmative Action: The Case for Colorblind
Justice. New York: Basic, 1996.

Kahlenberg, Richard D. The Remedy. New York: Basic, 1996.

Lederman, Douglas. "Persistent Racial Gap in SAT Scores Fuels
Affirmative Action Debate." The Chronicle of Higher Education 30
Oct. 1998: A36-38.

Lewis, Brian C. "An Ethical and Practical Defense of Affirmative Action."
1996. 18 Dec. 1998 <http://www.princeton.edu/~bclewis/action>.

Maguire, Timothy. "My Bout with Affirmative Action." Commentary 93
(April 1992): 50-52.

Matloff, Norman. "Why Not a Lottery to Get into UC?" Los Angeles Times
24 Jan. 1995, sec. B: 7.

---. "Toward Sensible Affirmative Action Policies." King Hall (UC Davis)
Law School Advocate Nov. 1994. 18 Dec. 1998
<http://www.heather.cs.ucdavis.edu/pub/AffirmativeAction/
Advocate>.

McWhirter, Darien A. The End of Affirmative Action. New York: Birch
Lane, 1996.

Ponterotto, Joseph G., et al. Affirmative Action on Campus. San Francisco:
Jossey-Bass, 1990.

Raspberry, William. "Despite the Myths, Affirmative Action Works."
Centre Daily Times 4 Oct. 1998: 9A.

Saha, Paula. "Panel Presents Perspectives on Diversity in Higher
Education." The University Record 26 Nov. 1997. 18 Dec. 1998
<http://www.umich.edu/~newinfo/U_Record/Issues97/Nov/
affac.htm>.

Sowell, Thomas. Preferential Policies: An International Perspective. New
York: Morrow, 1990.

Thernstrom, Stephan. "Farewell to Preferences." Public Interest 130
(1998): 34-49.

Zelnick, Bob. Backfire: A Reporter's Look at Affirmative Action.
Washington: Regner, 1996.

CHAPTER 17

APA Documentation

Disciplines in the social sciences (anthropology, government, linguistics, psychology, sociology) and in education most frequently use the APA (American Psychological Association) documentation style. This chapter offers a brief overview of the APA style. For a detailed treatment you should consult the *Publication Manual of the American Psychological Association*, fifth edition (2001).

The APA style has many similarities to the MLA style described in Chapter 16. Both styles use parenthetical references in the body of the text with complete bibliographical citations in the reference list at the end. The most important difference is the emphasis on the date of publication in the APA style. When you cite an author's name in the body of your paper with APA style, you always include the date of publication and the page number:

> By the end of the 1960s, the engineers were tearing down thousands of units of urban housing and small businesses to build expressways with a logic that was similar to the logic of mass bombing in Vietnam—to destroy the city was to save it (Patton, 1986, p. 102). Shortly the effects were all too evident. Old neighborhoods were ripped apart, the flight to the suburbs continued, and the decline of inner cities accelerated rather than abated.

Not everyone in the 1950s and 1960s saw expressways as the answer to urban dilapidation. Mumford (1958) challenged the circulation metaphor: "Highway planners have yet to realize that these arteries must not be thrust into the delicate tissue of our cites; the blood they circulate must rather enter through an elaborate network of minor blood vessels and capillaries" (p. 236).

Notice that unlike MLA, a comma is placed after the author's name and the abbreviation for page is included (Patton, 1986, p. 102).

 ## APA Reference List

The APA list of works cited is titled *References*:

Center "References"	References
Double-space all entries. Indent all but first line five spaces.	Bingham, J. (1996, September 3). Kids become masters of electronic universe: School Internet activity abounds. *Denver Post*, p. A13.
Alphabetize entries by last name of authors or by title if no author is listed.	Dyrli, O. E., & Kinnaman, D. E.. (1995). Telecommunications: Gaining access to the world. *Technology and Learning*, 16(3), 79-84.
Notice that author's initials are listed rather than first names.	Engardio, P. (1996, June 24). Microsoft's long march. *Business Week*, 52-54.
Notice that only the first words and proper nouns are capitalized in titles of articles and books.	The future just happened. (2001, July 29). *BBC Online*. Retrieved August 29, 2001, from http://news.bbc.co.uk/hi/english/static/in_depth/programmes/2001/future/tv_series_1.stm
Notice that article titles are not placed inside quotation marks.	Lewis, M. (1989). *Liar's poker: Rising through the wreckage on Wall Street*. New York: Norton.
Italicize the titles of books and periodicals.	Lewis, M. (2000). *The next new thing: A Silicon Valley story*. New York: Norton.
When there are two authors, alphabetize by the last name of the first author. Use an ampersand (&) before the second author's name.	Lewis, M. (2001). Next: *The future just happened*. New York: Norton.

National Center for Education Statistics. (1998, February). Internet Access in Public Education. Retrieved May 21, 1998, from http://nces.ed.gov/pubs98/98021.html

UK: A battle for young hearts and minds. (1996, April 4). *Computer Weekly*, 20.

When there are three or more authors, alphabetize by the last name of the first author. Use commas to separate the names and an ampersand (&) before the final name.

If an author has more than one entry, put the earliest publication first.

The reference list eliminates the need for footnotes. If you have your sources listed on notecards, all you have to do when you finish your paper is find the cards for all the sources that you cite, alphabetize the cards, and type your reference list. For works with no author listed, alphabetize by the first significant word in the title (ignore *a*, *an*, and *the*).

CITING BOOKS

The basic format for listing books in the reference list is

1. Author's name (last name first, initials)
2. Year of publication (in parentheses)
3. Title (in italics)
4. Place of publication
5. Name of publisher

Use the abbreviation for pages (pp.) for chapters in a book.

Book by One Author

Ellsworth, J. H. (1994). *Education on the Internet: A hands-on book of ideas, resources, projects, and advice.* Indianapolis, IN: Sams.

Book by Two or More Authors

Scribner, S., & Cole, M. (1981). *The psychology of literacy.* Cambridge, MA: Harvard University Press.

Translation

Martin, H.-J. (1994). *The history and power of writing* (L. G. Cochrane, Trans.). Chicago: University of Chicago Press.

Edited Book

Bizzell, P., & Herzberg, B. (Eds.). (1990). *The rhetorical tradition: Readings from classical times to the present.* Boston: Bedford.

One Volume of a Multivolume Work

de Selincourt, E., & Darbishire, H. (Eds.). (1958). *The poetical works of William Wordsworth* (Vol. 5). Oxford, England: Oxford University Press.

Selection in an Anthology or Chapter in an Edited Collection

Merritt, R. (1985). Nickelodeon theaters, 1905–1914: Building an audience for the movies. In T. Balio (Ed.), *The American film industry* (Rev. ed., pp. 83–102). Madison: University of Wisconsin Press.

Unpublished Dissertation

Rouzie, A. (1997). *At play in the fields of writing: Play and digital literacy in a college-level computers and writing course.* Unpublished doctoral dissertation, University of Texas at Austin.

CITING PERIODICALS

When citing periodicals, the necessary items to include are

1. Author's name (last name first, initials)
2. Date of publication (in parentheses). For scholarly journals, give the year. For newspapers and weekly magazines, give the year followed by the month and day (2001, December 13)
3. Title of the article
4. Title of the journal or magazine (in italics)
5. Volume number (in italics)
6. Page numbers

For articles in newspapers, use the abbreviation for pages (p. or pp.).

Many scholarly journals are printed to be bound as one volume, usually by year, and the pagination is continuous for that year. If, say, a scholarly journal is printed in four issues and the first issue ends on page 278, then the second issue will begin with page 279. For journals that are continuously paginated, you do not need to include the issue number. Some scholarly journals, however, are paginated like magazines with each issue beginning on page 1. For journals paginated by issue, you should list the issue number along with the volume (e.g., for the first issue of volume 11, you would put *11*(1) in the entry after the title of the journal).

Article in a Scholarly Journal—Continuous Pagination

Berlin, J. A. (1988). Rhetoric and ideology in the writing class. *College English, 50,* 477-94.

Article in a Scholarly Journal—Pagination by Issue

Kolby, J. (1988). The top-heavy economy: Managerial greed and unproductive labor. *Critical Sociology, 15*(3), 53-69.

Review

Chomsky, N. (1959). [Review of the book *Verbal behavior*]. *Language, 35,* 26-58.

Magazine Article

Engardio, P. (1996, June 24). Microsoft's long march. *Business Week,* 52-54.

Magazine Article—No Author Listed

UK: A battle for young hearts and minds. (1996, April 4). *Computer Weekly,* 20.

Newspaper Article

Bingham, J. (1996, September 3). Kids become masters of electronic universe: School Internet activity abounds. *Denver Post,* p. A13.

CITING ONLINE SOURCES

The *Publication Manual of the American Psychological Association* specifies that those citing Web sources should direct readers to the exact source page if possible, not to menu or home pages. URLs have to be typed with complete accuracy to identify a Web site. If you type an uppercase letter for a lowercase letter, a browser will not find the site. To avoid typos in URLs, load the page in your browser, highlight the URL, and copy it (Control C on Windows or Command C on a Mac), then paste it into the reference. You may have to change the font to match your text, but you will have the accurate URL.

The basic format for citing online sources is as follows:

1. Author's last name, initials
2. Date of document or last revision in parentheses
3. Title of document. Capitalize only the first word and any proper nouns.
4. Title of periodical (if applicable). Use italics and capitalize only the first word and any proper nouns.
5. Date of retrieval
6. URL or access path. Notice that there is no period after a URL.

Article in a Scholarly Journal on the Web

Agre, P. (1998). The Internet and public discourse. *First Monday, 3*(3). Retrieved July 10, 2001, from http://www.firstmonday.dk/ issues/issue3_3/agre/

Electronic Copy of an Article Retrieved from a Database

Schott, G., & Selwyn, N. (2001). Examining the "male, antisocial" stereotype of high computer users. *Journal of Educational Computing Research, 23,* 291–303. Retrieved from PsychINFO database.

Electronic Copy of an Abstract Retrieved from a Database

Putsis, W. P., & Bayus, B. L. (2001). An empirical analysis of firms' product line decisions. *Journal of Marketing Research, 37*(8), 110–118. Abstract obtained from PsychINFO database.

Article in a Newspaper on the Web

Mendels, P. (1999, May 26). Nontraditional teachers more likely to use the Net. *New York Times on the Web.* Retrieved September 19, 2001, from http://www.nytimes.com/library/tech/99/05/cyber/education/ 26education.html

Article from an Online News Service

Rao, M. (1999, February 10). WorldTel in $100 M community initiative for Indian state. *Asia InternetNews.* Retrieved April 15, 2001, from http://asia.internet.com/1999/2/1003-india.html

Article in a Magazine on the Web

Happy new Euro. (1998, December 30). *Time Daily*. Retrieved May 10, 2000,
from http://www.time.com/time/nation/article/0,8599,17455,00.html

Online Encyclopedia

Semiconductor. (1999). *Encyclopaedia Britannica Online*. Retrieved November
30, 2000, from http://search.eb.com/bol/topic?eu=68433&sctn=1#s_top

Document on a Web Site

Kaplan, N. (1997, December 17). E-literacies: Politexts, hypertexts and
other cultural formations in the late age of print. Retrieved July 2,
2001, from http://raven.ubalt.edu/staff/kaplan/lit/

Document on a Web Site of an Organization

National Audubon Society. (2001). Cowbirds and conservation. Retrieved
August 15, 2001, from http://www.audubon.org/bird/research/

Electronic Version of a U.S. Government Report

U.S. Public Health Service. Office of the Surgeon General. (2001, January 11).
Clean Indoor Air Regulations Fact Sheet. Retrieved February 12, 2001,
from http://www.cdc.gov/tobacco/sgr/sgr_2000/factsheets/
factsheet_clean.htm

Graphic, Audio, or Video Files

East Timor awaits referendum. (1999, August 31). *NPR Online*. Retrieved
August 31, 1999, from http://www.audubon.org/bird/research/
http://www.npr.org/ramfiles/atc/19990830.atc.10.ram

Electronic Mailing List Posting

Selzer, J. (1998, July 4). Ed Corbett. Message posted to WPA-L@lists.asu.edu

Newsgroup Posting

Brody, P. (1999, May 9). Chamax. Message posted to news: sci.archaeology.
mesoamerican

Personal Email

APA omits personal email from the list of references. Personal communication can be cited in parenthetical references in the

text. Provide a date if possible.

S. Wilson (personal communication, April 6, 2002)

Citing Other Sources

Government Report

U.S. Environmental Protection Agency. (1992). *Respiratory health effects of passive smoking: Lung cancer and other disorders.* (EPA Publication No. 600/6-90/006 F). Washington, DC: Author.

Film

Spielberg, S. (Director). (1998). *Saving Private Ryan* [Motion picture]. United States: Paramount Pictures.

Television Broadcast

Burns, K. (Writer). (1992, January 29). *Empire of the air: The men who made radio* [Television broadcast]. Walpole, NH: Florentine Films.

Television Series

Connelly, J. (Producer). (1957). *Leave it to Beaver* [Television series]. New York: CBS Television.

Music Recording

Glass, P. (1973). *"Low" symphony* [CD]. New York: Point Music.

Text Credits

Lance Armstrong, "A Defense of the Open Road" from *The Austin American Statesman*, February 11, 2001. Reprinted with permission.

Reprinted by permission from Kim Baer, Letter to the editor, *Sports Illustrated*, September 4, 2000.

William Bennett, excerpt from an open letter to Milton Friedman from *The Wall Street Journal* (September 19, 1989). Copyright ©1989 Dow Jones & Company, Inc. Reprinted with permission of the author and *The Wall Street Journal*. All rights reserved.

Grace Bernhardt, Balcones Canyonlands Preserve Web site. Reprinted with permission of the author.

Rachel Carson, "The Obligation to Endure," excerpt from *Silent Spring*. Copyright ©1962 by Rachel L. Carson, renewed by Roger Christie. Reprinted with permission of Houghton Mifflin Company. All rights reserved.

Chung-pei Hu, Sixth Street Safety & Awareness Web site. Reprinted with permission of the author.

"Common Sense," from *Commonweal* (September 13, 1991), p. 499. Copyright ©1991 by Commonweal Foundation. Reprinted with permission of *Commonweal*.

Robert H. Frank and Phillip T. Cook, excerpt from a summary of their book, *The Winner-Take-All Society*, from *Across the Board* 33:5 (May 1996). Copyright ©1996. Reprinted with permission of Professor Robert H. Frank.

Milton Friedman, excerpts from open letters to William Bennett from *The Wall Street Journal* (September 7 and 29, 1989). Copyright ©1989 Dow Jones & Company, Inc. Reprinted with permission of the author and *The Wall Street Journal*. All rights reserved.

Lani Guinier, excerpt from *The Tyranny of the Majority: Fundamental Fairness in Representative Democracy*. Copyright ©1994 Reprinted with the permission of The Free Press, a Division of Simon & Schuster, Inc.

Richard Handler and Eric Gable, excerpt from *The New History in an Old Museum: Creating the Past at Colonial Williamsburg*. Copyright ©1997 by Duke University Press. Reprinted with permission.

Advertisement courtesy of Harrison K-9 Security Services, Aiken, South Carolina.

Martin Luther King, Jr., excerpts from "Letter from Birmingham Jail." Copyright ©1963, 1964 by Martin Luther King, Jr., renewed 1991, 1992 by

Coretta Scott King. Reprinted with permission of The Heirs to The Estate of Martin Luther King, Jr., c/o Writer's House, Inc.

Donna Lopiano, "Title IX: It's Time to Live Up to the Letter of the Law." Reprinted with permission of Donna A. Lopiano, Ph.D., Executive Director, Women's Sports Foundation.

Scott McCloud, excerpts from *Understanding Comics*. Pp. 2–9 from *Understanding Comics* by Scott McCloud. Copyright ©1993, 1994 by Scott McCloud. Reprinted by permission of HarperCollins Publishers, Inc.

Meghann O'Connor, letter to Jim Cotner, Athletic Director, Lewisburg (Pennsylvania) Area High School (November 11, 1998). Reprinted with the permission of the author.

Natascha Pocek, "The Diet Zone: A Dangerous Place." Reprinted with permission of the author.

Anna Quindlen, "Clinic Visit," from *The New York Times* (February 21, 1991), p. A19. Copyright ©1991 by The New York Times Co. Reprinted by permission.

Rick Reilly, "Bare in Mind". Reprinted courtesy of *Sports Illustrated:* "Bare in Mind" by Rick Reilly, SI, September 4, 2000, Copyright ©2000, Time Inc. All rights reserved.

Leslie Marmon Silko, "The Border Patrol State," from *The Nation* (October 17, 1994). Copyright ©1994 by The Nation Company. Reprinted with permission of *The Nation*.

Edward R. Tufte, "Visual and Statistical Thinking: Displays of Evidence for Making Decisions," an excerpt from Chapter 2 of Visual Explanations, Copyright ©1997 by Edward Rolf Tufte. Reprinted with permission of the author and Graphics Press.

Chris Thomas, "Should Race Be a Qualification to Attend College?: An Examination of Affirmative Action." Reprinted with permission of the author.

Reprinted by permission from Elizabeth Vidmar, Letter to the editor, *Sports Illustrated*, September 4, 2000.

Excerpt from "Education" from *One Man's Meat*, text copyright ©1939 by E. B. White. Reprinted by permission of Tilbury House, Publishers, Gardiner, Maine.

YAHOO! Search. Text and artwork copyright ©1999 by YAHOO! INC. All rights reserved. YAHOO! and the YAHOO! logo are trademarks of YA-HOO! INC.

Photo credits are found on the copyright page.

Index